Global Perspectives of Human Resource Management

Global Perspectives of Human Resource Management

Oded Shenkar
Tel Aviv University and University of Hawaii at Manoa

PRENTICE HALL, Englewood Cliffs, NJ 07632

To Miriam

Library of Congress Cataloging-in-Publication Data

Shenkar, Oded.
    Global perspectives of human resource management / Oded Shenkar
        p.   cm.
    Includes bibliographical references.
    ISBN 0–02–409651–2
    1. Personnel management.   2. International business enterprises–
    –Personnel management.   I. Title
    HF5549.S54   1995
    658.3—cd20   94–11034
                                                                    CIP

Editor: Natalie Anderson
Production Supervisor: Anthony VenGraitis
Production Manager: Francesca Drago
Text Designer: Eileen Burke
Cover Designer: Eileen Burke

©1995 by Prentice-Hall, Inc.
A Division of Simon & Schuster, Inc.
Englewood Cliffs, New Jersey 07632

PRINTED IN THE UNITED STATES OF AMERICA

10   9   8   7   6   5   4   3   2   1

ISBN: 0-02-409651-2

Prentice-Hall International (UK) Limited, *London*
Prentice-Hall of Australia Pty. Limited, *Sydney*
Prentice-Hall Canada Inc., *Toronto*
Prentice-Hall Hispanoamericana, S.A., *Mexico*
Prentice-Hall of India Private Limited, *New Delhi*
Prentice-Hall of Japan, Inc., *Tokyo*
Simon & Schuster Asia Pte. Ltd., *Singapore*
Editora Prentice-Hall do Brasil, Ltda., *Rio de Janeiro*

Acknowledgments

An edited volume is as good as the contributions included in it. My first gratitude goes to the authors, both academics and practitioners, who have taken time off from their busy schedules to write a chapter in their area of expertise. Special thanks go to John Artise, vice president of Drake Beam Morin, whose enthusiasm for the project was infectious and who contributed to its launch and completion in numerous ways. Thanks also to my devoted assistant, Mang Mang Qiu, whose invaluable help carried me through this as well as other projects. Finally, I want to express my gratitude to Miriam, Keshet, and Joshua, for their understanding and support. This book hence represents a collective effort in more than one way.

Oded Shenkar

Contributors

Nancy J. Adler is Professor of Organizational Behavior and Cross-Cultural Management at the Faculty of Management, McGill University, Montreal, Canada.

John Artise is Vice President of Drake Beam Morin, Inc., New York City.

Elaine Bailey is Assistant Professor, College of Business Administration, University of Hawaii–Manoa, and is on the faculty of the Japan-America Institute of Management Science, Honolulu, Hawaii.

David C. Bangert is Assistant Professor, College of Business Administration, University of Hawaii–Manoa, Honolulu.

Alan M. Barratt heads the consulting firm Alan M. Barratt & Associates, London, England.

Richard W. Brislin is Senior Fellow and Project Director, Program on Education and Training, East-West Center, Honolulu, Hawaii.

Ronald C. Brown is Professor of Law at the Richardson School of Law, University of Hawaii–Manoa, Honolulu.

Mark C. Butler is Professor of Management at San Diego State University.

Wayne Cascio is Professor of Human Resource Management at the University of Colorado, Denver.

Thomas G. Dimmick is Human Resources Team Leader with O-Z/Gedney, Farmington, Conneticut. He is a former Senior Manager of Human Resource-Planning for Samsung USA Inc., Saddle Brook, New Jersey.

Ellen Drost is a Lecturer on Management at San Diego State University.

Dafna N. Izraeli is Professor of Sociology at Bar-Ilan University, Ramat Gan, Israel.

Mee-Kau Nyaw is Professor of Organization and Management and Director of the MBA program at the Chinese University of Hong Kong.

József Poór is the Managing Director of Hay Management Associates in Budapest, Hungary.

Manual G. Serapio, Jr. is Assistant Professor of Organization at the University of Colorado, Denver.

Oded Shenkar is with the Faculty of Management, Tel Aviv University, Tel Aviv, Israel, and Professor of International Management at the College of Business Administration, University of Hawaii–Manoa.

Mary B. Teagarden is Associate Professor of Human Resource Management at San Diego State University, California.

Mary Ann von Glinow is Professor of Management and International Business at Florida International University, Miami, and President of the Academy of Management.

Tomoko Yoshida is Director of Training, Japanese Programs, ITT Sheraton Hawaii/Japan Division, Honolulu, Hawaii.

Contents

Part II

Global Human Resource Management in Practice   61

Part III

Human Resource Management in Foreign Affiliates   195

Preface to Part III _____

Introduction

Oded Shenkar   Tel Aviv University, Israel
University of Hawaii-Manoa

Globalization has become, by now, one of the buzz words in business
and academic circles. Businesses have reckoned that without attention to
foreign markets and forces, their prosperity and very survival are at stake.
The evidence, supported by hard data, abounds. World trade's growth
continues to outpace the growth of global goods and services by almost a
two to one margin, and in 1990 it exceeded US $3.3 trillion. Foreign
direct investment (FDI) continues to register a growth level of approximately 30 percent yearly, reaching in 1990 an accumulated value in
excess of US $1.3 trillion. As a result, the number of wholly owned for-
eign subsidiaries and international joint ventures has been mushrooming.
In Hungary, for instance, more than 12,000 foreign invested enterprises
had been registered by 1992. In China, more foreign joint ventures were
registered in 1992 than in all previous years *combined*. And the wave of
foreign investment is growing, contributing to China's double-digit
growth rate, which now exceeds that of the "four tigers" of Taiwan,
Hong Kong, Korea, and Singapore. The "tigers" themselves, once only a
target for foreign direct investment, have become major foreign investors
with manufacturing affiliates in both developed and developing nations.
The Korean conglomerate Samsung, for instance, operates in 55 countries.

These tremendous flows of capital and technology are having a major
impact on how business is done, from strategy formulation to sales and
marketing. Yet, their impact is probably more pronounced and more revo-
lutionary in the human resource realm. Financing and technology transfer
issues nonwithstanding, the least easily transferable resource remains the
human one. Take, for example, Japan. A Booz, Allen & Hamilton survey
for the American Chamber of Commerce showed that the problem of hiring quality personnel ranked as one of the main factors inhibiting the
expansion of foreign investment in the country. The Japanese, on their part,

1

recently named conflict between expatriates and their local work force as their main globalization concern.[1]

Although businesses have had to confront the problem in the past, it was never on the same scale and magnitude as it is today. Consider the following: Close to 5 million Americans—roughly 5 percent of the business sector workforce—are already employed by the affiliates of foreign firms in the United States. At the same time, U.S. firms employ more than 6.5 million people in other countries: 3 million in Western Europe, 1.5 million (and growing rapidly) in Asia, and almost as many in Latin America. In Mexico alone, more than half a million people work for U.S. affiliates, a number sure to explode now that the North American Free Trade Agreement (NAFTA) has been ratified. At the end of this decade, roughly one out of every six workers in the United Kingdom will be working for a Japanese company.

As a result, employees will face choices not encountered before. An American executive will be able to choose between an American employer and any number of foreign firms operating in the United States; to stay in the United States or be stationed abroad; to work at a U.S. or a foreign headquarters, in an American or a foreign-owned subsidiary, or in one of the established or emerging cross-national alliances dotting the global landscape. With the European economic integration proceeding, nationals of European Economic Community (EEC) countries will be able to decide where they want to work and for whom. With increasing intra-Asian trade and direct investment, a Thai executive will be able to choose between an assignment in the home country, in Japan, or with a Thai/U.S./Chinese joint venture in China. Faster economic growth in Latin America will open up similar options for that region's employees.

This unprecedented openness will be perceived as an opportunity by some and a threat by others. With unemployment in Western Europe stubbornly high, East Europeans knocking on the EEC door are met with increasing opposition. In the United States, resentment is building against Mexicans and other immigrants and against Japanese investment. Ironically, free trade and foreign investment, which are most likely to help alleviate such pressures, are frequently singled out as the culprits. Our ability to overcome the fears of open economic borders will be crucial in determining the nature of the workplace as we know it.

The extent to which employers and employees around the globe will be able to take advantage of multiplying options also depends on a number of other developments. Japanese executives in large corporations are still assigned to overseas positions in subsidiaries and joint ventures with little regard to personal preferences and family constraints. Increasing opposition to the practice is noted nowadays, but it is too early to judge whether a fundamental change is taking place. In the United States, where executives are

---

[1] *The Wall Street Journal,* November 24, 1992, citing Towers Perrin.

more gently prodded to follow the company line, such choices are not necessarily less complicated. With more and more dual career couples, an overseas assignment can be a daunting challenge. And, with downsizing being the buzz word in the boardrooms the world over, assignees can no longer be assured of an appropriate position upon their return.

The social contract between employer and employee is changing, and executives have not been spared this time around. The last U.S. recession was the first in recent memory to hit the managerial level directly. Sober business magazines now advise their readers to forgo any allegiance to the corporation and focus on accumulating transferable skills. Large Japanese firms are rethinking their lifetime employment commitment to their employees, and the "salaryman" himself is increasingly questioning the value of this arrangement. Developments in various countries will not necessarily converge, however, nor will the practices maintained by corporations in their operations at home and abroad become uniform. Diverse circumstances will not only affect employee mobility but also the expectations and motivations of actual and prospective employees.

How likely are those expectations to be met in the international workplace? What do the foreign executives assigned to such subsidiaries expect from their local employees? And with the cost of expatriate assignment and failure soaring, how should executives be selected and assigned to their positions? How can they be trained to be culturally and socially sensitive, yet be counted on to introduce new work methods in a nonfamiliar environment? How can they be continuously coached to improve their performance on foreign soil? And how are the employees of local firms, sometimes suppliers to the foreign affiliates, affected by what they see? These are only some of the multitude of challenges faced by the human resource practitioner.

Joining a strategic alliance may be equally complicated. Having established a close relationship with a competitor-partner, an employee may be regarded as an asset—or as a threat, as a boundary spanner—or as someone with divided loyalties. Will it be possible to sustain employee development and growth against a backdrop of a deteriorating commitment between employer and employee, especially when each is anchored in a different national environment? And, given the freedom to do so, will the global work force move freely in pursuit of the most rewarding jobs, or will they stay put, possibly to fend off foreign workers and competition? There are no definite answers to these questions, but their implications are ominous.

A number of related developments are explored in this volume:

- An increase in the number and level of managerial positions occupied by women in general, and in international operations in particular.
- An increasingly complex legal environment cutting across national boundaries that forces globalization even on the most reluctant business players.

- Enhanced efforts toward localization of foreign affiliates and, at the same time, an enhanced impact of such affiliates on the operation of domestic business.
- A dramatic increase in the number and scope of strategic alliances that question the very concept of the corporation.
- A continuous increase in the proportion of part-time workers in developed nations.
- A growing disparity between the educated, skilled workforce and the nonskilled contingent.
- A threat to the part of the workforce whose employment was once considered a right of birth.

Increasing cross-border encounters make us aware of what we share as human beings but also of our significant diversity; of our need to cooperate but also of the competition underlying our relationships. Understanding these processes will determine whether the journey will be as successful and rewarding as it can and should be.

The book is divided into three parts: "A Framework for Analysis," delineating key frames of reference for understanding global human resource management; "Human Resource Management in Practice," where we discuss various functional human resource management (HRM) areas and their implemention in the global arena; and "Human Resource Management in Foreign Affiliates," where we focus on a number of countries and the HRM processes typical of their foreign affiliates. Each part begins with a preface that provides an integrative introduction to the chapters within the part.

Part I begins with a preface by Oded Shenkar that briefly examines the current perspectives on human resource management as they apply to the global era. A call for more interdisciplinary cooperation and the need to reach beyond traditional boundaries is made. In particular, the need to incorporate labor law and comparative/international management into the traditional human resource management area is emphasized.

Next, Wayne Cascio and Elaine Bailey present what the human resource management field has to offer the student and practitioner today in terms of knowledge, theories, and useful interventions. The field has gone through a transformation over the past decade. Globalization is no longer viewed as merely a specialized domain, left to a few experts; it now permeates all spheres of the field. This summary of what we know and what we don't know should serve us well in applying current knowledge as well as in planning further work and research in the years ahead.

The final chapter in this part, by Ronald C. Brown, brings us a critical, though often neglected perspective on global human resource management—the legal arena. Though human resource practitioners in the United States are probably more closely tuned to legal issues than are their counterparts in many other countries, they are not always fully aware of the legal implications of operating human resources across national boundaries. The U.S. labor and employment laws that apply to global operations, the ways international labor and employment laws affect such operations, and the legal issues that HRM practitioners must consider when operating abroad are some of the issues discussed in this chapter.

Part II of the book begins with a preface by Thomas G. Dimmick, the former Senior Manager of Human Resources Planning for Samsung–USA. Dimmick recalls what he went through as a "foreigner" in his own country. Assigned to the future site of South Korea's conglomerate Samsung in New Jersey, he soon discovered that what had to be constructed was not only the manufacturing plant but also the web of human relationships and practices that would make this a viable and successful workplace. The lessons as well as the questions raised by his experience serve as an introduction to the functional human resource management realms covered in the subsequent chapters of this section.

In the first chapter of Part II, John Artise discusses the selection, evaluation, and coaching of employees in international subsidiaries. He presents a three-phase process that is based on years of field experience with numerous foreign companies in the United States. This process can serve as the cornerstone of the acculturation effort in both the origin and target countries. Although the target cultures addressed are Japanese, Korean, French, British, and American, the model can be applied with relevant adaptations across countries and industries.

Using critical incidents from diverse cultures, Tomoko Yoshida and Richard Brislin show in the next chapter how to identify cross-cultural problems. They list the ingredients vital to successful cross-cultural training programs—awareness, knowledge, emotional challenges, skills, and behavior—and present a skill-streaming approach applied to cross-cultural training.

Next, Alan C. Barratt discusses the preparation of expatriates for overseas assignments. Focusing on the Arab countries of the Middle East, Barratt outlines the basic cultural expectations in this environment, and their origin. He then outlines a model for the effective training of expatriates about to be posted to overseas assignments.

In the following chapter, Elaine Bailey discusses another critical yet often neglected issue in global human resource management, namely, compensation. Using real-life examples, she shows the typical problems in this area and tells how to get a handle on them.

The final chapter of Part II, by Nancy J. Adler and Dafna N. Izraeli, describes the role of women in the global workplace. The authors examine the status of women in the executive suite, in particular women as expatriates in foreign lands, including those where women are seldom seen in an executive role. They debunk prevailing myths regarding the willingness of women executives to relocate abroad and their likelihood of success in their assignment. The promotion of women to key managerial positions around the globe is not strictly an equity issue but also a business one, the authors note. In an age of intense global competition, no company can afford not to choose the best person for the job.

The book's third and final part, "Human Resource Management in Foreign Affiliates," begins with a preface by Oded Shenkar addressing the general problems typically observed in managing human resources in foreign affiliates. The preface focuses on ownership and country-specific factors in the human resource management processes of such affiliates, distinguishing between wholly owned foreign affiliates and international joint ventures as well as assessing the role of country and other relevant variables in shaping the nature of these processes. This analysis prepares the ground for the four examples that follow.

Space limitations restricted this section to four chapters. The selection process, though difficult, was guided by the desire to provide both scope and diversity. Japanese affiliates in the United States have been targeted because the U.S.–Japan trade and FDI relationship is possibly the most important and perhaps the most problematic in the world today. Mexico was an obvious choice because of the NAFTA agreement and the hopes and fears that have been aired regarding its impact on human resources in the two countries. Hungary has managed so far to attract the lion's share of foreign investment in the emerging East and Central European democracies and thus is followed closely by investors and governments in other countries of the region. Finally, China has welcomed a tidal wave of foreign investment, with the number of foreign joint ventures registered in 1992 eclipsing not only that of all previous years combined but also that of its competitors for the investment dollars. This is despite continuous operational problems reported in many of those ventures, many of which apparently have related to the management of human resources.

In the first chapter of Part III, Manuel G. Serapio, Jr., presents the results of his study of Japanese affiliates in the United States. He looks at the extent of "localization" of such subsidiaries and its impact on the operation as well as the attitudes of the local workforce. On the basis of a five-year study of forty-seven manufacturing subsidiaries and several other Japanese affiliates, Serapio shows the staffing of such subsidiaries to be in a state of flux. His research suggests that despite public skepticism, management opportunities for Americans in Japanese subsidiaries are being created. The jury is still out, however, on whether these opportunities will materialize across the board or only in selected positions and industries.

Next, Mary B. Teagarden, Mary Ann von Glinow, Mark C. Butler, and Ellen Drost discuss the management of human resources in foreign affiliates in Mexico. With the impending post–NAFTA foreign investment looming large, the experience of existing affiliates is of vital importance. The authors show us how to prepare and what to pay attention to when launching foreign subsidiaries in Mexico.

David C. Bangert and József Poór then discuss the changing scene of human resources in Hungary—the leading target nation for FDI among the emerging countries of the former Eastern bloc nations. The authors examine the human resource innovations introduced in foreign affiliates, as well as the extent to which these foreign affiliates serve as role models for other enterprises struggling to adapt to the new market environment.

In the final chapter of Part III, Oded Shenkar and Mee-Kau Nyaw write about the clash of diverse cultures and environmental systems in Chinese–foreign joint ventures, a clash that makes the management of their human resources a daunting task. Relying on examples from both successful and unsuccessful ventures, the authors highlight the vital role of human resources in the performance of such ventures, and what it takes to steer a successful course along the human resource mosaic that is typical of a foreign joint venture.

A FRAMEWORK FOR ANALYSIS

Preface to Part I

The Globalization of Human Resource Management: The Interdisciplinary Challenge

Oded Shenkar   Tel Aviv University, Israel
University of Hawaii-Manoa

To the extent that it can be generalized, the "traditional" response to the emerging globalization of human resource management has been to extend our current knowledge from its domestic base into foreign lands. This process has been largely channeled in two directions. The first is an attempt to question the universality of domestic (i.e., United States) human resource practices in light of the realities found in foreign nations. The second is the development of a specialized field of study focused on human resource issues unique to international business, such as the selection of U.S. employees for overseas assignments. Although both directions of inquiry have made considerable progress in enhancing our understanding of major processes in global human resource management, a number of key areas remain unexplored.

To a great extent, we are still unfamiliar with the influence exerted by major sectors of the environment over human resource management. Cultural, political, social, economic, and technological sectors of the environment are still insufficiently explored in terms of their potential impact on human resource management practices, their effectiveness, and their transferability. An enhanced understanding of the organization–environment interface across these sectors is, however, vital to the understanding of the dynamics of human resource management in the global era and must be gained if we are to reach beyond the confines of the domestic treatment of the field.

One of the most important of the environmental sectors in terms of its implications for global human resource management is the legal field. Although studies of domestic human resource management, especially in the United States, have greatly emphasized the legal angle, relatively little has been done in terms of exploring the legal aspects of human resource management in the global arena. This is surprising, because the interface between the two fields seems to be critical. The applicability of the U.S. labor and employment laws to global operations as well as the effect of international labor and employment law on global operations are two legal domains with far-reaching implications for the management of human resources in the global age. These domains are explained in detail in the final chapter of Part I, though their relevance clearly extends to the functional human resource management areas discussed in Part II, as well as the foreign affiliates discussed in Part III.

Other developments in global human resource management also call attention to the need to incorporate the perspectives of disciplines that have long been regarded as existing outside the traditional domain of the field. The internationalization of business beyond the operations of giant multinational enterprises implies a greater role for comparative and international management in analyzing human resource processes. For instance, the clustering of countries in terms of the relative similarity of work-related values (e.g., Hofstede, 1980; Ronen & Shenkar, 1985) has obvious implications for various human resource practices, yet these implications have only recently been considered.

The proliferation of foreign affiliates suggests bringing not only strategic management but also the more specialized strategic literature on FDI into human resource management in a much closer fashion than is the case at the present time. After all, human actors are making the FDI decision, and individual career and other human resource considerations play a role in the choices made (Tallman & Shenkar, 1994). And human resources will eventually determine the success of the affiliates with considerations of "strategic fit" now dominating the literature on FDI.

An interdisciplinary approach is essential if we are to provide the human resource practitioners with the tools necessary for their success, as well as put them in a better position to tap that knowledge. Challenged by the realities of the global business environment, practioners in fields ranging from international selection and performance evaluation to expatriate compensation and taxation have accumulated a substantial body of knowledge from which we could all benefit. For the mutual learning process to take place, however, we must remove the barriers currently dividing academic camps as well as academics and practitioners.

Learning from the practitioners is of vital importance. Arguably, the global human resource practitioner is frequently a step ahead of the academician in having to tackle problems for which research or theory-based answers are not yet available. To be aware of those questions as well as to be able to provide answers, we should do a better job of collecting, processing, and analyzing the vast amounts of data and experience accumulated by the practitioners, at the same time extending the scope of our theoretical reach in a way that will make such responses both timely and accurate.

References

Hofstede, G. 1980. *Culture's consequences.* Beverly Hills, CA: Sage.

Ronen, S., and Shenkar, O. 1985. Clustering countries on attitudinal dimensions: A review and synthesis. *Academy of Management Review* 10, 435–454.

Tallman, S., and Shenkar, O. 1994. A managerial decision model of international cooperative venture formation. *Journal of International Business Studies,* 25(1), 91–114.

International Human Resource Management: The State of Research and Practice

Wayne Cascio, University of Colorado at Denver

Elaine Bailey, University of Hawaii-Manoa

John Artise's frequent tip to Japanese managers—"Don't ask a job applicant personal questions"—is often greeted with surprise. Without information on an employee's religion, upbringing, or home life, Japanese managers ask him, "How are we going to know them and trust them?"

Artise conducts seminars for Japanese managers about the American workplace. Along with lawyers, other consultants, and corporate officials, he says that clashes in custom, culture, and management style have been a growing source of legal embroilments for Japanese companies doing business in America. Although litigation on employment issues also plagues their American counterparts, Japanese managers in the United States may be less sensitive to a multiracial society and unfamiliar with the legal constraints on employment practices. Statistics bear out these concerns. "Japanese firms commonly have at least one employment lawsuit pending against them . . . when a company loses a case, it can expect to pay at least $20 million in damages and litigation costs" (Jacobs, 1990).

Cultural blunders by well-meaning but misinformed managers have led to major problems in international operations, not just for the Japanese but for Europeans as well. Britain's Grand Metropolitan, for example, angered Pillsbury's minority employees in the United States when, as the new owner, it fired several black middle managers (including the head of its affirmative action program). In another case, a European firm lost a talented employee when it purchased an American company and expected a female executive to start serving coffee at the board meetings. Finally, a Brazilian executive created major problems for his firm when he treated his American secretaries as personal servants. Not only did he ask them to do his personal shopping, but he even asked them to mend his clothes!

15

As these few examples illustrate, human resource management practices that may work domestically do not necessarily work when transported across national borders. Different cultures require that companies take different approaches. Managers need to understand local business protocol, employment laws and governmental policies, and labor practices. A minor misunderstanding can easily lead to a major blunder, just as the wrong person on the job can lead to disaster (Ricks, 1993).

Cultural differences significantly influence management approaches and performance of employees within organizations. General principles of management and specific human resource practices evolving out of management theories are currently being seriously questioned in various cross-cultural settings. For example, it has been found that human resource management practices different from those used in the United States must be used in Mexico to effectively manage maquiladora alliances (Teagarden & Von Glinow, 1990). In a study of employee performance control approaches, it was found that effective practices in Japan were very ineffective when applied in U.S. companies (Eshgi, 1985). Practices that have evolved out of American management theories are even more difficult to transplant in non-Western countries.

One of the most critical determinants of an organization's success in the global business arena is the effective management of its human resources. This chapter addresses some major issues that managers face daily as they attempt to manage human resources across national boundaries. It incorporates an overview of current international human resource management (IHRM) research with organization examples. Specific topic areas include the traditional human resource management (HRM) functions, as well as issues that evolve from the globalizing of these processes. Our primary emphasis is on employees at the managerial level. However, we also address issues related to employees at the technical and professional levels, largely as a result of the increasing requirements placed on the management of human resources growing out of new technologies.

Human resource management has escalated to the forefront of organizational attention because of the transformations taking place in social, political, economic, and educational environments around the globe. Expanding business operations beyond national boundaries while continuing the commitment to local markets requires more complex business structures. The increasing need for businesses to provide information and services while making productive use of new technology demands a well-educated and well-trained work force. As we move through the 1990s, the world's work force has become even more mobile, thus requiring labor, at least highly skilled labor, to be viewed in terms of a world market.

As the European Economic Community, Eastern and Central Europe, and the Commonwealth of Independent States relax restrictions on the rights of citizens to travel and work outside their countries, more geographic, national, cultural, and ethnic boundaries are being spanned. In countries where educational systems have outperformed economic development, human resources have become a major export commodity. These dynamic forces demand that employees at all levels of the organization be able to change rapidly as well as be prepared for continuous learning throughout their careers. The "learning organization" is a reality of effective HRM and one of the most critical processes contributing to an organization's ability to respond rapidly to change.

Trends in International Human Resource Management

In a recent study, 110 senior human resource and industrial relations managers from multinational companies in a variety of industries located in North America, South America, the Middle East, Asia, Europe, and Australia responded to a survey designed to elicit their opinions of the most compelling issues in international human resource management for the 1990s. Of the multinationals surveyed, 57 percent were owned by U.S. companies; and 43 percent were owned by companies in other countries (Cascio, 1993).

The following three *within-firm* issues were identified as most salient:

1. The role of human resources in international operations
2. Managing a multicultural work force
3. Developing management talent in a global business environment

Three other issues were seen as critically important *external* challenges:

1. Human resource aspects of international alliances
2. The impact of the social dimension of the new Europe
3. The future role of Japan in Asia and the world.

These issues were identified as critical in terms of their strategic and managerial implications. In the following section the interplay between corporate strategy and effective HRM is examined.

Strategic International Human Resource Management

Effective strategic planning requires the integration of human resource planning into an overall planning process for the organization to be able to realize its goals and objectives. Strategic international human resource management can be distinguished from human resource management and strategic human resource management by the degree to which it has an impact on the strategic activities of the international concerns and goals of the organization (Schuler, Dowling, & Cieri, 1993). The degree of effort expended to understand the country's culture(s) and socioeconomic environments in which a firm operates is a critical element of the strategic international human resource process (Milliman, Von Glinow, & Nathan, 1991). The success of the integration of the planning process can be represented by the degree of integration among HR functions throughout the international operation.

A number of researchers have identified flexibility as being critical to successful strategic management. Flexibility may be defined as the ability to cope with change and continual adaptation to the changing internal and external organizational environments (Miles & Snow, 1984). As HR functions change over the life of the organization (development of the organization), internal and external integration as well as flexibility are critical to successful strategic HR decisions.

United Airlines (UA) illustrates the necessity for rapid internal organization change and the requirement for internal and external integration. United Airlines began as a domestic airline, serving the United States mainland and, beginning in the 1950s, Hawaii. In the 1960s it added service to two international destinations, Vancouver and Toronto. Until the 1970s, that was the extent of United's international network. In the late 1970s it began to serve Mexico (Cancun and Cozumel), and in 1986, after it acquired routes formerly owned by Pan American World Airways, United immediately began service to destinations in Asia and throughout the Pacific. Shortly thereafter, it acquired the rights to serve cities in western Europe. United currently spans the globe completely, providing air transportation to and from five continents (Bauserman, 1992).

As the United Airlines example illustrates, large, worldwide businesses tend to evolve from domestic to international to multinational to global organizational structures (Zeien, 1991). The structures, in turn, have significant implications for the management of people within them. The first issue to be addressed is how the various types of organizational structures differ. An *international* company transports its business outside of its own country although, in general, each of its operations is a replication of the company's domestic experience. Typically, an international company is structured geographically and involves subsidiary general managers. A *multinational* company, by contrast, grows and defines its business on a worldwide basis but continues to allocate its resources among national or regional areas. Companies with multiple product lines often find it difficult to remain geographically organized for a variety of reasons, such as the need to have a common accounting system, common financial and management controls, and interrelated marketing programs. As a result, such companies tend to evolve into multinational structures, with combinations of product-line and solid-line responsibilities (Zeien, 1991).

Global organizations treat the entire world as though it were one large country. The global organization may be the entire company or one or more of its product lines. Some firms operate with a mixture of two or even three of these models of organizational structure simultaneously. The choice and combination of structure have a direct impact on all human resource management functions from recruitment through retirement.

Changes in organizational structure have important implications for the management of people within those existing structures. As an example, consider the business system of Japanese-owned global organizations. The system is comprised of five interlocking parts (Campbell, 1991):

1. *Borderless structure and bottom-up decision-making processes* that encourage communication and information flow among all components of the company and extend the network to its key suppliers, distributors, and other business partners.
2. *Custodial leadership* that emphasizes values and vision and is skillfully unassertive, while energizing and challenging middle managers with demanding targets.
3. *Human resource management,* including socialization, training, and promotion by means of a hierarchy of ranks, job rotation, and appraisal systems that promote hard work, commitment, and competition among peers.
4. *Incremental planning and control* that help a company expand little by little, focusing on new products and the relentless pursuit of operating improvements, rather than grand designs for competitive advantage.
5. *An extended family model* that encourages and rewards commitment.

As these five practices illustrate, Japanese global organizations are actively trying to enhance the quality of human relations, thereby maximizing the effectiveness of their human resources. The five practices generate broad networks and an appreciation for total business needs horizontally and vertically throughout the organization. In fact, they illustrate a point often made by academic researchers, which is that effective human resources management does not exist in a vacuum but must be integrated into the overall strategy of the organization. The human resources policies of the company and the HR function itself must relate to the goals of the organization. The match between Japanese practices and the expectations of the workforce has not always been consistent. Although they operate according to the five-step system in Japan, Japanese organizations have sometimes opted for different practices with host or third-country personnel. This lack of consistency has been a source of discontent for foreign employees of Japanese corporations.

Thus far, we have described activities and organizational structures within individual firms. International strategic alliances represent collaborations between or among companies that span national borders. As we shall see shortly, such arrangements are becoming more and more common. The HRM implications are even more complex.

International Strategic Alliances

Traditionally researchers have tended to focus on characteristics of multinational firms on the basis of their country of origin, such as Japan, the United States, or Europe. Comparative approaches across countries tend to emphasize "us versus them" thinking. Today, more and more multinationals are forming strategic alliances. Such alliances have become an important feature on the landscape of international business.

Most major U.S. multinationals maintain numerous international cooperative agreements. According to *Fortune* magazine, U.S. companies entered into some 2,000 alliances with European countries in the 1980s alone (Main, 1990). This trend results from the rapid development of technology and the globalization of markets and products. Not even the largest multinationals can acquire from their own laboratories all the technology that they need. In many cases, alliances are formed to secure access to new technologies or to share the risks associated with the huge capital investments that some technologies require (Cascio & Serapio, 1991). An excellent example is the multicultural alliance among IBM, Toshiba, and Siemens, to create memory chips sixteen times as powerful as any existing at the time ("If You Can't Beat 'Em," 1992).

At a broader level, consider the fast-paced field of personal communications, with its intersection of wireless telephone, portable computing, and information services. There "no one can go it alone anymore," says John Sculley, former chief executive of Apple Computer. "We can't do without the Japanese and they can't do without us." Apple has manufacturing pacts with two Japanese companies, Sharp Corporation and Sony Corporation, for handheld computers and laptops. In Sculley's opinion, U.S. companies, typically strong in systems design and software, are foolish if they do not take advantage of Japan's capabilities in such commodities as memory chips and monitors, especially in view of limited domestic sources (Zachary, 1992).

An international alliance allows multinational companies to pursue common goals based on collaboration between the parties involved. This type of arrangement allows all partners to maintain their individual identities and engage in other activities outside the alliance. Joint ventures, research and development arrangements, marketing and distribution agreements, and licensing provide some of the means by which international alliances are formed.

The implications of such alliances diminish the debate over who is ahead technologically, as it becomes more difficult to identify the national origins of many high-tech products. Second, *many such alliances require* sustained contact among employees and managers of collaborating firms. These are alliances of people as much as alliances of technology. As such, human resource management issues that include, among others, mergers of company and national cultures, staffing, training and development, performance appraisal, and compensation are fundamental to their success (Cascio & Serapio, 1991). One of the most salient forces driving the need for continuous learning, one that affects virtually all companies, both domestic and international, is the management of new technology (Zammuto & O'Connor, 1992).

New Technology: What Are the Implications for Managing People?

Global competition requires organizations to use information and communication technology to accommodate rapid and complex changes in global markets. The advent of new approaches to management (e.g., from command and control to self-direction and self-managed work teams), coupled with computer and information technologies that expand a firm's links to its wider environment, have created an increasing concern for the management of technology. Manufacturing companies are adopting advanced manufacturing technologies (AMT) to improve quality, reduce cost, and speed processes.

Managers have been slow to adapt to this new and dynamic organizational environment that is human resource driven. Many nontechnical managers are averse to technological concepts, and some suffer the same kinds of stress, fear, and frustration as do lower-level employees when new technology is introduced. Methods of adopting new technology are influenced by culture; therefore, successful international ventures require that technology be adapted and introduced in ways consistent with the cultures of the employees involved (Gattiker, 1990).

However, many firms are experiencing a 50 to 75 percent failure rate when attempting to implement new technology, due mainly to neglect of the critical interface between technology and human resources in the workplace (Saraph & Sabastian, 1992). Managers are finding their jobs being redefined or eliminated as technology assumes more functions and fewer personnel are required to perform tasks. This trend has created the need for management development programs that relate specifically to the interface between technology, culture, and the work force (Bailey & Cotlar, 1993).

The various levels of technical competence of the work force require different styles of managing coupled with technical competence on the part of managers. The demands of new technology require equally new approaches to developing and managing human resources as well as reorganizing business processes. Cross-cultural differences limit the ability of managers to use standardized strategies for the introduction and integration of technology. As rapid technological change redefines work roles, individuals need reassurance as much as retraining. Japanese industries report fewer difficulties in introducing new technology than do American companies. However, the job security and retraining provided by Japanese companies could account for this difference. The core of these new approaches should be a synthesis of technology and culturally sensitive management practices (Brod, 1984; Gattiker, 1990).

Within international high-technology companies, the human resource management function is given considerable attention and resources. A survey of 200 companies revealed that 100 percent of the high-technology firms in the sample had formally established HRM departments, as compared to 71 percent of the medium-technology firms. Regarding the importance attached to the various human resource activities, managers in high-technology firms generally rated human resource activities higher than did their counterparts in medium-technology companies. High-technology firms also practiced a wider spectrum of human resource activities. In addition, they placed significantly greater emphasis on activities that were likely to contribute to the building of morale and satisfaction, incentive systems and pay structure, and the proper selection and development of their employees (Yuen, 1991).

Human Resources: The Key to Cultural Literacy

Marquardt and Engel (1993) emphasize the significance of national and corporate cultures on international human resource practices in their recent book, *Global Human Resource Development*:

> International HRD practitioners must be able not only to operate on a global scale but also to work effectively in the myriad of distinct local cultures they encounter. They need to learn from the best of each nation's HRD programs as well as from the best of the global HRD technologies, ideas, and visions. In short, the successful HRD professionals of the nineties and beyond must be able to integrate globally what they practice locally. (p. xii)

Culture can be defined and described in numerous ways. It is not the intent of this chapter to address this issue in depth but merely to alert the reader to the need to ensure consistency between organizational practices and cultural norms. Among newly internationalizing companies, it is not an unusual assumption that "what works at home will work elsewhere." Unfortunately, that assumption almost never holds up in practice. Start-up obstacles are by no means the most serious problems newly internationalized companies face in expanding beyond local markets. Far more serious is cultural illiteracy.

As an example, consider the comparison between the operational and cultural problems United Airlines encountered after it acquired the entire Pacific Division of Pan American World Airways on February 11, 1986. Virtually overnight, United began serving thirteen cities in ten Pacific Rim countries—with no prior experience in this fastest-growing region of the world. Not surprisingly, United Airlines made a number of mistakes that reflected its lack of cultural knowledge about its new customers in the Pacific Rim (Zeeman, 1987):

- The map United inserted into its sales brochure left out one of Japan's main islands.
- United's magazine ad campaign, "We know the Orient," listed the names of Far Eastern countries below pictures of local coins. Unfortunately, the coins didn't match up with the countries.
- Imagine how Chinese business people felt taking off from Hong Kong during the inauguration of United's concierge services for first-class passengers. To mark the occasion, each concierge proudly wore a white carnation . . . a well-known oriental symbol of death.
- Perhaps United's most embarrassing mistake was its in-flight magazine cover that showed Australian actor Paul Hogan wandering through the Outback. The caption read, "Paul Hogan Camps It Up." Hogan's lawyer was kind enough to phone United long distance from Sydney to let the company know that "camps it up" is Australian slang for "flaunts his homosexuality."

Americans often assume that the folks Down Under are just like Americans because both groups speak English. As the Paul Hogan story illustrates, cultural ignorance can lead to most unhappy customers. United learned a great deal during its early days in the Pacific, and it incorporated this knowledge into an eighteen-month training program for 28,000 of its employees. Since the average air fare across the Pacific exceeds $2,000, United had to learn to speak the language and to understand the culture of its customers if it wanted to prosper. It did. Today United's Pacific service is second to none, and it serves more customers in that region than any other airline.

As the United Airlines example illustrates, careful attention to human resource management can make a significant contribution to the implementation of business strategy. If United had staffed its expansion with individuals knowledgeable about the various countries' logistical and cultural issues, many of the initial crises would have been eliminated or at least minimized. The lesson? It is critical for organizations to develop policies and practices that align their employees with their global strategies. It also is critical to understand and to respect cultural norms in the areas in which companies wish to do business.

Staffing for Global Success

In multinational corporations (MNCs), the difference between business failure and success often depends on how well organizations select, train, and manage their employees. International staffing is becoming more common as companies become more global in their operations and strategic thinking. Although some companies view expatriates as the embodiment of the emerging global workforce, others see foreign national and third-country employees (e.g., a German working for a U.S.-owned company in Spain) as another recruitment source from which to fill jobs, especially in areas of low unemployment.

One of the distinguishing characteristics between international and domestic HRM is the complexity of the workforce mix. The type of organization structure has a direct impact on the complexity of the mix of employees. A wholly owned subsidiary operation may employ only expatriate and host country personnel, whereas a strategic alliance may have a far more complex workforce. Research to date has basically categorized human resources into three or four of the following groups of employees: (1) foreign parent(s) expatriates; (2) host parent(s) transferees; (3) host-country nationals; and (4) third-country employees.

Employees can be classified further using the following three criteria: (1) country of origin; (2) recruiting entity; and (3) country of employment (Zeira & Shenkar, 1986). There are many possible combinations that result in a variety of far more descriptive categories of employees. Shenkar & Zeira (1987) identified eight categories of employees; however, six categories of employees require attention in each functional area of HR (e.g., recruitment, staffing, training, performance appraisal, and compensation) to maximize their effectiveness in the complex global venture (Bailey & Shenkar, 1993). A striking feature of the classification scheme is that four of the six categories involve expatriates. This is no accident. Indeed, a trend that has accompanied the internationalization of organizations is the increase in the number of managers and technical and professional employees who work outside of their home countries. Foreigners hold top management positions in one-third of large U.S. firms and in one-fourth of European-based firms (Cascio, 1992). At the same time, more than 4.6 million workers are employed by foreign companies in the United States. British-owned companies employ almost twice as many U.S. workers as Japanese-owned companies do, and Canada and Germany also rank ahead of Japan (Hoerr, Nathans, & Armstrong, 1990). In developing countries of the world this number is even larger. A study of four large European MNCs revealed that 80 percent of all international transfers were into developing countries and only 20 percent into Europe or North American (Galbraith & Elstrom, 1976).

A study of U.K. multinational firms' international staffing practices revealed that, although almost 50 percent of the companies surveyed had formal policies favoring host-country managers, in practice two-thirds used expatriates to manage their foreign operations. Although lip-service is given to using fewer expatriates, in practice firms are actually making greater use of them. The principal reasons given for this practice are weak pools of available local management talent and maintenance of control in key foreign businesses following acquisitions (Scullion, 1991).

The failure rates of expatriate personnel are well documented. A key reason for failure is the lack of predeparture and postarrival training and orientation for the employee and other family members (Black, 1989; Black & Mendenhall, 1991; Mendenhall & Oddou, 1988). However, recruitment and selection criteria have as much impact on success of an expatriate as do orientation and training. Employee selection criteria based on technical competence alone will not lead to success in the global organization. Personality characteristics that predict success in overseas assignments include perseverance and patience (for when everything falls apart); initiative (because no one may be there to indicate what one should try next); and adaptability and flexibility (to accept and try new ways) (Cascio, 1991; Tung, 1981). However, on-site visits that provide genuine insight into the foreign experience allow for a realistic evaluation before departure.

On-site support programs are proving successful by lowering early return rates. Corporations are beginning to provide on-site mentoring support programs by using employees who have completed other foreign assignments. The mentor is a link to formal as well as informal organizational information. Japanese corporations have gone so far as to provide schooling and retail outlets for food and merchandise "from home."

Repatriation is the stage of the foreign assignment that is most often neglected when, in fact, it should be a critical component of the HR global strategy. In a survey of more than 135 expatriates, only 39 percent said that their firms had taken advantage of the skills learned from their experiences (Oddou & Mendenhall, 1991). The recently repatriated employee or manager is a source of information about the most current state of the organization and the external environment of the country and region from which he or she has just returned. This individual can assist in the strategic planning, the HR planning, the selection, and the training and preparation of staff for upcoming foreign assignments.

For the repatriated employee or manager, a meaningful, responsible job upon return to the home country is essential to readjustment and sense of contribution to the organization. The unique experience, expertise, and information the employee has acquired is used immediately by the organization; this, in turn, provides significance to the past assignment and assists in adjustment to the current assignment.

Gillette International is an example of a corporation that recruits foreign talent. Gillette's International Graduate Trainee Program has groomed local foreign talent in the developing nations in which the company has business operations. This type of program helps weave an international human resource thread into the organization at the entry level and at a cost much lower than would be needed to recruit and hire senior-level foreign executives or to ship expatriate employees abroad (Laabs, 1991).

Human Resource Training and Employee Development

Companies that compete in the global marketplace are finding that they need to develop an in-house pool of managers with international experience and an international perspective. Strategically orchestrating cross-national assignments provides firms with an opportunity to develop this talent. However, training is only one part of an overall human resource development system.

A careful selection process sets the stage for tailoring a program to integrate the person into the position and the culture. Then, a development program can be constructed to prepare the person for the demands of the new setting. As we noted earlier, consideration also needs to be given to having a plan in place to support the person during the period of adjustment and reentry.

What are the benefits of such a system? The establishment of an ongoing program for managing global assignments provides a mechanism for continuous improvement, and maintaining a database for such information avoids having to rely on the anecdotal expertise of staff with experience.

Specific training topic areas for the global workforce include multicultural team building and strategies for cross-cultural conflict resolution. Critical skill-building areas include problem solving, decision making, communicating, negotiation, performance appraisal, and leadership styles. Global career paths for employees that identify assignments as well as competencies associated with successful completion of assignments provide on-the-job dimensions of training.

In its new global role, United Airlines is serving approximately 200,000 people per day in eighteen countries. United is competing not only with TWA, American Airlines, and Delta but also with Lufthansa, Singapore Air, British Airways, and a host of other international carriers. United has embarked on an eighteen-month training program to instill international awareness and a commitment to world-class service in every customer service and in-flight employee. The program, called "Best Airline—The Global Challenger," eventually will provide training for 28,000 United employees. The airline prepared a 200-page pretraining workbook to help equalize the skill level among employees, and thus to provide a common baseline from which to begin training, because some employees already have extensive international experience. In addition to employee training, United is investing $125 million in such areas as new meals, headsets, check-in areas, and world-class products to enhance the international air-travel experience of its customers.

Recent research shows that the foreign assignment is perceived as being of less importance and out of the mainstream of decision making. Therefore, the link between the true and perceived career benefits of the international assignment must be made clear to the expatriate. Training and inclusion in the decision-making processes, even though at a distance, appear to have an impact on job satisfaction. The perception that career benefits will result from the international experience tend to lead to greater job satisfaction among expatriates (Naumann, 1993). Therefore, it becomes critical for the human resource management department to link career development and career progression to international assignments.

Companies such as Minnesota Mining and Manufacturing and AT&T appoint a "career sponsor" to link the expatriate to corporate headquarters in their absence. The sponsor acts as mentor and informant and in some cases conducts performance appraisals and gives input on compensation increases for the expatriate. Informal training programs of this nature have been highly successful and are becoming common practice in companies with high expatriate failure rates. Comprehensive formal training programs for the expatriate and family members combined with a mentor program appear to lead to increased expatriate success rate (Cascio, 1992).

In summary, the performance of global organizations can be enhanced greatly by employee training at all levels but especially among managers. Failure to provide such training perpetuates a "stand-still" mentality when in practice the pace of change is accelerating year by year. Indeed, it is not an exaggeration to say that training is a key component of international HR systems and that such systems are critical for implementing global business strategies.

Performance Appraisal in the International Context

"Where do I stand?" "What does my boss think of my work?" These are common questions from almost all employees and managers. The answers, however, are likely to be communicated (if at all) in very different ways in different parts of the world. As we shall see, the process of performance appraisal varies considerably across countries and cultures: in its objectives, in the characteristics and style of the appraiser, in the frequency of the process, in assumptions made about the process, in how criticism and praise are communicated, in opportunities for the employee to respond, and in the kinds of factors used to motivate subsequent performance.

Perhaps the most basic issue, however, is this: "What should be evaluated?" In response, most managers would answer, "The kinds of things that make the difference between success and failure in the international assignment." Some of those things include such characteristics as cross-cultural interpersonal skills, sensitivity to foreign norms and values, understanding differences in labor practices and customer relations, and ease of adaptation to unfamiliar environments (Dowling & Schuler, 1990). At least this is true of expatriates. However, other factors that count include the tasks that an individual is assigned to accomplish, as well as the characteristics of the environment that make those tasks relatively more or less easy to accomplish.

A key characteristic of the environment is the culture that defines it. The cultural environment varies enormously. Table 1 illustrates such variation by examining characteristics of performance appraisal in a western culture (the United States), a Middle Eastern culture (Saudi Arabia), and a Far Eastern culture (Korea). Perhaps the most important lesson of Table 1 is that a foreign manager could be misled completely by assuming that the approach that works in his or her own culture will work elsewhere.

In Western cultures, we tend to focus on *outcomes* or results. This tends to imbue the process with a short-term focus. In the Middle East and Far East (to the extent that they can be generalized), however, the *process* or ways that results are accomplished are just as, if not more, important. Hence, these cultures tend to take a longer-term view of the performance appraisal process. Indeed, Korean middle-level managers often do not really know exactly how their performance is viewed until roughly five years after joining their companies. At that point, some are promoted from entry-level positions, and others are not.

Performance appraisal practices vary considerably around the globe. Appraisal practices also are likely to vary for expatriate managers as opposed to host-country nationals. Understanding three key variables is crucial to success in this area: task, environment, and process. Now let's consider some important aspects of international compensation.

The Complex Components of International Compensation

Economic globalization is increasingly challenging employers to provide benefits to all categories of employees worldwide. Although some employers have made strides in determining the best approach to provide benefits to employees, some still have complex issues to resolve. When a firm has employees in various countries, a typical first step is to categorize all employees and then to determine the type and level of each benefit to be extended. Each category of employee requires close scrutiny to determine

TABLE 1
Some Characteristics of Performance Appraisal Systems in the United States,
Saudi Arabia, and Korea

Issue	United States	Saudi Arabia[a]	Korea
Objective	Administrative decisions, employee development	Placement, organizational development	Develop relationship between supervisor and employee
Done by?	Supervisor	Manager several layers up who knows employee well	Mentor and supervisor
Authority of appraiser	Presumed in supervisor role	Reputation (prestige determined by nationality, age, sex, family, tribe, title, education)	Long tenure of supervisor with organization
Style	Supervisor takes the lead, with employee input	Authority of appraiser is important; never say "I don't know"	Supervisor takes the lead, with informal employee input
Frequency	Usually once a year	Once a year, as well as a continuous process	Developmental appraisal once a month for 1st year; annually thereafter
Assumptions	Objective—appraiser is fair	Subjective appraisal more important than objective; connections are important	Subjective appraisal more important than objective; no formal criteria
Feedback	Criticisms are direct, may be in writing	Criticisms more subtle; not likely to be given in writing	Criticisms subtle and indirect; may be given verbally
Employee acknowledgment and possible rebuttal	Employee acknowledges receipt; may rebut in writing	Employee acknowledges receipt; may rebut verbally	Employee does not see or sign formal appraisal; would rarely rebut
How praised?	Individually	Individually	Given to entire group
Motivators	Money, upward mobility, career development	Loyalty to self, family, village, tribe, concentric circles outward	Money, promotion, loyalty to supervisor

[a]Characteristics of the Saudi Arabian approach to appraisal come from Harris & Moran (1990).

all legally required benefits (e.g., by country), as well as the equity of benefits as measured against other similar categories of employees both internal as well as external to the organization (Block, 1992). Corporations must carefully examine their underlying compensation philosophy and objectives. For example, what is the compensation system trying to accomplish? What are employees truly rewarded for doing? The challenge is to design a program that is consistent with the philosophy and objectives of the organization.

Tax effectiveness is becoming a major consideration in international employee benefit and compensation planning. Multinational corporations must follow economic and legislative issues in all their countries of operation and must provide valuations and related information to ensure compliance with domestic and local regulations. Most global corporations provide many benefits and incentives to employees who work on foreign assignments (e.g., hardship allowances, housing and utilities differentials, education allowances for children, cost-of-living adjustments). However, foreign countries usually tax income earned by expatriates and third-country personnel within their jurisdiction. This practice means that employees may be taxed twice on the same income and also taxed on all allowances.

To deal with the tax jeopardy issue, the two most common types of income tax policies that employers use are tax *equalization,* in which employees pay a fixed tax amount, and tax *protection,* in which an upper limit is set on the tax employees must pay. Companies can save tax money by changing the way compensation is administered (e.g., current versus deferred), the source of compensation (country of payment), and the timing of compensation (Stuart, 1991). The issue of retirement benefits for international transferees must be considered as an integral part of the compensation and benefits strategy designed to foster the globalization process.

A synthesized international compensation policy might provide a percentage of home country salary, plus the higher amount either of a percentage of host country salary or of the amount required in host country currency to maintain a home country standard of living in the host location. A funded, tax-deferred foreign service allowance calculated to reflect the difference between host country and home country pay levels may also be provided. In addition, some multinationals offer a long-term benefits plan for initial transfers or an international long-term benefits plan for long-term transfers that is related to the home country (Anderson, 1990).

The taxation laws and regulations of the host country play an important part in human resource management. Countries that extended tax equalization privileges for a limited number of years may force organizations to repatriate experienced employees prematurely.

Although most companies have not attempted to force all their employees worldwide into the same compensation package, there has been an increased interest in extending stock ownership of the parent company to worldwide employees. It is difficult to extend a U.S.–based, qualified employee stock ownership plan (ESOP), with its favorable U.S. tax consequences, to foreign employees because of the varying laws in each country. However, many foreign employees would rather face the adverse tax consequences in their local jurisdictions than not have company stock offered to them. As a result of such demand, several U.S.–owned multinationals have established U.S.–based ESOPs and offered them to employees in Europe and the Far East. In general, however, a U.S.–owned multinational is willing to extend such benefits only if it receives a U.S. tax benefit either directly or indirectly from its ESOP contributions (Gibson & Burmeister, 1990).

If incentive compensation continues to prevail in the United States, and we fully expect that it will, many companies will export these plans overseas to cover their expatriates, third-country nationals, and local nationals. Doing so could prove to be an expensive mistake. Before implementing any plan, firms need to resolve questions that may arise because of foreign securities laws, foreign exchange control laws, income taxes for the employee, and income taxes for the employer. Incentive plans must be designed to reinforce common global or regional strategies and objectives. Again, what do you want your compensation plan to accomplish?

Compensation plans must also be consistent with the culture of the workforce. In some (perhaps many) foreign cultures, U.S.–style incentives based on the performance of individual employees run counter to traditional norms concerning acceptable behavior (that is, group orientation).

Rewards, including incentives, are only one component of the international human resource management system. Moreover, it may be that the more successful an organization is with its other human resource functions, the less attention it needs to give incentives. The organization that hires the best available workers, provides training when and where it is needed, and provides a sound compensation package and quality management may not need an incentive program. Individuals may already be working at maximum productivity levels. Two final issues we address very briefly are the emerging trend toward company involvement in work and family and the involvement of the HR function in responding to external crises.

Increasing Company Involvement in Work and Family

To attract and retain employees, global corporations need to address several demographic and sociological changes in the altered nature of their workforces (Howard, 1991). To remain competitive, businesses need to focus on specific segments of their workforce. Demographic studies worldwide show increasing numbers of women and racial and ethnic minorities entering the labor force. Many of these new entrants are immigrants or migrant workers. For example, events such as the collapse of the former Soviet empire in

Central and Eastern Europe, the civil war in the former Yugoslavia, and the large disparity in standards of living even within the twelve countries of the European community (e.g., Spain, Portugal, and Ireland compared to Germany, Denmark, and the Netherlands) have accelerated cross-border migration. Thousands of Russian Jews have emigrated to Israel, and as a result of the Persian Gulf War, large numbers of emigres have streamed into such countries as Jordan and Turkey. Large numbers of refugees, many of whom are fleeing political persecution in Latin America (e.g., El Salvador), Southeast Asia (e.g., Cambodia, Vietnam), and China, continue to arrive in the United States every year.

Although balancing work and family life always has been a problem for working women, only recently have organizations begun to recognize the need to develop new work structures and policies to assist employees in integrating their work and family roles more effectively (Zedeck, 1992). As more organizations acknowledge the reality of the changing workforce and its changing values, rigidity is giving way to flexibility. The most popular family-responsive programs and policies in the United States fall into four major categories: (1) dependent care, (2) parental leave, (3) spouse relocation and job locator programs, and (4) flexible work arrangements such as alternative work schedules and locations, flextime, job sharing, and part-time work. Responsiveness to family concerns of employees is not simply a matter of social justice but an essential investment in the bottom line (Maier, Thompson, & Thomas, 1991). The ability of the organization both to satisfy and to motivate the workforce depends on human resource practices and benefits being consistent with the social and family values of the employees.

Crisis Management and the HRM Function

When Iraq invaded Kuwait in 1990, human resources professionals employed by multinationals operating in the Middle East were placed in new key roles for which few were prepared. They were required to concentrate on the well-being of their workforces, but they also needed to address compensation and benefits issues, reassignment and legal matters, as well as health, safety, and security issues. The primary crisis-management roles of all human resource professionals were those of record keeper, crisis management team member, communicator, and contributing writer to the emergency plan. In a survey of companies operating in the Middle East at that time, all companies reported providing professional counseling to assist employees and their families deal with psychological problems associated with a hostage or evacuation situation (Williamson, 1991). Global corporations spend approximately 1 to 2 percent of their revenues on protection against terrorism. It is critical for international human resource managers to be prepared for this crisis management role.

Conclusion

We began this chapter by pointing out that a critical determinant of an organization's success in international business is the management of its human resources. At a more fundamental level, there is a perpetual need for closer links between corporate strategy and human resource management. Changes in strategy have significant implications for staffing (e.g., international strategic alliances), training and development, performance appraisal, and compensation (including benefits). New technology, for example, has accelerated the need for managing effectively the interface between technology, cultural differences, and human resources in the workplace.

We also noted that a major difference between domestic and international human resource management is increased involvement by the organization in the personal lives of employees. Although this affects almost all functional areas within HRM (e.g., orientation, staffing, compensation), it is nowhere more obvious than in the final two sections of this chapter: (1) increasing company involvement in work and family issues, and (2) crisis management by human resource managers. In closing, it is appropriate to keep in mind the words of a senior international executive: "Virtually any type of international problem, in the final analysis, is either created by people or must be solved by people. Hence, having the right people in the right place at the right time emerges as the key to a company's international growth. If we are successful in solving that problem, I am confident that we can cope with all others."[1]

References

Anderson, J. B. (1990, July/August). Compensating your overseas executives, Part 2: Europe. *Compensation & Benefits Review* 22: 25–35.

Bailey, E. K., and Cotlar, M. (1993). Managing globally with technology. *Leadership and Organizational Development Journal* 14: 21–24.

Bailey, E. K., and Shenkar, O. (1993). Management education for international joint venture managers. *Leadership and Organizational Development Journal* 14: 15–20.

Bauserman J. (1992, August 4). Instructor Training Manager, United Airlines, Denver. Personal communication.

Black, J. S. (1989). Locus of control, social support, stress, and adjustment in international transfers. *Asia Pacific Journal of Management* 7: 1–29.

---

[1]Quoting Dueer, in Greene, P. E. & Walls, G. D. (1984). Human resources: Hiring internationally. *Personnel Administrator, 29*(7), p. 61.

Black, S., and Mendenhall, M. (1991). A practical but theory-based framework for selecting cross-cultural training methods. *Academy of Management Journal* 15: 113–136.

Block, L. (1992). Benefits abroad a vexing problem. *U.S. Business Insurance* 26: 23–25.

Brod, C. (1984) *Technostress.* Boston, MA: Addison-Wesley.

Campbell, N. (1991, 4th Quarter). How Japanese multinationals work so well. *PRISM,* 61–69.

Cascio, W. F. (1991, September). *International assessment and the globalization of business: Riddle or recipe for success?* Keynote address prepared for the National Assessment Conference, Minneapolis, MN.

Cascio, W. F. (1992). *Managing Human Resources: Productivity, Quality of Work Life, Profits.* New York: McGraw-Hill.

Cascio, W. F. (1993). International human resource management issues for the 1990s. *Asia-Pacific Journal of Human Resource Management* 30: 1–18.

Cascio, W. F., and Serapio, M. G., Jr. (1991, Winter). Human resources systems in an international alliance: The undoing of a done deal? *Organizational Dynamics:* 63–74.

Culture shock at home: Working for a foreign boss. (1990, December 17). *Business Week:* 80–84.

Dowling, P. J., and Schuler, R. S. (1990). *International Dimensions of Human Resource Management.* Boston: PWS–Kent.

Eshgi, G. (1985). Nationality bias and performance evaluations in multinational corporations. *National Academy of Management Proceedings,* p. 85.

Galbraith, J., and Elstrom, A. (1976, Summer). International transfer of managers—Some important policy considerations. *Columbia Journal of World Business:* 44–55.

Gattiker, U. E. (1990). *Technology Management in Organizations.* London: Sage Publications.

Gibson, V. L., and Burmeister, E. D. (1990, July). America-Based ESOPs get a worldwide look. *Pension World* 26: 22–23.

Greene, P. E., and Walls, G. D. (1984). Human resources: Hiring internationally. *Personnel Administrator* 29: 61.

Harris, P. R., and Moran, R. T. (1990). *Managing Cultural Differences* (3rd ed.). Houston: Gulf Publishing.

Hoerr, J. P., Nathans, L., and Armstrong L. (1990, December 17). Culture shock at home: Working for a foreign boss. *Business Week,* 80–84.

Howard, P. D. (1991). World shrink. *HR Magazine* 36: 42–43.

If you can't beat 'em. (1992, July 27). *Time,* p. 23.

Jacobs, D. L. (1990, September 10). U.S. culture trips Japanese firms. *The Denver Post,* p. A10.

Laabs, J. (1991). The global talent search. *Personnel Journal* 70: 38–42, 44.

Maier, M., Thompson, C., and Thomas, C. (1991). Corporate responsiveness (and resistance) to work-family interdependence in the United States. *Equal Opportunities International* 10: 25–32.

Main, J. (1990, December 17). Making global alliances work. *Fortune,* 121–122.

Marquardt, M. J., and Engel, D. W. (1993). *Global Human Resource Development.* Englewood Cliffs, NJ: Prentice Hall.

Mendenhall, M. S., and Oddou, G. (1988, September-October). The overseas assignment: A practical look. *Business Horizons:* 78–84.

Miles, R. E., and Snow, C. C. (1984). Fit, failure, and the hall of fame. *California Management Review* 26: 10–28.

Milliman, J. F., and Von Glinow, M. A. (1991). Strategic international human resources: Prescription for MNC success. In K. Rowland (Ed.), *Research in personnel and human resources management,* Supplement 22: 21–35. Greenwich, CT: JAI Press.

Milliman, J. F., Von Glinow, M. A., and Nathan, M. (1991). Organizational life cycles and strategic international human resource management in multinational companies: Implications for congruence theory. *Academy of Management Review:* 318–339.

Nauman, E. (1993). Organizational predictors of expatriate job satisfaction. *Journal of International Business Studies* 24: 61–80.

Oddou, G. R., and Mendenhall, M. E. (1991, January/February). Succession planning for the 21st century: How well are we grooming our future business leaders? *Business Horizons* 34: 26–34.

Ricks, D. A. (1993). *Blunders in International Business.* Cambridge, MA: Blackwell.

Saraph, J. V., and Sebastian, R. J. (1992). Human resources strategies for effective introduction of advanced manufacturing technologies. *Production & Inventory Management Journal* 33: 65–70.

Schuler, R. S., Dowling, P. J., and De Cieri, H. (1993). An integrative framework of strategic international human resource management. *International Journal of Human Resource Management* 4: 711–764.

Scullion, H. (1991). Why companies prefer to use expatriates. *Personnel Management* 23: 32–35.

Shenkar, O., and Zeira, Y. (1987). Human resources management in international joint ventures: Directions for research. *Academy of Management Review* 12: 546–557.

Stuart, P. (1991, October). Global payroll—A taxing problem. *Personnel Journal* 70: 80–90.

Teagarden, M., and Von Glinow, M. (1990). Contextual determinants of HRM effectiveness in cooperative alliances: Mexican evidence. *International Management Review* 30: 23–36.

Tung, R. L. (1981) Selection and training of personnel for overseas assignments. *Columbia Journal of World Business* 16: 68–78.

Williamson, H. (1991, November). In harm's way. *HR Magazine* 36: 55–59.

Yuen, E. C. (1991). Human resource management in high- and medium-technology companies. *International Journal of Manpower* 12: 10–20.

Zachary, G. P. (1992, July 29). Getting help: High-tech firms find it's good to line up outside contractors. *The Wall Street Journal,* A1; A6.

Zammuto, R. F., & O'Connor, E. J. (1992). Gaining advanced manufacturing technologies' benefits: The roles of organization design and culture. *Academy of Management Review* 17: 701–728.

Zedeck, S. (1992). *Work, Families, and Organizations.* San Francisco: Jossey-Bass.

Zeeman, J. R. (1987, November 14). Service, the cutting edge of global competition: What United Airlines is learning in the Pacific. Speech presented at the Academy of International Business, Chicago, IL.

Zeien, A. (1991, 4th Quarter). International, multinational, and/or global? *PRISM,* 85–88.

Zeira, Y., and Shenkar, O. (1986). Personnel decision-making in wholly owned foreign subsidiaries and in international joint ventures. Working Paper No. 45, Geneva, Switzerland, ILO.

Employment and Labor Law Considerations in International Human Resource Management

Ronald C. Brown   University of Hawaii at Manoa

Introduction: The Legal Aspects of Global Labor Management

The CEO had just returned from the new overseas project. Among the waiting list of phone calls for him to return were several to the company's labor lawyer. Although he had been gone only two weeks, a spate of messages stated that the overseas activities had already generated personnel questions under U.S. law and under foreign law. Specifically, management in the overseas operation reported that a sex harassment complaint would soon be filed by an employee who held a U.S. "green card," and it wanted to know whether U.S. Equal Employment Opportunity (EEO) laws applied to those operations.

Also, the overseas management is about to hire a number of local employees in preference to U.S.-based employees (who had requested to transfer per contractual seniority rights) because of its inability to obtain a sufficient number of visas to permit the transfer. The U.S. union is claiming this would violate the seniority and transfer provisions of its collective bargaining agreement. Additionally, the overseas operation reports that local authorities claim that under local law these newly hired local employees could not easily be terminated or have their employment rights modified by a negotiated settlement or arbitration.

And finally, the overseas management reports that news stories are suggesting that its operations and its suppliers are involved in using prison labor to keep down the labor costs. It is asking whether this is only a P.R. problem or whether it has legal implications?

These questions are real and involve such companies as Sears, United Airlines, and Sheraton Hotels; however, the kinds of legal questions arising under international human resource decisions are even more varied and can affect any size company involved in an overseas operation.

Employers increasingly are establishing operations and relationships throughout the world and looking to make international HRM decisions so as to remain globally competitive. The answer by affected employees, such as in a United Airlines case in which the employer allegedly gave hiring preference to Paris-based *employees* over U.S.–based *employees* with greater seniority rights under a collective bargaining agreement, was to go to court to enjoin the hiring decision. The union leadership stated "[W]e will continue to pursue all available avenues—whether in the courts, arbitration, at the bargaining table or in the political arena—to ensure that United's global desires do not provide an excuse for exporting jobs and depriving flight attendants of their legal rights."

Global competition drives business into every reach of the world. Choices made by foreign direct investors are often influenced by labor costs and government regulations. International human resource managers are increasingly confronted by foreign regulations that apply to their expatriate and local employees, as well as the U.S. labor regulations, which may bind them even in the overseas operation.

Just as U.S. labor laws are an important factor in operating a business in the United States, the increasing legalization occurring overseas, particularly in Asia, also affects operations on foreign soil. This blend of business necessity and legal requirements and the legal issues generated by global management decisions are discussed in this chapter. Within the legal framework of international human resource management there are recurring employment and labor relations issues that managers must identify and address. In this chapter, employment and labor relations regulations in the United States are considered as they apply to HRM policies of U.S. and foreign companies operating overseas and in the United States. Foreign labor regulations involved in FDI, particularly in Asia, including illustrations from Japan, South Korea, and the Peoples' Republic of China.

Businesses operating in the United States know very well the numerous labor laws and regulations that shape and influence human resource management decisions here. However, when these businesses are part of global operations—even in just one foreign country—these same issues can multiply potential legal concerns by a factor of at least four or five times. For example, the U.S.-based company must know and comply with (1) the U.S. labor laws; (2) the foreign laws as they may apply to U.S. citizens working on foreign soil; (3) the foreign laws as they may apply to foreign employees working for the parent and/or the foreign-based company; (4) the U.S. labor laws applied extraterritorially to U.S. citizens working for the foreign operation; (5) and finally, management must consider the applicability of the labor laws to its U.S.-based employees as equitably contrasted with the personnel policies accorded to the overseas-based employees working for the foreign-based operation. The 1991 Civil Rights Law's extension to extraterritorial locations and its provision for damages (including punitive damages) highlight the types of legal and management issues of increasingly vital concern to managers of international human resources.

Furthermore, "going global" raises many HRM–related business decisions that have legal implications. For example, foreign direct investors decide the business form—local incorporation, joint venture, branch office, and so on—and each form may invoke a different applicability of labor laws, as will be discussed. Likewise, the type of business operation (licensing, manufacturing, etc.) can affect the scope of applicable laws. Also, the choice of country, whether its status is that of an industrialized, developing, or socialist country, will invoke consideration of external factors that will influence and determine whether meaningful laws exist and how they will be applied to foreign operations.

However, meeting the requirements of foreign laws first necessitates assessment of how the parent company's global personnel policies and decisions are established and how they will be administered, so as to meet U.S. labor laws as they apply to foreign-based employees *and* how that relates to home-based employees' rights and benefits. For example, coordinating staffing opportunities, compensation, and benefits to induce and retain the "right" employees to work overseas may well have an impact on personnel at home operations, as will be discussed. The fact that the male manager of a Chrysler plant in Beijing makes 25 percent more than a female manager in Newark should be reviewed before the EEO office makes an inquiry.

Therefore, going global requires knowing the United States and foreign legal environment and how business decisions invoke legal regulations, whether their source be domestic, international, or foreign. Knowing these laws raises issues that affect HRM decisions. Informed international human resource managers understand that these legal considerations can be factored into the business decisions to provide fairness and to avoid unnecessary litigation in the United States and overseas. The key is to be informed, know the legal issues that need to be addressed, and to accommodate the law with the needs of boards of directors, management, employees, labor unions, and foreign governments.

A checklist or agenda items of the recurring variables affecting the legal issues and to which labor laws may apply include the following:

1. Who is the *employer*? What is the type of business entity established overseas (e.g., a joint venture), the type of operations (e.g., manufacturing or a representative office), and, its relationship to the U.S.–based operation (e.g., a controlled subsidiary).
2. Who is the *employee*? Not only is the nationality of the employee possibly significant but also the actual employment relationship. For whom does the employee actually work (e.g., one of the parties to a joint venture [foreign or local] or the joint venture itself)?

3.   What are the types of HRM practices in question and what is *the applicable* labor law—U.S. or foreign? For example, recruitment and selection, performance evaluation, training and development, compensation, and labor relations may normally involve foreign law where the overseas operation is located, yet as indicated, they may also involve U.S. laws.

Depending on the type of international HRM activity and who the *employer* and the *employee* are, U.S. laws may apply extraterritorially or only to the U.S.–based employees. Or U.S. laws, in relationship with international laws and treaties, may be affected. This could undermine the continued economic feasibility of such overseas operations. For example, using prison labor could help bring about the forfeiture of a country's most favored nation (MFN) import preference status and the elimination of U.S. government subsidies, thus removing much of the competitive advantage for locating there. These same legal issues likewise can be raised about the possible applicability of foreign labor laws to overseas operations.

U.S. Labor and Employment Law Applied to Global Operations

To identify items of legal importance under foreign law when doing business overseas, a brief overview of U.S. labor and employment law is described in three parts: (1) U.S. labor regulatory system applicable to U.S. businesses; (2) the regulatory system's application to foreign direct investors in the United States; and (3) the extraterritorial application of U.S. labor laws applied to U.S. companies doing business overseas.

United States Labor and Employment Law

United States labor law affecting human resource management largely arises from two sources: common law and statutes (with corresponding government regulations and enforcement agencies). Business corporations are incorporated under statutes and enter into contractual relationships enforced by the courts under principles of common law. Likewise, they may enter into employment contracts with employees at all levels and geographic locations of the business. In addition, local, state, and federal labor statutes provide certain rights, protections, labor standards, and benefits to employees, sometimes depending on their positions. These labor laws may also place obligations on employers, sometimes depending on the size or type of business.

These labor and employment laws are implicated in overseas operations in at least two ways. First, there are always parity and fairness issues about whether disparate group or individual benefits for employees in both foreign and host locations meet legal requirements. For example, pay, hiring, promotion, training, or travel reimbursement disparities between managers of foreign and local operations may demand that the employer justify the differences, sometimes by validated tests, under EEO laws.

Likewise the National Labor Relations Act (NLRA) protects collective bargaining and the contract rights arising thereunder. For example, there may be contract rights for pensions and benefits or transfer rights to overseas locations. In the United Airlines case mentioned earlier, such rights were arguably violated when the number of French visas were restricted and the employer bypassed contractual seniority limitations. Also, the NLRA may require the U.S. employer to bargain to impasse before moving a significant portion of its operations to an overseas location. Of course, the applicability of these laws may vary depending on the relationship between local and foreign operations and whether the overseas operation falls within the proper legal definitions of "employer."

U.S. Labor Laws Applied to Foreign Direct Investors

Choices as to the form of business determine whether and to what extent U.S. labor laws apply to foreign direct investors in the United States. In 1982 the U.S. Supreme Court in *Sumitomo Shoji America, Inc.* v. *Avagliano* (457 U.S. 176) held that a foreign wholly owned subsidiary *incorporated in the United States* was subject to the U.S. labor laws. It further held the Friendship, Commerce, and Navigation (FCN) Treaty between the United States and Japan (similar to that with many other nations), which removed certain executive personnel decisions from application of antidiscrimination laws, was inapplicable because by locally incorporating, the corporation was no longer a "foreign" corporation that qualified.

The decision by the Supreme Court, however, left open many related questions, such as the potential defenses or liabilities, if any, of the foreign parent corporation (or the local corporation's ability to raise defenses on behalf of the foreign parent), and what application of U.S. labor laws, if any, there would be over certain foreign executive positions if the foreign direct investor used a business form other than local incorporation. For example, an unincorporated division of a U.S. corporation, wholly owned by a Japanese company, was able to use the FCN Treaty defense of its foreign parent (*Fortino* v. *Quasar,* 950 F.2d 389 [7th Cir. 1991]. Therefore, questions remain as to the full applicability of U.S. labor laws to foreign direct investors who use the business forms of unincorporated divisions, branches, and representative offices of foreign companies.

Likewise, a global employer setting up operations overseas can be similarly affected by local laws providing or removing the applicability of local labor laws, depending on the business *form* used, such as a representative or branch office, or locally incorporated. However, often most important is the *actual* relationship that exists between the home-based parent employer and the overseas operation and whether the parent actually controls those operations.

A related business decision affecting the scope of U.S. labor laws applied, deals with the *type* of required business operation; that is, whether, for example, it is in manufacturing, licensing, or sales. United States labor laws apply differently depending on the nature of the business. For example, a licensing operation may involve executive employees who are exempt from the overtime or minimum wage laws; OSHA may be irrelevant, and there may not be nonmanagement "employees" to qualify for unionization under the NLRA. The point is that even though U.S. labor laws are technically potentially applicable to the foreign direct investor, as a result of management decisions regarding the type of business operation, many U.S. labor and employment laws may not be of concern. Global managers likewise can, to some extent, control and anticipate issues of applicability of foreign labor laws, depending on their business choices, when doing business globally.

Of further concern to foreign direct investors in the United States may be the geographic location of the business operation. Location is often dictated by marketing and business necessity, but some foreign investors have sought to locate in regions of the United States, such as in "Right to Work States," where the labor laws, although permitting unionization, likely will not be used because of perceived local antiunion attitudes.

Last, foreign direct investors consider the likely enforceability of a country's laws. How serious is the government's restriction on the use of foreign labor or the monitoring of child labor, overtime, and OSHA requirements? Whether the government or complainants can easily litigate and secure sizeable remedies is certainly viewed as a cost of doing business. Therefore, not only the law but also its likely enforceability are of concern to foreign direct investors in the United States and to U.S.–based global managers doing business abroad.

Extraterritorial Application of U.S. Labor Laws

Although some U.S. labor laws extend to certain global operations and provide legal rights and obligations for employees and employers operating in foreign locations, most do not. Generally speaking, most U.S. laws regulate only the U.S. operations of the U.S.–based parent company, although, as a practical matter they may strongly direct the human resource managers to coordinate and create generally parallel employment packages for its employees at home and abroad, particularly if overseas employees rotate back into the parent company's operations. For example, the National Labor Relations Act requires unionized employers to bargain over management decisions to relocate and shift work from U.S. locations when such shifts substantially displace U.S. workers. In addition, the 1988 Worker Adjustment and Retraining Notification Act (WARN) requires advance notification to affected employees of U.S. plant closures. This again underscores the legal significance of whether the overseas connection is part of the global U.S. employer's operations or merely a foreign corporation with whom it is doing business.

Notable exceptions exist in the area of antidiscrimination legislation that is extended extraterritorially. Laws that prohibit discrimination on the basis of age, race, color, sex, handicap, national origin, or religion are applicable to certain employees working in global operations. In 1984, the Age Discrimination Employment Act (ADEA) defined *employee* to include citizens of the United States employed by an employer in a workplace in a foreign country. *Employer* was defined to include (1) a U.S. firm, (2) a foreign branch of a U.S. firm, or (3) a foreign corporation controlled by a U.S. firm. Furthermore, where an employer controls the foreign corporation, even the acts of the foreign incorporated entity are deemed to be the acts of the employer.

This legislation thus seeks to prevent the American parent company from circumventing the law by incorporating its subsidiaries in foreign countries. In determining whether the U.S. company controls the foreign entity, tests for common law control are used including (1) interrelationship of operations, (2) common management, (3) centralized control of labor relations, and (4) common ownership or financial control. An interesting legal question is whether a complaining employee can directly sue not only the U.S. firm but also the controlled foreign entity, either solely or as a codefendant. The law on this point does not provide obvious guidance or limits.

Congress did, however, place limits on the law's extraterritorial application by limiting it to *U.S. citizens* (though, arguably, noncitizen employees can be counted for purposes of attaining the required minimum number of employees for the law's application). Also, its application is limited if compliance would violate the laws of the country in which the workplace is located.

The primary U.S. labor law extended extraterritorially is the Civil Rights Act of 1991 (CRA) and also the Americans with Disabilities Act of 1990 (ADA). Overturning a recent U.S. Supreme Court case that did not extend Title VII of the Civil Rights Act of 1964 (as amended), the law, by Section 109, explicitly paralleled the ADEA and applied the law to citizen–employees working in extraterritorial locations for the covered "employer," including foreign companies controlled by the U.S.–based company. It too is limited in its application where compliance would violate local laws. Perhaps the point of greatest interest to global employers is that these laws explicitly permit an increased scope of remedies including attorney fees, expert witness costs, and punitive damages.

A final substantive implication of the extraterritorial application of U.S. discrimination laws is its impact on U.S.–based operations. Because the laws apply to both locations, there is the obvious need to approach international

HRM decisions in an evenhanded and fair way and to have documentable reasons for selection and assignment of personnel to foreign locations. Also, there must be justifications for compensation disparities between employees at the U.S. location versus the overseas location. The legal issues thicken as one considers the impact of U.S. legal obligations on foreign operations when disparities are created with host country nationals in terms of selection, opportunity, or compensation. Does this create violations under foreign law? Can U.S. citizen employees also sue under the foreign laws? How does one decide whether the foreign law will be violated by compliance with the U.S. labor law? And finally, when will the U.S. law be excused when there is "compliance" with the foreign law?

These thorny and multiple legal issues raised by U.S. labor laws, as applied to parent company operations and to extraterritorially controlled foreign operations, raise the need for international human resource managers to consider carefully how the business choices and labor and personnel policies of global business have an impact on or are directed by U.S. labor laws—even and, especially, overseas. As mentioned, even the choice of extending business overseas can trigger application of U.S. labor laws. The National Labor Relations Act obligates unionized employers to bargain over management's decision to relocate to overseas locations if such decisions will displace U.S. workers. Likewise, choosing the business entity, using subsidiaries, engaging in joint ventures, involving third parties, investing capital, changing operations—all will affect how the U.S. labor laws apply and obligate the global employer to direct its operations.

International Labor and Employment Law Affecting Global Operations

International Labor Law and Labor Standards

As the hands of foreign direct investment reach out into various regions of the globe, serious consideration must be given to how law outside the United States, either international or foreign, may affect global operations. Business managers must understand what "law" is and is not, and what the "legal cultures" are, and the legal influences, obligations, and practical restraints affecting regulation of operations. Particular local legal sources can include influences from historic or colonial periods (such as American labor law in Japan), traditions of civil versus common law, as well as secular versus religious laws.

In addition to these local sources of foreign law, there are also international and regional sources of law, labor standards, and influences affecting global operations. The primary sources of international labor law standards, in addition to treaties, are those emanating from the International Labor Organization (ILO), a specialized agency of the United Nations (UN), and the United Nations itself, which has established basic human rights covenants applicable to all member nations.

The ILO has adopted more than 170 conventions establishing labor standards dealing with numerous labor issues such as health and safety, unemployment, migrant workers, collective bargaining, social security, freedom of association, and employment of women and children. The conventions of the ILO are not binding obligations, however, until they are ratified by member states and thereafter enacted into local law.

The labor standards may also be indirectly enforced by particular trading countries under the international agreement of GATT (General Agreement on Tariffs and Trade). The GATT system establishes both administrative rules and a forum within which contracting parties may conduct trade negotiations and resolve trade disputes. It (1) requires these parties to conduct their trade on a nondiscriminatory basis; (2) requires, as between member parties, special tariff preferences—that is, the MFN (most favored nation) treatment; and (3) submits them to mechanisms for dispute resolution for adjudicating trade issues.

Some restrictions on international trade may be based on international labor standards not being met by particular countries. For example, Section 20(e) of GATT permits contracting parties to place restrictions on imports of products produced by prison labor. Although GATT has not yet accepted international fair labor standards as criteria for GATT trade restrictions, the matter continues to be debated. By contrast, the United States, through its Trade Act of 1974, permits the United States to decide whether to grant tariff preferences—generalized system of preferences (GSP)—based on a number of criteria, including the foreign trading country's maintenance of certain conditions pertaining to human rights and other labor standards.

Global operations may also be affected by the laws, regulations, labor standards, and practices of *regional organizations,* a notable example being the European Economic Community (EEC). Also, organizations such as the Organization for Economic Cooperation and Development (OECD) provide influential voluntary guidelines for multinational enterprises on a number of topics, including specific guidelines respecting enumerated labor standards.

Again, business managers must determine the applicability of these labor standards originating in regional or organizational institutions and decide whether they, like ILO conventions, require local adoption and implementation, or whether they, like U.S. federal law, apply automatically to all the covered states.

In sum, international labor law standards are a factor that must be considered when a company is operating in foreign countries. For example, if the raison d'être for FDI in the People's Republic of China (PRC) is to establish a cheap labor manufacturing base to export products from the

PRC to the United States and take advantage of the MFN reduced tariff rates, it is significant to know and understand international labor standards and their relationship to GATT, the Trade Act of 1974, and so on. That is, although the international labor standards established by the ILO and the UN will not be locally enforceable, because of absent acceptance and implementing legislation, these same standards may be used in treaties and under arrangements like GATT to create de facto economic restrictions on companies doing business in or with those countries that violate the standards. The result is that legal violations by the country can eliminate the tariff advantage that was the reason for operating there in the first place.

There is also the possible nonlegal effect of a real marketplace impact of such practices, as was discovered by Sears in the early 1990s when they were alleged to have a connection with the production and sale of prison-made goods. This led to a U.S.–PRC Memorandum of Understanding on August 7, 1992 that addressed the issue (and left the MFN provision intact). In 1994, President Clinton "de-linked" human rights (including many labor standards) with MFN considerations for China.

A final matter to consider, even when international labor standards are implemented by local law, is whether the local government administration meaningfully enforces the law inside the foreign country. It is not uncommon for some countries, especially developing countries, to adopt international standards for prestige and to gain international trading advantages but then to provide underfunded and lax enforcement of those laws and labor standards.

U.S. Laws Enforcing Internationally Recognized Labor Standards

U.S. laws that grant or deny trade preferences, guarantee overseas investment, permit trade sanctions and import restrictions conditioned on local recognition and observance of internationally recognized labor standards clearly and directly affect the global operations of private overseas business investors.

The primary law in this area is the U.S. Generalized System of Preferences (GSP), which is designed to promote international trade and economic development through increased exports from foreign countries by granting favorable tariff and custom rates to qualifying countries over specified products.

Another law promoting and supporting international development through overseas investment is the Overseas Private Investment Corporation Amendment Act of 1985 which created OPIC, an autonomous federal corporation that provides assistance, financial incentives and guarantees, and political risk insurance to overseas investors. The law prohibits OPIC assistance to investors in countries whose governments fail to adopt and implement internationally recognized labor standards as defined under the GSP Renewal Act of 1984. Also in an effort to meet the concerns of U.S. unions and to curb "capital flight" and loss of employment opportunities in the United States, the law further limits the availability of assistance in several instances: if the overseas investment is likely to cause a significant reduction in the number of employees in the United States or if it is likely to cause the investor to significantly reduce the number of its employees in the United States because of effective replacement of domestic production with foreign production of substantially the same product for the same market. Those limitations are of obvious concern in global operations and are an additional agenda item for overseas investors seeking financial support under OPIC. The limitations also raise a host of possible labor-related legal issues under the law as to their applicability and enforceability.

Other U.S. laws and agencies involved in enforcing internationally recognized labor standards that can affect overseas investors in global operations include the Export-Import Bank of the United States (Eximbank), an independent federal corporation that assists exports of U.S. origin or manufacture by providing financial aid (loans, credits, guarantees) to foreign buyers (governments or private entities) of certain products. Restrictions on assistance include prior certification by the U.S. State Department of a country's compliance with, or movements toward, certain internationally recognized labor standards.

In sum, international labor standards must be taken into account when operating under a foreign jurisdiction. Foreign investments can be significantly affected not only by local laws and conditions, but also those locally favorable business conditions may be used as a reason for U.S. laws to intervene to undermine and cut off investment services, loans, and guarantees under OPIC or Eximbank, or cause tariff preferences to be lost—all because of failure of the foreign country to meet the international labor standards.

Role of the Host Country's Laws

The most important law to consider in deciding whether to locate operations overseas is the law of the host country. Legal requirements imposing financial obligations for employee hiring, layoffs, or plant shutdowns; restrictions on management decisions on hiring, disciplining, and firing staff; and the difficulties of immigration laws permitting expatriates from the home country to work on foreign soil—all are important labor law considerations in successfully establishing operations in a foreign location.

Though each country is different, a common legal agenda can create a checklist of areas of inquiry that should be evaluated before commencing operations.

Begin by comparing local conditions with international labor standards. Although corporate human resource management practices normally do not raise legal liabilities under international labor standards, practical liabilities can befall a company that takes advantage of "too good a deal" in, for example, production or supply. The list of U.S.–based companies who have operated in China to reap the advantages of cheaper labor includes such familiar names as Sears and Nike. Events in the early 1990s suggesting that some companies may have been involved in production or supply from prison labor caused an international furor and raised a number of "legal" issues regarding MFN status and problems of importing such goods into the United States. These incidents generally created havoc with stockholders and customers "back home."

It is axiomatic that the choices of the global manager as to the type of business entity in the host country will invoke the applicability of different sets of that country's laws. As in the United States, the applicability of labor laws to a licensing operation may vary considerably from those affecting a branch office or a locally incorporated operation or a joint venture. Host country investment laws may require certain types of business entities, such as joint ventures or companies, to be 51 percent locally owned. The legal implications of these requirements is that a different labor law can apply to different business entities or to employees of each side of the joint venture—one for host country employers and employees and one for the FDIs. Or the labor law might cover foreign nationals under one set of labor laws and locals under another. Issues can arise as to who is the employer under the law—the local host country company, the foreign company or the joint venture entity—and what of their parent companies' liability? Related problems can arise in recruiting, hiring, and firing employees. Will the host country's immigration laws allow "expats" to enter the country and work (recall the possible extraterritorial application of U.S. laws to such persons).

These questions must be resolved to know who can be hired and whether disparate compensation systems are permitted, to name but two of many HRM problems.

In the PRC, though different legal entities may be established, specific labor laws normally attach to Chinese employees and another set to foreign employees. This situation can arise, for example, in a joint venture in which the Chinese partner supplies the local labor. Although the joint venture laws govern the joint venture itself and provide compensation minimums (150% of local rates) to the local employees, expatriates normally are not subject to all the domestic labor laws as are their Chinese co-employees. China's central government has promulgated a comprehensive new labor law, effective January 1, 1995, which will affect and reorder the labor law requirements for domestic and foreign employers. Even so, some flexibility remains with provincial and SEZ lawmakers, though their laws will require reexamination in view of the new labor law.

Interesting legal issues arise regarding non-Chinese employees as to (1) the applicability of domestic labor laws, and (2) the availability of the law and courts to resolve employment disputes under labor contracts. For example, under Guandong Province labor provisions, Article 2 states that it applies to "foreign investment enterprises" (FIE, including the "wholly for-eign-owned enterprise" or WFOE) and "to such of their employees as are hired from the Chinese party to the venture." Inasmuch as the FIE is the employer under Chinese law, discussed earlier, does that not mean that a WFOE as an FIE has no "Chinese party" and thus Article 2 is inapposite as to employees? Article 36 further states that foreign nationals need a work permit, and that "matters such as the employment, dismissal, work [pro-duction] task, labor remuneration and labor insurance of such employees shall be provided for in labor contracts," which are to be submitted to the local labor department as a matter of record.

Zhejiang Province labor regulations, Article 20, require foreign nationals of equity joint ventures to have their employment terms determined by the Board of Directors and provided in their labor contracts. Again, questions of the choice of law (and interpretations of applicable law) and the legal forum for employees who are also foreign citizens will be legal agenda items requir-ing attention under law and contract. In that regard, there are general central government laws that may decide many of these issues, such as the Foreign Economic Contract law (not to be confused with the domestic economic contract law) and the Civil Procedure Law (governing some settlements).

Beyond employer and employee concerns, recent Chinese laws and policies at the national level permit increased managerial choices in many of the traditional HRM areas of recruitment, wage determination, employee performance, and the like. Also, local regulations permit more discretion than at the national level. For example, Guangdong Province labor regula-tions state: "Foreign investment enterprises may determine on their own the establishment of their organization, the size of their staff, their labor wage scales and wage distribution plans."[1] In these situations, applicable Chinese law will be used for FIE employees (or at least for employees who are Chinese citizens) in enforcement of the labor contracts, which incorpo-rate domestic labor law requirements such as labor standards, labor insur-ance, the requirement of having a labor union. Of course, these laws will need to be reexamined under the new 1995 labor law.

In South Korea, as in other foreign locations, methods and choices of business operations and entities exist, each with their different legal implica-tions. Korean laws allow foreign investors several methods by which they may do business, such as by using a local agent, a representative office, a branch office (which constitutes a legal presence in South Korea), or by establishing a "company." Under South Korean law, four types of compa-nies are recognized, though the first two are closed by law to foreigners: partnership (*Hapmyung Hoesa*); limited partnership (*Hapcha Hoesa*); stock company (*Chusik Hoesa*); and, limited liability company (*Yuhan Hoesa*).

Nearly 90 percent of South Korean companies are stock companies, and foreign investors often choose this form of organization because it is similar

---

[1]Guangdong Province, Enterprise with Foreign Investment Labor Management Provisions, Article 4, effective May 1, 1989, vol. III, 6CLP, July 10, 1989, p. 50.

to U.S. corporations. There are no legal limitations on the percentage of foreign ownership, though government approval procedures are more stringent when ownership is over 50 percent, and certain industries are prohibited or restricted in permitting foreign investment.

The labor laws in South Korea apply to employers and employees in much the same way as in the United States. Therefore, a foreign investor may become an employer as a joint venturer, as a foreign subsidiary, or as a local corporation. Questions of whether U.S. labor laws apply extraterritorially are resolved through the usual control tests. Questions of whether and how labor laws apply to U.S. or foreign employees are resolved through application of South Korean labor law.

Even though one has an understanding of the applicable local labor laws, other legal problems can arise as to whether variations exist. For example, in the PRC, how do the relaxed special economic zones' regulations relate to those of the central government? Are treaty immunities to applicable labor laws available—such as the Friendship, Navigation, and Commerce Treaty's exception for certain executive personnel? Are those immunities available only to parent company nationals or also to third-country nationals employed by the parent company? The liability of the local company versus the liability (if any) of the parent company must also be resolved in terms of both labor issues and nonlabor issues such as taxes.

Regarding the extraterritorial applicability of U.S. labor laws, certain defenses exist—for example, if local law is inconsistent. Therefore, familiarity with local law becomes important for several reasons. Also important is knowledge that some inconsistent local laws may not be used as a defense. For example, products made by prison labor, a practice that may be locally permitted, still cannot be imported into the United States.

Last, consideration must be given to the level of enforcement of local labor laws. To what extent do nonlegal considerations affect legal enforceability in such areas as cultural (e.g., traditional role of women), political (e.g., influence of the dominant political party in judicial outcomes), or economic (e.g., as a developing country, economic development may be favored over labor standards or at least over their enforcement)? As stated earlier, some countries may pass labor laws to qualify for special tariff treatment under GATT or other treaties, but in fact they do not meaningfully enforce the laws. Japan may enforce labor laws by custom and by "administrative guidance" (e.g., the Sex Discrimination law omits enforcement provisions because "it expects" employers to obey the law. In South Korea, there is legal authority to establish minimum wages by industry, yet it is seldom used. And, unexpected paradoxes may exist; for example, in South Korea the law limits the regular work week to 44 hours, *unless* there is a labor-management contract that allows a 56-hour work week. As a further illustration, developing countries may permit labor unions but carefully regulate them to limit their power.

In conclusion, there are many agenda items on the list of labor laws to consider when operating in a foreign country. To some extent business choices can be made so as to invoke different sets of labor laws, but understanding and complying with the myriad of requirements will be by far the larger task.

Legal Considerations in International HRM

Which Laws and Legal Issues?

Global operations, like any business venture, cannot successfully operate without due consideration of the law and legal issues. Examining global legal issues should be like examining a diamond from all sides and realizing that flaws on one facet will diminish the value of the whole. Laws, like diamonds, have many faces. In deciding which laws are relevant, one can look primarily to two sources: the home country law and that of the foreign location.

Home country laws in the United States stem from several sources. First, the usual labor laws regulating employment and human resource management are dually applicable to all U.S.–based operations, both directly—including employees rotated or transferred abroad—and indirectly—in the comparison of benefits between home-based versus foreign-located employees of the U.S. global employer. A second source of U.S. labor law are those laws that have extraterritorial application, such as the civil rights laws, though such obligations might lawfully be displaced by applicable foreign laws. The third source of U.S. laws affecting global operations are those U.S.–based laws with international effect or influence. Examples are granting or denying financial assistance and guarantees to the overseas investor, permitting favorable tariffs to imported items from the foreign-located U.S. investor (among others), or giving government support to overseas buyers of U.S. products. The application of these laws to the global employer depends on the government in the foreign country where the employer is located, and using and regulating labor and labor conditions to meet international labor standards as embodied in some of these U.S. laws.

The labor and employment laws of the foreign country where the global employer is located also is a source of applicable laws. The laws may apply differently to different forms of business entities, distinguish between local and foreign citizens in granting rights and benefits, and where applicable, present possible defenses to the applicability of U.S. labor laws applied extraterritorially.

The *general* approach of Japanese law is to apply the same laws (as contrasted with the PRC's use of different laws), including labor laws, to foreign and Japanese business entities, including definitions of "employer" and "employee." However, this equal treatment approach can be affected by applicable immigration laws, visa limitations, and treaty provisions.

Similar to the U.S. approach, Japanese labor laws usually accord obligations and rights to employers and employees. The Japanese laws tend to have a more expansive view of "employees." They include numbers of positions that in the United States (e.g., under the NLRA) would be categorized as management or supervision. The legal implications of such categories on HRM is worth serious consideration because it has an impact on EEO, labor relations, and so on, as well as on the basic concept of authority as to who speaks and acts for the "employer."

Determining the sources and coverage of labor laws and employment regulations is no small undertaking; however, even that task can be dwarfed by the need thereafter to consider the applicability of the laws, their conflicts, and the legal issues they generate. These legal issues must be understood before global employment and HRM policies may effectively be placed into operation. After deciding *what* laws apply (i.e., whose law and which laws?), attention must be turned to the content and likely enforceability of those laws and the legal issues they generate within the usual categories of HRM: recruitment and selection, performance evaluations, training and development, compensation, and labor relations.

Legal Issues and Agenda Items of International HRM

Recruitment and Selection. Finding the right personnel for foreign assignments involves several issues depending on the variables of size, nature of operations, and so on, as well as the type of foreign country—industrialized, developing, and the like. For example, FDI in the PRC likely will take advantage of cheaper labor costs, and a local work force may be hired with an emphasis on a largely local supervisory staff. To establish a representative trading operation, an FDI in Japan may involve more management personnel from the home country.

Selection, recruitment, and performance evaluation are areas of HRM in China that were early perceived to be obstacles to successful foreign investment. Complaints were heard about Chinese worker discipline and worker productivity cutting against the advertised benefits of cheap labor and the historic practice of the "iron bowl," which traditionally provided continuing employment notwithstanding work performance. Legal regulations evolved, particularly after 1986, which to an increasing degree and in various forms of business entities, permitted greater managerial control over recruitment and selection. Advertising, raiding other employers, using local labor bureaus, and even conducting open interviews and testing have become more usual. Recent government regulations have sought to outlaw the "secret laws," which were often nonexistent or brought out to influence negotiations. However, bureaucratic realities of using government labor bureaus, of finding skilled workers, of obtaining the "release" of trained workers from other work units, and being able to discipline and possibly discharge an employee are all issues to be dealt with under a layer of legal regulations. China's new labor law, effective January 1, 1995, will clarify as well as increase some of the obligations of employers regarding human resource decisions.

The rules and regulations can vary by province, special economic zone, (SEZ), coastal city, or municipality. For example, Guandong labor regulations provide in Articles 4–8 the recruitment procedures to follow, the sources that can be tapped, the uses of labor, and the requirements and conditions of those employed, including training and probationary periods. The practical aspects of working with appropriate government agencies, trade unions, and other organizations have been performed quite successfully by some companies, notably, Kentucky Fried Chicken in Beijing.

Of course, foreign employees can be brought in by the locally based enterprise, but regulations normally require a work permit and appropriate immigration status. The importation of foreign employees can be a sensitive local issue, and it is often an area covered in initial negotiations under the appropriate business entity law and resulting contracts.

In local operations in Japan, recruitment and staffing issues must first fit into the global management's decisions regarding business entity and coordination with parent company policies. However, in implementing those decisions within the obligations of local labor laws, some differences in approach from those used in China will be required. For example, open recruitment by newspaper ads may be regarded as only "inviting strangers." Emphasis on word-of-mouth referrals, hiring only men, or recruiting on the right college campuses might be the local practice. The ultimate selection may necessitate background checks and determinations about attitudes of potential employees regarding work habits, unions, family plans, and so on.

Most of these approaches are common in Japan and do not violate Japanese labor laws. For example, the sex discrimination law applies not to applicants but to employees. However, even then there may not be meaningful enforcement mechanisms for most of its provisions. Still, concerns can be raised about the possible impact such HRM decisions might have under U.S. labor laws—as applied to U.S. citizens at home or those based extraterritorially. Selection of local managers on the basis of citizenship, national origin, age, sex, and union preferences may provide business advantages, but it may also raise legal issues under Japanese and U.S. labor law.

Personnel choices are often divided into management and labor; the latter are usually hired locally. An important number of home country management staff may need to be recruited depending on business requirements, but how those choices are made, the incentives provided, and the compensation awarded are all governed by U.S. labor laws. Whether local customs regarding choices of personnel, such as religious, racial, or sexual preferences may be considered, may also depend on the foreign law (as a possible defense to U.S. law) and the extent to which it mandates discrimination of this kind. If expatriates are to be used, requirements of foreign immigration laws must be met. Also, some executives and professional staff may be exempted from certain foreign labor laws under treaty provisions, such as the Friendship, Commerce, and Navigation Treaty (FCNT) discussed earlier.

When promotions, transfers, and other benefits, including travel, compensation, and the like, are held out in the recruitment process as available to all "employees," considerations must be given the U.S. EEO laws, as well as local laws, at least as applied to the U.S. citizen employees. When overseas relocation of operations adversely affects the level of employment in the home-based operations, certain U.S. labor laws may be triggered, such as those of the NLRA and WARN.

When hired employees—U.S. and foreign—work side by side doing similar work, questions can be raised as to which country's legal standards apply. These issues are resolved by examining the laws and by determining how the employment relations are structured. That is, who is the "employer" and who are "employees" under the various applicable laws?

Managers of international operations obviously are trying to select the best qualified people on the basis of nonlegal considerations of personality, ability, family situation, compensation need, and proper mix and interface with host country nationals. However, it should be underscored that there are monetary as well as moral incentives to give legal consideration to staff selection (e.g., the new civil rights law of 1991 permits far-reaching remedies, including punitive damages).

Performance Evaluation. An integral part of HRM is performance evaluation, and coordination of domestic and foreign employment policies is required. The key to understanding the legal issues in this area involves performance *standards* and *uses* of the evaluations based on the standards, both in the foreign location and in comparison with home-based operations. Again, ultimate decisions will depend on legal definitions of "employer" and "employee."

The legal issues raised by standards for performance evaluations depend on *whose* standards are applied *where?* Does the foreign operation use its own standards, those of the home company, or a global operations standard? And to whom are they applicable—home country versus foreign nationals, management versus workers? The main factors to be used, from a legal point of view, are those of fairness and defensibility. That is, are there legitimate, provable reasons upon which standards are based and used? When productivity of managers is not measured by merit because of local conditions, are the same or similar criteria used at the U.S. plant locations? And, if not, are the differences justifiable?

In foreign countries, customs regarding age, seniority, and sex of employees may affect labor pools and the selection process and may become a factor in evaluation, especially when foreign managers are used. One must determine the degree to which U.S. and local laws control those employees. The effect of any decisions taken under those laws on other employees located in both the host country and the United States must be considered.

Performance evaluation can also raise legal issues, largely under EEO laws, when one uses the results of performance ratings to see who needs training, discipline, compensation increases or decreases, and qualification for promotions or transfers. These business choices can affect basic interests and rights of employees. If favoritism or unfairness is perceived, disputes will arise under local and U.S. labor laws.

Therefore, who establishes the standards and who evaluates them can be legally significant. Employment tests in the United States under civil rights laws may need to be validated if there are adverse effects on legally protected employees. Are the same or different tests to be used overseas? What role, if any, is played by the home office or the local labor union in creating standards or using them? Are there local legal limitations, and is there an employment contract or labor union agreement that affects their use? Does a local government labor bureau perform the testing function before an applicant is referred to the employer?

An example of how such legal concerns can appear and possibly be bypassed by overriding business considerations is as follows. A global company has operations in several overseas locations to enhance its flexibility and competitive advantage. Because of declining sales, cutbacks in operations are called for, and a choice must be made about whom to lay off. If laws, regulations, and contracts in one country require large severance payments or unemployment compensation benefits, the employer may well choose the cheapest alternative, notwithstanding performance evaluations of the respective work forces. Does that violate any local legal requirements? If employees have strong unions and are likely to strike, labor relations considerations will also play role.

Where individual cutbacks are required, performance standards, seniority, and legal requirements will all play a part in the decision, with possible legal issues arising along the way. For example, what are the legal obligations of the U.S.–based parent "employer" when a Beijing "employee" of a subsidiary in a PRC–based joint venture argues that she was laid off because of her gender?

Training and Development.   A number of variables affect management's choices regarding training and development programs. Basic among them are whether the overseas programs will be integrated with or separate from that of the parent company. There will be questions about career development opportunities and techniques of training, about who does the training, who receives the training and where, and who pays for it. The important point here, from a legal perspective, is that training and development programs almost always create expectations, rights, and benefits. When expectations are frustrated, legal demands may be made.

First, one must decide how to coordinate or separate training "tracks" for personnel. U.S.–based personnel who are "rotating in" may have needs different from those of "borrowed" third-country nationals from another subsidiary operation or those of host country nationals who are performing the same job functions but who may have different future expectations and who therefore have different training needs. Local host country employees will be concerned how trainees are chosen and who gets the opportunity? For example, if it turns out that management trainees are predominantly of one gender and of one ethnic background, does that raise questions under either local or U.S. law? The answer is yes. And, to know which obligations to meet the global employer must take care in setting up the employment relationship so as to carefully define "employer," "employee," and "parent–subsidiary" relationships.

As for the content of training programs, in addition to work performance training, it is also useful to educate personnel about pertinent legal requirements—local and United States—regarding EEO, safety and health, dispute resolution, and the like. Properly trained personnel, both management and staff, is still the best way to deter legal problems.

A large practical issue with legal implications involves labor relations and how to dovetail these training programs into existing relationships with labor unions, contracts, and involved government agencies (e.g., immigration, if training will occur in the United States).

Lastly, another legal issue can arise with selected jobs. For example, there may be requirements for licenses or for locally required training or certification. From skilled workers, such as electricians, to accountants and lawyers, there may be special restrictions that must be met and perhaps, in the case of skilled workers, that could be integrated into training programs or linked with existing local programs.

Compensation.   Money most easily attracts the interest of personnel. Financial discrimination that is, or is perceived to be, unfair can trigger legal claims under U.S. and local laws. Although the uses of salaries and fringe benefits to attract and retain needed employees are well known, in the global context, the legal ramifications are more complex. For example, if a global company brings into Beijing, China, managerial staff from Singapore and the United States, how may one justify any comparative compensation differentials or the fringe benefits, including housing and travel.

There are many business explanations that will determine and perhaps justify compensation differentials—but will they satisfy applicable laws, United States or local—and not just the tax laws but also the labor laws? Foreign managers can often point to local laws or joint venture or contract obligations in seeking some parity in compensation and fringe benefits. Questions again arise—whose "employees" are they and what legal obligations apply? Legal concerns under U.S. EEO laws can also be raised regarding justification for compensation differentials while employees are overseas *and* upon their return, when higher (comparatively) compensation levels are maintained. Clever and appropriate uses of "overseas allowances" can usually lessen legal concerns.

With respect to the foreign-based work force, compensation-related opportunities and benefits, including training, travel, bonuses, vacations, housing, and other "fringes," can raise EEO issues and questions whether there has been compliance with local legal requirements regarding social insurance, job security, severance, and layoff funds or procedures, worker injuries, housing subsidies, redundancy, and so forth. Questions recur about who is the "employer" with the obligation—the local joint venture, the respective subsidiaries who have joined, or their parent companies—and who are the "employees" who are entitled to such benefits? Understanding and complying with these laws and coordinating them, to the extent necessary, with U.S. laws, is a tedious but necessary task. Global employers usually deal with these issues when first going into a foreign location, but changing and ongoing relationships with local suppliers, contractors, or partners often requires constant monitoring.

Labor Relations.   No area of HRM is more important than the labor relations environment of the foreign location. This area more than ever crosses lines and mixes practical realities with legal requirements. The key to success in this area is twofold: preparation and execution. The employer must know and understand the history and the socioeconomic factors at work, primarily the current power bases and players of the government, business, and labor unions. The employer must then use this knowledge in executing and implementing his goals within the local rules and within the local power balances.

The specific factors to consider are as follows. In first formulating employment policies, a decision must be made as to the coordination and the allocation of decision-making authority over labor relations between the U.S.–based parent and the foreign-based subsidiary. Is it delegated, centralized, or handed over to local control? This has practical as well as legal significance on the potential extraterritorial application of U.S. civil rights laws. Important attention is paid to the control factor in assessing employer status. The extent to which local managers are empowered to make real decisions also affects the applicability of various labor laws concerning employment status, for purposes of coverage or noncoverage.

The type of employment relations and the manner in which they are derived is significant. Are wages, terms, and conditions fixed by statute, by collective negotiation, or on an individual basis? What role does a labor union have, if any? Are there rights of collective bargaining? Can a union be ignored? Would a strike be legal? Can replacement employees be found and used? What alternatives for dispute resolution are permitted and used?

All of these aspects of employee relations raise a myriad of legal questions upon which local law must be consulted and understood. Here, also, a practical understanding of how the law is used and enforced is absolutely required. If management under the law has a right to determine bonuses and their method of distribution, it may not want to use its right if local custom and a powerful local union have a tradition of making those determinations within employee committees and the labor union. Under such circumstances, it may be unnecessary and foolish to blindly adhere to legal "rights." Such an example may be true in the PRC. On the other hand, even where legal rights of employees exist, such as the right to strike, knowing the likely local reaction of law enforcement officials may guide the employer in its legal deliberations.

Finally, it is obvious that employee relations are complex and vary with local conditions. Even in a location with certain government attitudes toward worker protections or lax enforcement thereof (e.g., in health or safety standards), there may be some other areas of great concern, such as payment of workers, social insurance, and other legally required worker subsidies. Balancing legal requirements with the practical realities of labor relations requires much attention by human resource managers.

Japan provides an illustration. Much of the mystery about Japan has been lifted by U.S. presence and involvement in Japanese business and society for the past fifty years. To many it remains a truism that the United States and Japan labor laws are about 96 percent alike, yet different in almost every way. The laws and bureaucratic institutions are often similar (e.g., the U.S. labor law, the Wagner Act, is also closely reflected in Japanese law), but their administration and the law and practices under them are quite different.

The difference in operation and application of similar-appearing laws is due to the pervasive influence of culture on a rather homogeneous country and the degree of economic and "legal" control and guidance the government and related organizations exert over Japanese companies. Thus, the very close cooperation and the more than an implied social covenant among government, business, and labor unions have given rise to the stereotypical designation of Japan, as "Japan Inc." This is a useful aid in understanding Japan, at least as it connotes the heavy coordination undertaken by government, labor, and business and its acceptance by society. It should also alert the foreign investor to the clear fact that "outsiders" will probably remain just that. When foreign business locates in Japan, there is little doubt that to succeed it must accommodate local requirements, whether they be laws, culture, or human resource management practices.

In conclusion, legal implications abound in most decisions in labor relations, not only in the United States, but also on foreign soil. Decisions in international HRM covering all the areas of recruitment and selection, performance evaluation, training and development, compensation, and labor relations raise complex legal issues that can be largely eliminated by key legal planning. Careful consideration can be given to structuring "employer" and "employee" status which, if business values permit, can affect the applicability of laws. Careful assessment of the local legal requirements in foreign locations can result in employer policies compatible with U.S.–based policies that go a long way in complying with the law and practical realities.

Clearly, as in all personnel situations, United States or foreign, no amount of planning can eliminate every legal dispute; but by anticipating them, they can be dealt with under a designed plan while also maintaining the global employer's business interests.

Thus, it can be seen that the legal agenda concerning the potential applicability of U.S. labor laws, the possible interplay of international labor obligations and foreign law, and the foreign labor law itself, all provide a significant area of concern affecting business choices and international human resource management.

References

Amato, T.A. (1990). Labor Rights Conditionality: United States Trade Legislation and the International Trade Order, 65 *N.Y.U.L. Rev.* 79.

Ballon, X.X. (1987). The Implications of Making the Denial of Internationally Recognized Worker Rights Actionable Under Section 301 of the Trade Act of 1974, 28 *Va. J. Int'l L.* 73.

Carr W., & Kolkey D. (1984). Labor Relations for Multinational Corporations Doing Business in Europe, 7 Loy. L.A. *Int'l & Com. L.J.* 1.

Cherian, J. (1989). Current Developments in Transnational Employment Rights, 40 *Lab. L.J.* 259.

Dowling P., & Schuler R. (1990). *International Dimensions of Human Resource Management* (PWS–Kent, Boston).

Doyle, F. (1990). People Power: The Global Human Resource Challenge for the '90s, *Columbia J. of World Bus.* 36 (Spring–Summer).

Holton, R.M. (1990). Human Resource Management in the People's Republic of China, 30 *Management Int'l Rev.* 121.

Kelley, L., & Shenkar, O. (1993). *International Business in China* (Routledge, London).

Khambata, D., & Ajami R. (19XX). "International Staffing and Labor Issues," ch. 19, *International Business,* pp. 474–506 (Macmillan, New York).

Litka, M. (1991). *International Dimensions of the Legal Environment of Business* (2nd ed.) (PWS-Kent, Boston).

Mendenhall, M., & Oddou G. (1991). "International Executive Compensation Practices," *International Human Resource Management,* pp. 375–383 (PWS–Kent, Boston).

Phatak, A. (1992). *International Dimensions of Management,* 3rd. ed. (PWS–Kent, Boston).

Shenkar, O. & Zeira, Y. (1990). International Joint Ventures: A Tough Test for HR, *Personnel* 26 (January).

Silver, G. (1989). Friendship, Commerce and Navigation Treaties and United States Discrimination Law: The Right of Branches of Foreign Companies to Hire Executives "Of Their Choice," 57 *Fordham Law Review* 765.

Whitehill, A. (1991). *Japanese Management: Tradition and Transition* (Routledge, London).

GLOBAL HUMAN RESOURCE MANAGEMENT IN PRACTICE

Preface to Part II

Human Resource Management in a Korean Subsidiary in New Jersey

Thomas G. Dimmick O-Z/Gedney

When I first joined Samsung in June 1984, I was given the assignment of the start-up of Samsung's color television manufacturing plant in Ledgewood, New Jersey. It was a rare opportunity. There were no production employees. They were to be hired. There were no benefits. They were to be designed and implemented. There was no building. We worked on the second floor of a nearby bank while construction continued. As I worked with my Korean co-workers to get those things completed in the days before we began manufacturing televisions, I was struck with the overwhelming realization that I was totally unprepared to interact in any effective way with the people around me. As time passed and my understanding of Korea, its people, its history, and its culture increased, I began to realize that my Korean co-workers were as unequipped to deal with the vastness of America (by Korean standards), the diversity of its cultures, and the complexity of its society and language as I was to deal with them and theirs.

My career before joining Samsung was not ordinary. In 1968 I graduated from a small, all-male preparatory school located in New Jersey. I think I was the only one in my class who was not immediately destined for college. Instead, I joined the Air Force and was placed on active duty in December of that same year. This was the year when President Lyndon Johnson announced to the American people that he would not be seeking reelection as president. The draft was still blowing its cold wind on those young men not in college, and the Tet offensive had shattered our confidence in the truthfulness of our politicians and the military. Columbia University had been taken over by student rioters, and the Democratic convention in Chicago seemed to indicate to everyone that our worst fears

63

about the assassinations of Martin Luther King, Jr. and Bobby Kennedy were justified. I spent the next four years in the USAF learning how to repair the automatic flight control systems of multiengine cargo aircraft. A one-year sojourn in Southeast Asia in a rescue squadron did little to prepare me for cross-cultural business relationships.

In 1973, I began working in a specialty gas manufacturing plant in Rahway, New Jersey. Wages were low and the risks of gas poisoning were high. I helped to convince the production, laboratory, warehouse, and maintenance employees of the firm into affiliating with the International Chemical Workers Union (ICWU), which was granted exclusive bargaining rights following National Labor Relations Board (NLRB) election. I became the shop steward of the facility and the vice president of the composite local into which the ICWU had assigned our thirty-five person unit. I began taking college courses at night at Rutgers University College.

After three years and two contracts, I had risen in the ranks of the union to be elected to the position of second vice president of the Eastern Regional Conference. My college major was labor studies, and I was a believer in the trade union movement. However, as the next two years passed and I had more and more opportunities to see the trade unions from the inside out, I began to question whether or not unions were truly the means or methods by which working people were going to better themselves. In 1978, after the plant's clerical staff had been added to the union, the facility closed. I became convinced that the best way to serve the needs of the working people was through enlightened management. I chose to credential myself with a masters degree in HR/IR, also from Rutgers, completed in December 1979.

When in Spring 1984, the call came to me at my home from a Mr. Han-Il Lee, I had never heard of Samsung. Korea was, as far as I knew then, a land of mountains and cold weather. Interestingly, he began our conversations with references to his friendships with Rutgers professors whom I also had known, most of them while I was in the labor movement. It seemed that Han-Il Lee had also attended the Rutgers graduate program a few years before I did. The significance of that conversation and the use of our common college experiences did not dawn on me for several years. I had no idea that in a Confucian society those shared relationships had a value far beyond what would have been their coin in western business transactions.

The hiring process was unique. Many people attended the interviews. Side conversations in Korean were the norm. Decision making inched forward as consensus was painstakingly achieved. The senior people did not commit themselves to a position until their respective staffs had fully and freely expressed their support or concerns for my candidacy. Personal issues were critical. Those items went beyond my wife and me. They penetrated into the realms of what my father had done for a living, whether or not my mother had worked outside of the home, and what my brothers and sister were doing. They all seemed to have a significance I could not fathom.

On my third day in my new position, at a management meeting presided over by my boss, the president, and attended by the seven Samsung Korean staff members and the Korean consultant, the controller demanded that the organization be changed so that I would report to him. This was contrary to the conditions of my employment as stipulated in my written offer letter. I was to report to the president. However, I seemed to be the only person who felt that the controller's suggestion was out of line. After several all-Korean meetings and in about one week's time, I was told that my reporting relationship to the president was affirmed as a policy of the management committee. This seemed to affirm my value to the organization. However, because I never did find out what the true issues surrounding the confrontation were, I was never certain why it became an issue or the basis for its resolution.

I had been very concerned about the intentions of the controller. I didn't know that in Korean organizations, the human resource function is typically a part of the finance/control (FC) sections. Additionally, I had no knowledge that the FC sections exercised power and influence well beyond their usual scope in American firms. Typical of the broad authority given the FC sections, within several weeks of this confrontation between the controller and me, we were thrown together in the all-out effort to finish the construction of the Ledgewood manufacturing facility. That construction, ultimately costing US $7.4 million, was something with which neither of us had ever had any experience.

The HR function in a Korean organization operating in Korea has very broad authority. The HR function hires, fires, promotes, demotes, and develops all salary transactions. In a Confucian society, a superior would never directly confront a subordinate with the subordinate's substandard work performance. To do so would cause both of them great humiliation— the superior for having to admit that a subordinate was less then perfect and the subordinate for having forced the superior into a confrontation through his poor work performance. The HR function therefore provides the means to accomplish the discipline without the direct superior being blamed.

The balance of 1984 passed with a great deal of work being accomplished but without anything remarkable happening. The plant dedication ceremony held on December 4 of that year might be considered an exception. I was appointed the master of ceremonies. On that day, there was a catered luncheon for all employees. Gifts were given to all 1,500 guests. There was a fifteen-minute multimedia presentation that had finally been approved, with the final changes, at 11:00 o'clock the night before. I used six slide projectors to backlight two 10 by 15 foot screens. The presentation portrayed the elements of Samsung Electronics for all the guests to see. The New Jersey governor cut the ribbon, assisted by the commissioner of the New Jersey Economic Development Authority, the president of the plant, the president of Samsung Electronics in Korea, the president of Samsung Consumer Electronic Sales in the United States, the Korean consul general, and the junior U.S. senator from New Jersey. Thereafter was a plant tour and fully catered cocktail party in an area of the 238,000 square foot facility dedicated to expansion. To say that it was exciting, lavish, extravagant, and exhausting would be an understatement.

Beginning in the spring of 1985, there were about 175 plant, warehouse, quality control, and engineering employees. As a result of management's efforts to reduce absenteeism by reducing the amount of paid time-off benefits the employees were to enjoy, the United Steel Workers Union began an organizing drive of the Samsung employees. Samsung was determined to remain free of the union. When the USWA finally managed to collect sufficient cards to make a reasonably successful election attempt, it notified the company and petitioned the NLRB for a representation election. The board granted the petition and we estimated that the union probably had about 55 to 65 percent of the population represented by signed cards. Initially, the Korean management advocated firing all the suspected union supporters. After many discussions, the company set about running a legal campaign that incorporated a broad range of supervisory training, employee training and small group discussions. These efforts were supported by some slick advertising efforts and constant discussions with line supervision.

The company's efforts were successful. In December 1985, after nearly eight months of campaigning, the union was soundly defeated by a ratio of three to one. Furthermore, the hard-won lessons of the campaign were incorporated into ongoing HR programs such as supervisory audits, plant job evaluations, open door policies, and regular meetings between the employees and management. These efforts proved to be vital in 1987.

One of the results of the union campaign was the establishment of a point factor analysis plan using the National Metal Trades (NMT) standards. The Korean method for monetary compensation of employees was to increase their salary on an annual basis, everyone at once, by a fixed amount. Incentives were typically accomplished with bonus payments. If you are familiar with the manner in which the U.S. military compensates people, the similarities to the Korean fixed increases are striking. The employees perceived the NMT standards to be both fair and reasonable in making pay distinctions between different jobs. Two length-of-service increases were established to satisfy Korean management, one was at one year and one at three years of service. These boosted an employee's salary grade one and two pay grades, respectively, beyond the NMT established job grade.

Another and perhaps the most significant results of the 1985 union drive was the decision to continue the group meetings that had proven to be so successful during the campaign. These group meetings reached the peak of their effectiveness in subsequent years. They were especially helpful in keeping the president of the Ledgewood facility, Hai-Min Lee, in front of and in touch with the employees.

The plan work force proved to be very productive. So productive in fact, that management installed and staffed a third color television assembly line by midsummer 1986. By November of that year, a seasoned manufacturing professional, Clayton Senecal from General Electric's Consumer Electronics Division, was hired to bring the Ledgewood operation up to world-class standards. The production, engineering, quality control, and warehouse work force hovered at the 260 persons mark, and the support staff had grown to nearly forty people. The Human Resource and Administration Department had grown to a total of twelve. That included an administration clerk, a building mechanic and an assistant, two security guards, and two cleaners. It was significant that the number of Samsung's rotating staff members in the management group remained constant at between seven and nine men.

Beginning in early 1987, Hai-Min Lee, Clay Senecal, and I formed a task force whose purpose was to boost production quantity, reduce in-process defects, and consolidate the production supply operations. A variety of programs affecting the human resource function were initiated. A major part of this process was the enhancement of the existing communication efforts with the employees. Each month, the three of us decided upon a topic. A script was drafted by me and critiqued by Clay and Mr. Lee. After revisions incorporating their inputs, a final form was given back to Mr. Lee. He practiced the delivery of the presentation for several days before its delivery to the employees. All employees were required to attend the meetings. That included all office staff and managers. At the conclusion of the twenty or twenty-five minute speech, Mr. Lee would open the meeting to questions from the floor.

In support of President Lee's monthly meetings, there were focused, small group meetings with Clay. The selected subject was always either the same or consistent with the message Mr. Lee had delivered. Employees were selected to attend these early morning sessions on the basis of their work behaviors. Those who were supportive of the president outnumbered those who had indicated their opposition to it. A free exchange of ideas was encouraged with Clay's role being limited to that of moderator. Minutes were kept. Edited and typed editions were posted on a special bulletin board in the cafeteria.

Also in support of President Lee's meetings were three communications vehicles under the control of the Human Resources Department. They were the company newsletter, the employee social activities groups, and the complaint/suggestion box. The company newsletter was produced on a monthly or twice-monthly basis. It consisted of material written by employees, was generally about eight pages long, and had articles with a topic that reflected what President Lee had mentioned in his monthly speech. Employees voluntarily composed each article. It was finally edited by the Human Resource Department. Questionable articles were reviewed by the task force members.

Social activities were proposed, planned, and executed by employees. General oversight was provided by the Human Resources Department. Themes for the company picnic, Halloween Costume Day, Christmas party, Dedication Ceremony Anniversary, as well as bus trips to Atlantic City and elsewhere were, if possible, loosely built around the monthly meeting topics. Just before each year's Christmas shutdown, employees had a Christmas tree decoration competition, a luncheon, and a gift exchange. The company supplied the trees for each functional area of the company. The employees in that area supplied the decorations. The social committee judged the results. The food was provided by employees and represented the foods served in their native lands with Korean food in a prominent position. The company permitted an extended lunch period, and employees were free to sample the foods from each area.

The complaint/suggestion box was a direct line to the task force. A locked box and forms were located in the cafeteria next to the bulletin board. The box was checked weekly, and responses were posted on the bulletin board monthly.

The efficiency of these communications programs was proven in the spring of 1987 and again in the fall of 1991. In the spring of 1987, the International Union of Electrical Workers (IUEW) began to handbill the plant. They held meetings, distributed flyers, wrote letters, and in short, took nearly every legal action available to them in their efforts to have enough authorization cards signed to petition the board for an election. This effort began about March and lasted until about August.

The big difference between 1987 and 1985 was the ease with which the employees, their supervisors, and the management of the company were able to communicate with one another. Before the union could make an issue over an event that the company had handled badly, the employees had already taken appropriate corrective actions. The union simply could not make any inroads. As August passed, they simply gave up the campaign and walked away. A few of the most vocal of the employees who had supported the union also left the company. Their peers made their lives very difficult.

In September 1991, Samsung announced that, effective the Wednesday before Thanksgiving, it would cease production of color televisions at the Ledgewood facility. The work was to be transferred to other assembly plants located throughout the world, including in Tijuana, Mexico. The production levels had been decreasing steadily since 1988. By the fall of 1991, there were only about fifty production employees. The facility had been transformed into a warehousing and distribution center with after-sales service filling the bulk of the office areas.

The employees continued to perform their assigned tasks to the same high degree of competence that they had demonstrated since 1987. As the final sets were being assembled during the week before Thanksgiving, a supply problem arose. Because the production machinery was scheduled to be disassembled and sent out of the country commencing the week after

Thanksgiving and because the sets then on the production line as work-in-progress had already been sold, it was essential that the units be built before Thanksgiving.

The management of the unit called the employees together and asked if they would be willing to go home and then come back later that night when the supply truck had arrived. You must remember that the employees already knew that they were going to be terminated. They already knew what their separation benefits were going to be. There was simply no way that the company could have required them to work had they declined to do so. So management asked them. All of them returned. All the sets were built and shipped on time and in conformance with the existing quality standards. Later, when some of the employees were asked why they did it, the answer was, "Because it was our work to do."

Reflecting on my experience in both domestic and foreign operation in the United States, I must say that some of the lessons I have learned are not unique to either a local or an international context. Listen to everyone in the organization, reason with unreasonable employees, include employees in all aspects of the business, treat everyone with respect and concern; these seem to be universal recommendations, though they may be more difficult to implement in a foreign subsidiary.

At the same time, selection, training, coaching, performance evaluation, and compensation may require a radically different approach in a foreign subsidiary. My hiring process at Samsung, for instance, was radically different from anything I have experienced in an American company. These processes also tend to vary substantially from one country to another, so what we developed at Samsung would not necessarily be relevant for a Japanese affiliate here. This is what makes global HRM complex but also challenging. How important is "face" in providing feedback? What is the role of silence? What are the host and foreign attitudes toward women and minority executives? What are the applicable pay and benefits practices? These are just a few of the relevant questions to be asked by the practitioner engaged in human resource management.

In this section, techniques for the selection, evaluation, and coaching of employees in foreign subsidiaries are delineated, followed by training methods to develop intercultural skills and behaviors useful not only to the foreign expatriate but to anyone who, like me, had to work and manage in a global organization. Compensation and the emerging role of the woman expatriate follow. Understanding the issues and, in particular, how to identify and resolve them, will go a long way toward making the work of the global human resource practitioner more effective and rewarding.

Selection, Coaching, and Evaluation of Employees in International Subsidiaries

John Artise   Drake Beam Morin, Inc.

Introduction

This chapter specifically focuses on a *three-phase* process that I recommend be part of every international corporation's acculturation efforts both in the home country and abroad. This process involves separate yet complete systems prioritized as follows: selection, coaching, and evaluation. Each of these systems must also adhere to the sequential process of planning, implementation, and follow-up. These systems directly consider the acculturative factors of language differences, values, belief systems, social customs, and cultural behaviors that are characteristic of the employee population whether homogeneous or diversified.

Each of these systems in the three-phase process is treated with the intention of universality of application to all international companies in all industries. However, the target cultures addressed here are Japanese, Korean, French, British, and American. Pertinent cultural issues, questions, and problems are addressed regarding each of the five cultures respectively in each phase of the three-phase process. Practical recommendations for modifications or alterations possibly needed in each phase, according to the requirements of the target culture, are considered.

Bear in mind that the three-phase system presented here is applicable to a company's home base and outpost operating facilities, regardless of the variances in employee population ratios: foreign vs. home country.

I. The Selection System

Over the years many attempts have been made at creating the most appropriate employee selection methodology for multinational companies that would allow for an accurate identification of a candidate's competencies, motivation, and fit within the target company culture. By and large, these attempts have proven to be only moderately successful. One key reason for this is management's failure to do the following:

1. Consider *all* the pertinent factors of acculturation with respect to hiring foreign and domestic personnel.
2. Devise a structured yet flexible selection schema that can be used *consistently* both in the home country and in the foreign outposts.

Foreign managers, especially those who have not been acculturated to the target country in which they are operating, have not been adequately trained in selection techniques and therefore encounter difficulties later on in managing their personnel. It is quite startling that even in organizations that practice rigid protocols of operating procedures there is a glaring lack of attention paid to selection and a scarcity of managerial acumen in this regard on the part of both line and staff management.

What is needed is, first, a generic selection schema that is then carefully worked into an operating system to which acculturative techniques corresponding to the respective target cultures of the applicants are applied. In this way, a viable balance can be struck between the *objective* and *subjective* aspects of the selection process which is necessary for its success.

I provide here such a selection schema that can be superimposed on any cross-cultural environment whether in the home country or in the outpost. The three universals of the selection of employees in any industrialized culture are the following:

1. *Can* the individual do the job? This is the competency issue relating to the technical phase of the interview. Does the applicant have the skills, knowledge, and depth/diversity of experience to perform the given job function?
2. *Will* the individual do the job? This refers to the issue of *motivation* and figures into the nontechnical phase of the interview. Is the applicant motivated to perform, and what are the origins of that motivation?
3. *How* does the applicant *fit* the organization's culture? The focus here is on the sociobehavioral and sociopolitical issues of the applicant's acculturating to the organization's mission, its value system, the preferred management and work styles of the organization's members. What are the critical success factors for a good fit?

When these three elements of the selection process are, with cultural modifications, rolled into a consistent system, the probability is high that an appropriate match between the applicant's background and the job requirements will be accomplished.

If we first consider the job's technical and competency issues (*can* do?) in the selection process, there is a useful interviewing method called "**ASK**," which meets the manager's requirement for inquiry in this first phase. "**ASK**" is a handy acronym for

Accomplishments

Skills

Knowledge

The manager should "**ASK**" questions of the applicant pertaining to these three aspects of job competency in order to ascertain the following:

1. The depth/diversity of major achievements and their relevance to the prospective environment. What value do these accomplishments have if they are repeated in the new environment?
2. The consistent, well-honed, practical skills that are transferable to the new job function.
3. The depth and breadth of the applicant's knowledge of the job function, the state-of-the-art of the technology in the field, and the current issues and trends in the industry.

Before the manager can ask the appropriate questions pertaining to these categorical areas, he or she must have a reference point to serve as a guideline.

Résumés, vitae, and profiles have been the usual forms of documentation used in job interviews on an international basis. But because of the diversity of the formatting of these documents along with the selectivity of information entailed in the content, which can vary greatly from culture to culture, it is best for the manager not to use any of them as the focal point of the interview. They should be used as ancillary sources only, which may enhance the selection process.

What is recommended instead is a Job Model, which through its structure and content *characterizes* the job in five specific components rather than just listing duties, as job descriptions are solely designed to do. The five components of the Job Model are: I. Results Achievable, II. Priorities, III. Obstacles, IV. Environment, V. Management Style.

The line of questioning the interviewer engages in using "**ASK**" focuses on categories I, II, and III. Categories IV and V are relegated to the *cultural fit* line of questioning (Phase II) of the interview.

Thus, the Job Model reflects the nature of the position the applicant will be involved in. This model should be constructed well in advance of the beginning of the selection process and is used in a *comparative* or *contrastive* way in the interview.

A typical Job Model for a project engineering manager is designed as follows:

I. Results Achievable

1. Create eight-member project team.
2. Plan two-year telecommunications project in Sydney, Australia.
3. Hire outside consulting firm to assist in construction of satellite communications headquarters in Brisbane.
4. Completely outsource all project budgeting and capital expenditures on an ongoing basis.
5. Complete within one year a global computer network linking the Hawaiian islands with all of Asia, North America, and Central and South America.
6. Serve as team leader in a joint venture with France to commence a five-year transatlantic fiber optic telecommunications project.

II. Priorities

1. Identify, screen, select, and train engineering and technical professionals to comprise a project team of eight high-quality personnel.
2. Analyze current budget process for projects to convert to outsource maintenance.
3. Establish joint venture with French engineering team to commence a projected five-year transatlantic telecommunications project.
4. Undertake trans-Pacific global computer network project (Hawaii, North, South, and Central America).
5. Hire outside consulting firm to assist in international construction projects.
6. Plan Australian telecommunications project.

III. Obstacles

1. Currently limited financial resources to support proposed projects.
2. New top management team will be on board within ninety days. May have a different philosophy and approach to the business.
3. Recent change in French government's regulations regarding joint venture projects with the United States and Canada.
4. *Excessive* worldwide travel.
5. Tight bureaucratic reporting protocols and required "stepladder" approval for all project proposals and midstream changes during project roll-out.

IV. Environment

1. Seventy percent out-of-home-office work. No permanent office space.
2. Reactive; time-sensitive.
3. Project teams numbering from eight to 200 persons.
4. Heavy computer network communication.
5. Diverse geographic project locations.

V. Management Style

1. Logical thinker/planner.
2. Creative visionary.
3. Hands-on, proactive team builder/leader.
4. Quick, accurate decision maker.
5. Detail oriented.
6. Aggressive communicator.
7. High energy level; mission oriented.

Although the interviewer has already seen the applicant's vita and/or résumé, the Job Model is presented to the applicant within the first five minutes of the interview and is introduced as follows:

INTERVIEWER:
Mr. Stockton, this is a model of the job you'll be engaged in should you be hired for the position. While I have indeed read your résumé and I certainly will be asking you questions about certain aspects of your background, please review this model for a few minutes, comparing it to your most recent and past positions. Then be prepared to ask *me* questions regarding any part of the job model as to how it compares favorably or unfavorably with your experience. I will, of course, be sure to clarify any aspect of the model you are unclear about.

The interviewer leaves the room and allows the applicant to scrutinize the document. Thus, the Job Model serves as the focal point of the interview, coupled with the résumé or vita, and avoids the need for the interviewer's asking extraneous or noncontextual questions that are not related to the job.

Typical Format for the "ASK" Portion of the Job Model

Accomplishments

The interviewer should focus on two critical lines of thought in questioning the applicant about significant achievements:

1. What did you exactly achieve that was influential in one or all of the following:

   Improving efficiencies?

   Reducing costs?

   Generating value (money, quality, etc.)?

2. *How* did you achieve these things? (through what means)?

The interviewer should be looking for *two* key measures of the applicant's value regarding accomplishments:

1. *Depth.* How much hands-on involvement did the applicant have in the process of accomplishing, and how much was covered in a short space of time?
2. *Diversity.* How many different areas of experience were tapped to produce individual accomplishment *and* how diversified are the total number accomplishments in terms of their covering a *broad spectrum* of endeavor.

Skills

The interviewer should be addressing the skills issue with following line of thought:

1. How sharp are these skills? What is their degree of acumen?
2. Have the applicant's skills been consistently tested?
3. Are the skills readily transferable to the prospective work environment?

Knowledge

The primary focus of the questioning here must be on the following two factors:

1. *Depth.* How much does the applicant really know about:

   The industry?

   The business as an operating entity?

   The field or discipline in which he or she is functioning?

2. *Ectocentricity.* How much of the applicant's knowledge base is drawn from sources outside of the domain of the job yet having an important impact on the job?

From a strictly acculturative point of view the interviewer should have little difficulty asking *open-ended* questions that address "ASK." The majority of applicants, even from diametrically opposite cultures, respond favorably to open-ended questions such as the following:

"How did you manage to complete that turnkey project in just five months?"

"Please tell me as much as you can about your role as a team leader in your experience while in France?"

"Explain your reasoning behind proposing to build a satellite substation in the middle of the North Pacific Ocean?"

"Describe the combination of skills you used in building that twelve-member project team consisting of professionals with diverse backgrounds from six different countries?"

Typical Format for Motivation/Style Performance Issues

In addressing the "Will do?" and "How fit?" issues of the applicant's candidacy, we are looking at the personal attributes that comprise an individual's management and work style and motivation to perform.

Motivation

Does the applicant really *want* to do the job? Will she or he find it rewarding? Of course, cultural differences among applicants may obviate the asking of certain of these questions, but we discuss that later on in this section. Motivation questions should be asked *before* asking questions regarding cultural fit in order to minimize the applicant's rendering biased answers should the questions be asked in reverse order.

Sample questions might be formulated as follows:

"What incentives have you found to be the most valuable to you in your career?"

"If you require a motivational boss, how do you prefer that that person motivate you?"

"How important are employee benefits as an incentive?"

"On a motivational scale of one to ten, ten being the highest, where would you place 'quality of worklife' as a motivational factor in your career?"

"Why are you attracted to this position?"

By allowing applicants to speak in an open-ended manner, the interviewer is able to obtain a more complete picture of the applicant's perception and attitude toward the motivational aspect of the job.

Management Style

Of all the aforementioned Job Model categories, this one requires the most critical questioning by the interviewer to determine the applicant's cultural fit within the prospective company culture. Because job applicants already have an established management/work style that can be evidenced only by their observable behavior on the job, it is important for the interviewer to use a probing method of interviewing to obtain as clear a picture as possible of how this applicant is likely to perform on the job.

Here are examples of generic categorical questions that can be asked. Later, more specific acculturative issues are addressed focusing on the five key cultures already mentioned at the beginning of this chapter.

(A) *Communication*
"Describe the reporting relationship you prefer with your subordinates? Superiors?"

"Describe your management (work) style?"

"How often do you conduct meetings with your team?"

(B) *Workplace Philosophy*
"What values do you espouse in the workplace?"

"What is your definition of accountability?"

"How would you characterize yourself as a leader?"

(C) *Influences*
"What is your technique in managing (working with) employees from diverse cultures?"

"How would you rate your ability to make important decisions?"

"Have you ever influenced anyone or any event without having the authority?"

(D) *Motivating Others*
"How do you motivate your subordinates?"

"What incentives have you used to motivate a team?"

"Do you use performance coaching as a motivational tool?"

Again, these questions serve only as guidelines to formulating more customized inquiries sensitive to the diversity of applicant cultures the interviewer will encounter.

Decision to Hire

Simply put, the decision to hire or reject a job candidate when using this selection system is best accomplished by a *consensus approach,* requiring input from the other interviewers involved in the process (see Figure 1).

To sum up thus far in this chapter:

1. A selection *system* is recommended to hire applicants from diverse cultural backgrounds.
2. A Job Model should be created to serve as the focal point of the interview.
3. The **"ASK"** method of questioning should be used to determine the applicant's technical competency (*can* do).
4. Open-ended questioning should be employed to determine the non-technical aspects of the applicant's background that concern motivation/style performance.

The following is a selection interviewing schema designed for a large Japanese trading company in the United States.

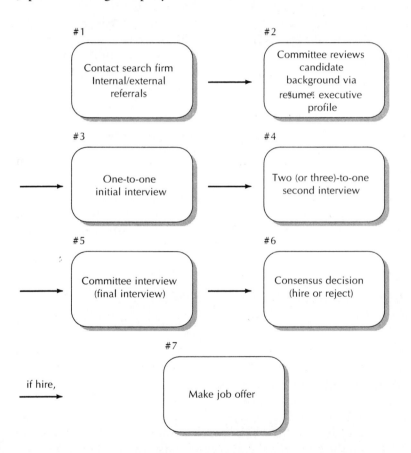

FIGURE 1
Executive Selection (General Manager Level)

Content Outline

Selection Interviewing at a Large Japanese Trading Company in the United States

Introduction
- Overview of interview process/common mistakes
- Discussion of key Japanese and American differences in this area

Preparing for the Interview
- Obtaining a thorough understanding of the job
  - Can Do
  - Will Do
  - How Fit?
- Reading the résumé

Rapport Building
- Meeting and greeting/names
- Small talk
- Nonverbal behavior—eye contact, smiling, and so on
- Positive feedback

Interview Structure/Making Transitions
- Opening
- Work experience
- Education
- Outside activities/interests
- Summary of strengths
- Summary of shortcomings
- Close

Types of Questions
- Open-ended vs. closed-ended
- Behavioral questioning
- Neutral questions

Handling Difficult Interviewees
- Nervous
- Quiet
- Talkative
- Glib

Senior Executive Hiring

The selection interview process at the senior executive level requires much more attention and scrutiny than hiring at lower levels.

The key concern among interviewers should be to determine the strength of *leadership* and the full understanding of *responsibility* and *accountability* on the part of the senior level candidate.

It can be assumed that senior candidates have a high regard for *stability* in the organization and are themselves an example of that. Their desire for longevity with the company is a natural by-product of their sense of stability, and this provides a reliable groundwork from which to conduct a thorough, meaningful interview.

Senior level executives, at this point in their careers, usually have *broad-based* skills and knowledge which are *transferable* from one business environment to another. This makes them more versatile in general management applications.

Senior Executive Sourcing

Candidates for a senior level position generally come from two key sources:

a. Executive Search Firms
b. Internal/External Referrals

Executive search firms conduct searches for the candidate whose profile most closely matches that position you want to fill.

Professional search consultants scrutinize every detail in the candidate's background regarding your **MUSTS** and **PREFERREDS** *before* referring that candidate to you.

They are a good, reliable source in identifying senior candidates.

Internal/External referrals are also widely requested, since the senior candidates recommended to you come from known, reliable people with whom you have contact inside and outside the company.

Keep in mind that you should begin your selection interviewing process with **NO MORE THAN THREE CANDIDATES** from any one or all of your sources.

If the sourcing has been conducted well, you should be able to make the best selection among three candidates.

Reviewing a Candidate's Background

It is wise to call a meeting with all those who will be interviewing the candidate to jointly review background information in the form of a résumé, vita, or an executive profile.

During the meeting, it can be determined among the members *what questions should be asked of the candidate* regarding the critical aspects of the job.

Also, this pre-interview review of credentials helps the consensus decision-making process (post-interview) avoid any unanticipated surprises.

The Senior Executive Interview—One-to-One

(In Practice)

Here are some helpful protocols and procedures to follow when interviewing the senior level candidate:

1. **NEVER** have a senior candidate fill out an application form. It can be perceived as rather demeaning and unprofessional, especially when considering higher level persons for a place in the company. All application form information can be taken care of *after* the candidate is hired.

    The résumé, profile, and information from the search firm will be all that is necessary at this point.

2. Be sure that the interview setting is a professional one. Your office or the board room is perfectly adequate.

    If you prefer, you can take the candidate to a nice restaurant. However, this setting is usually reserved for the second or third interview. Your aim is to impress the candidate and keep the company's image in high esteem.

3. Your communication style should be congenial and, at first, informal. This is to establish a comfort level between you and the candidate. The tenor of the interview becomes more businesslike and focused when you begin delving more deeply into the candidate's experience.

4. Remember to ask open-ended questions, allowing the candidate to elaborate on each response.

5. It is advisable *not* to take notes while interviewing senior candidates. It can be disconcerting to them and can also take your attention away from the flow of the interview.

6. Avoid interruptions during the interview. Tell your secretary to hold all calls until after you are finished. Distractions can detract from your professional image and the company's.

Questions to Ask Senior Candidates

Interviewing senior level candidates requires that you select your questions carefully.

Avoid asking closed-ended questions that can be answered with a "yes" or "no," and equally avoid questions that will oblige the candidate to reach way back in the past in order to give a plausible answer.

In other words, pay close attention to the *relevancy* of your questions to what the job requires of an individual who has thus far performed at a senior level in his or her career.

An intelligent way of interviewing the senior candidate is to target the following areas of senior managership and formulate questions based on them:

Leadership

Decision-making

Planning and Strategizing

Management Style and Philosophy

Communication Skills

Examples of Rational Thinking

Handling a Crisis

Keep your questions open-ended, that is, *ask* the candidate to "tell," "elaborate," "expand," "explain," "describe," and so on.

Remember, you are looking for *depth* in each answer.

Suggested questions:

Leadership

1. Give me an example of how you led a team to a successful end result when faced with a major business challenge.
2. What are your five hallmarks of leadership as a senior executive?
3. Who in your opinion is the best role model of a leader who influenced you in your career?
4. What sets you apart from other peer managers with regard to leadership?
5. Give me an example of the greatest risk you ever took in your career?

Decision Making

1. Describe your process for making an intelligent business decision.
2. What is the most difficult decision you ever made?
3. When have you relied on sheer intuition to make a decision? Describe the circumstance.
4. If you had the following situation presented to you, what would you do?
    (Describe a real, job-related situation.)
5. When did you ever feel it necessary to reverse your decision? Describe the circumstance.

Strategizing

1. Give me an example of how you employed strategic vision in leading your staff.
2. What are the key elements of a sound business strategy? How have you employed these in your experience?
3. Give an example of the most successful strategy you ever witnessed.
4. How do you teach someone to be a good strategist?
5. Using a major project you managed as an example, explain how you strategized the outcome.

Philosophy of Management and Management Style

1. Describe your style of management.
2. What, in your view, are the key elements of good management?
3. What is your philosophy of management?
4. Describe the management style you find most difficult to contend with. In a peer. In a superior.

5. Describe the most difficult project you ever managed. How did you handle the challenges?
6. What is your expectation of your role in this company?

Rational Thinking

In this line of questioning there are no typical questions to ask. Instead, you pose *realistic* and hypothetical situations for the candidate to comment on. For example:

> If you were faced with a situation involving _____,
> how would you approach the problem in order to produce a positive end result. Explain your steps.

Experienced senior candidates are usually prepared to answer these *situational questions* with ready responses. Be sure to listen carefully to follow the rationale.

Communication Skills

Throughout each interview the candidate's professional communication skills are judged.

It is not difficult to determine the level of sophistication of a candidate's communication style, since his responses to open-ended questions will allow him to speak at length—at least 50 percent of the time.

To provide a short checklist, keep these stylistic components in mind during the interview:

Is the candidate:

articulate (Good command of English grammar and pronunciation)

projective (Does she or he get the point across assertively, in a direct manner?)

In command of an educated vocabulary?

Energetic in communication (Emphatic body language, facial expressions that enhance verbal communication)

A good listener (Does the candidate listen attentively when it is not his or her turn to speak?)

The Second Interview (Senior Executive)

Two-to-One (Three-to-One)

If you feel that the candidate deserves a second interview, make sure that at least two interviewers are present for the second round.

Three interviewers are strongly recommended.

Usually the same line of questioning as in the one-to-one is used.

However, each interviewer will have a preset list of interview questions focusing on a specific theme or themes to determine the professional *balance* of skills the candidate provides with regard to the position and the fit within the company culture.

When one interviewer asks a question, the others listen and observe the candidate's behavior closely. Notes are usually not taken by the interviewers.

This second interview usually lasts longer than the first interview. A good ninety minutes should be devoted to the second interview to establish a valid impression of the candidate to determine whether she or he should be invited to the final interview.

Remember, the purpose of asking the same type of questions in the second interview that were asked in the first is to check on the *consistency* of the candidate's answers.

The Final Interview (Committee Type)

The final interview is the most critical. It is after this interview that a hiring decision is made.

The setting for this interview is typically a committee or panel arrangement. The physical location should be a meeting room *or* a restaurant.

It is required that all of those managers who will have a *peer* relationship with the candidate in his or her immediate circle of influence on the job and those to whom the candidate will be reporting be present at the final interview. As many as ten managers may take part in the interview process.

Customarily about two to three hours are set aside for this interview.

Procedure:

1. The candidate is introduced to the committee by his or her prospective boss (or boss's boss) who serves as the moderator.
2. Each interviewer will focus on a respective topical line of questioning and maintain that focus until the end of the interview.
3. The committee *should not* engage in random, rapid-fire questioning. This is disconcerting to the candidate; it deters quality responses and gives the impression that the committee is disorganized and not well prepared.
4. Each interviewer should be prepared to follow a colleague in a line of questioning, just in case an important question was inadvertently left out.
5. When the interview is over, the mediator thanks both the candidate and committee for their time. The candidate is told when to expect a decision. After the candidate leaves, the committee remains convened to deliberate on the hiring decision.

The Consensus Decision

Needless to say, the hiring decision will be made by consensus among all committee members after the final interview.

The usual Japanese style of decision making by consensus (*ringi-seido*) should be employed.

The committee should feel comfortable with the decision whether or not it is in favor of hiring or rejecting the candidate.

Making the Job Offer to a Senior Candidate

Because senior candidates have higher expectations of professional business relationships, it is important to extend an offer in the following manner:

1. Phone the candidate and extend the offer verbally. Indicate that a formal letter outlining the terms of the offer will be forthcoming.
2. Be sure to indicate that you and your company are proud to have chosen the candidate for the position.
3. Ask if the candidate has any questions.
4. Agree on a start date.

Figure 2 summarizes the basic sequence of the selection process. Cultural considerations and adjustments will follow next.

Observing Cultural Difference in the Selection Process

Once a selection interview schema has been established, the task now is to address the cultural subtleties and nuances in the process in order to increase the probability of making a good hire.

The Selection of Japanese Managers by American Managers (at the Japanese outpost in the United States)

Although the direction of hiring is usually Japanese vs. Japanese, even in long-term Japanese outposts in the United States, more responsibility for interviewing Japanese will be assumed by acculturated American managers in the coming years.

Format.   A one-to-one interview format is appropriate because the Japanese require privacy and confidentiality in the rendering of information

Figure 2. Selection System

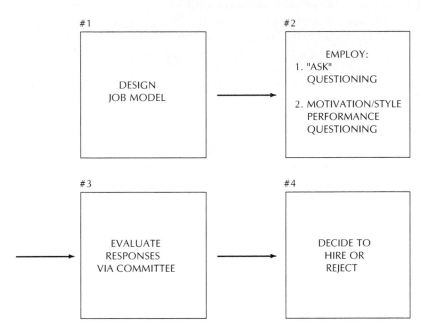

FIGURE 2
Selection System

during the engagement. A committee interview arrangement, even on the third interview, would not be appropriate, although this is a quite customary setup for western interviews.

Use of Job Model.   When presenting the Job Model to the Japanese manager, it is necessary to explain its purpose fully. If the manager is not a new rotational and is familiar with American job descriptions, it will be easier to explain the use of the Job Model. For the new rotationals, the American manager must begin the interview by asking the applicant a few questions of a personal nature about his family, childhood education, philosophy of life, social relationships, hobbies and interests, and so on. While these topics are *not* recommended as content core issues, they are indispensable in the Japanese interview. In fact, Japanese interviewers may spend as much as two hours with a Japanese applicant covering these topics only and later delving into his work experience.

When explaining the nature of the Job Model to the applicant, be certain to reassure him that this is a *necessary* step in the interview process to determine the depth and breadth of his technical skills but that it is *only one* criterion that will weigh in the decision to hire. The Japanese abide by a culturally prescribed behavior referred to as *kata* ("form") in which the environment is perceived as operating in a compartmentalized fashion. Therefore, any structured process that is new or unfamiliar must be explained in terms of where it fits in the *kata*-based system. A detailed explanation of each component of the "ASK" system is necessary for the interview to proceed smoothly and logically.

After the applicant has reviewed the Job Model, begin by asking questions about his SKILLS that relate to the prospective job. The reason for this is clear. Japanese are very modest about speaking about their achievements. They feel uncomfortable explaining things they view as a *normal duty* rather than a meritorious effort. The applicant may be visibly reluctant to speak about accomplishments so early in the interview. That is why SKILLS should be addressed first.

As is typical with Asians as a cultural protocol, they do not prefer eye contact during a face-to-face meeting, so it is important to keep eye contact sporadic—that is, do not maintain a steady fixation on the applicant's eyes. This will only deter him from answering open-ended questions with the completeness you require.

Some sample questions regarding SKILLS that have been successful with Japanese applicants:

1. From the time you were in high school and through your university training, which skills did you identify that caused you to excel academically?
2. In what facets of your job do you use these skills consistently?
3. What skill or skills have you acquired during the past five years?
4. Please give me an example of how you used a well-developed skill of yours to overcome a great challenge?
5. What additional skills do you believe you need to acquire to promote your career?

Each of these questions has been worded to be consistent with the cultural mindset of the Japanese manager relating to his skill base.

One should not expect a lengthy, comprehensive response to any of these questions, because most Japanese prefer not to take inordinate risks with the English language, fearing that the longer the answer, the less they will be *exactly* understood. It would also not be a surprise to detect almost immediately that non-Westernized Japanese engage in vagueness in their answers, which is also culturally based. The indication is that his relative unfamiliarity with the Western approach to interviewing leans toward the culturally comfortable response made in vagueness. In this case, it is perfectly acceptable for the interviewer to probe for an answer a little more deeply to obtain a clearer picture of the applicant's experience relating to his skills. It is certainly not out of line to request an example of his experience rendered in scenario form, since this request, coming from the interviewer as "conversation leader," gives "permission" to the applicant to refrain from vagueness and be more explicit. Following up probes such as:

"Could you please explain a bit further the application of those skills in the context of that project you just mentioned?"

"It would be helpful to me if you could give me a little more detail regarding how you use these skills on a daily basis."

are useful in obtaining more information. The interviewer should refrain from asking questions such as:

"How do you compare your skill level with that of your peers?"

This question is perfectly acceptable in most Western business cultures, but it is *not* perceived as culturally appropriate in Asian cultures, especially Japanese. The Japanese do not like to openly compare themselves to peers, especially when speaking to outsiders. Although there certainly is internal competition among Japanese in their corporations, overt comparisons of skills, power, and influence are not articulated. Self-aggrandizement is frowned upon in Japanese culture, and the asking of a question in this manner would most likely be met by a long silence or an outright circumlocutory answer.

A question such as, "On a scale of one to ten, ten being the highest rating, how would you assess your skills?" also invites the applicant to rate himself on a comparative basis, and this brings him discomfort because it is acultural.

When Japanese applicants are asked to enumerate their skills quickly, they will rarely give a short answer. The mention of each skill will usually be accompanied by a sometimes intricate explanation of the *circumstances* under which the skills were applied. They will usually not get to the interviewer's desired point until they have set the proper stage. This is another example of *kata-ization*, or the compartmentalized mindset of the Japanese that is so much a part of their culture that it has been extended into corporate culture in particular.

After skills have been covered, the interviewer should now focus on KNOWLEDGE. Most Japanese feel comfortable talking about what and how much they know, especially those who have gone through very rigorous academic training from childhood through the university level. It is customary in Japan for the interviewer to know in advance all the details of the applicant's educational successes, and this is not a major focal point in the interview. But for the Western interviewer it is indeed helpful to enter into a substantive dialogue with the applicant to cover the KNOWLEDGE component of "ASK" schema, since the applicant may very much want to talk at length about his knowledge of his field, the industry, the business, etc. Contrary to the popular Western belief that the Japanese are merely dutiful technocrats with no real "depth," in their knowledge of the world, one would be amazed to discover how much they *do* know about the world outside of Japan.

Sample questions regarding KNOWLEDGE are:

"What current trends in your field have you discovered will have a considerable impact on the company's business?"

"Describe your working knowledge of _____ in your daily tasks."

"How did your study of [academic subject] at the university prepare you to enter this field?"

"What sources of knowledge did you apply to that project you were involved in two years ago?"

"What additional knowledge would you like to acquire on this new job, and how would you consider using it to help you in your career?"

The latter question can be tricky for an unacculturated Japanese. Although there is now a trend in Japan toward adopting more *Westernized* thinking regarding self-promotion, career advancement, and a breaking of the bonds of a rigid sociocultural structure based on relatively unchallenged protocols (led especially by the *shinjin rui* or "new breed" of forward-thinking young professionals), long-held traditions remain relatively strong.

The applicant may be reluctant to indulge in a lengthy discourse about his personal strategy for career advancement. However, Westernized, acculturated Japanese immediately adapt to this question, and they are likely to give a fairly open and thorough answer.

Finally, the ACCOMPLISHMENTS component will be the subject of the interviewer's questioning that will put into clearer focus the complete perception of the applicant's technical competency. According to the "ASK" schema, the logic follows that when *KNOWLEDGE* is applied to a set of *SKILLS*, the result is an *ACCOMPLISHMENT*.

The following material suggests the types of questions that are preferred when using the "ASK" schema with Korean, French, British, and American applicants.

Korean

Accomplishments

"How did you lead your team to successfully completing the project one month ahead of schedule?"

Rationale.   Since Koreans have proven to be more aggressive managers than their Japanese counterparts, and they tend to demonstrate individual leadership without concern for breaking cultural protocols, the question positioned this way is perfectly appropriate.

"Describe an action you took that involved substantial risk."

Rationale.   Korean managers tend to be greater risk-takers than the Japanese and are prone to "seizing the moment" if achievement of success is the likely result.

"What was the most difficult decision you ever had to make on your own without your boss's input?"

Rationale.   Korean managers, especially those responsible for individual output of their respective business units, are sometimes called upon to make independent decisions in their boss's absence, particularly in a crisis. Not so with Japanese managers, who must confer with a higher authority first, or at least involve the immediate team in an impromptu *ringi-seido*, or *consensus process*, before any action can be taken.

Skills

"Try to describe how you combine different skills to accomplish difficult tasks."

Rationale.   Like the Japanese, Koreans have a problem demonstrating versatility when they manage their work and that of others. This unidimensional mode of operating is very similar to the Japanese philosophy and practice of *kata* or *paradigm* which dictates, "this task must be done *this* way, with *this* motion, using *this* tool, etc." In other words, both Koreans and Japanese (and including the Chinese) operate out of "sets" or "forms" (Japanese, *shikata*) with little or no deviation. This stems from the the way they were taught their respective writing systems as children, the martial arts, and so on. The question phrased in this manner attempts to elicit information from the applicant that may reveal indications of a timely breaking of the paradigm. This would provide the interviewer with an insight into the potentiality of performance coaching the prospective employee toward skill diversity and versatility in operating style.

"What skill do you most enjoy using?

Rationale.   In contrast to Japanese employees, who do not really consider "enjoyment" as a part of their performance at work, the Koreans are much more in tune with their feelings in the workplace. It's part of their cultural *kibun* or *good feeling* associated with working with others, learning from others, and deriving satisfaction from their labor. This *kibun* is a strong self-motivational force that must be identified in the applicant in the pre-hire phase of selection. Connecting it with their application of key skills will help the interviewer to identify motivational factors, which will enhance performance coaching later on.

Knowledge

Questions regarding both *content* knowledge (that which is derived from self study, training) and *process* knowledge (that which is derived from on-the-job experience) should be phrased in such a way as to allow the Korean applicant to express the *depth* and *diversity* of his knowledge base, which can later be cross-used.

> "Tell me how much you know about (*identify discipline, field, process, etc.*)."

Rationale. Allow the Korean applicant to reveal his knowledge in an *open-ended* fashion (a way he is probably not used to but will definitely attempt to accommodate) in order to probe the depth and diversity of his knowledge. Although the applicant may respond in a somewhat demure manner, he will reveal facets of his knowledge that the interviewer can probe more deeply.

> "How extensive has your training and education been in (*area of endeavor*)?"

Rationale. To identify the extensiveness of preparation the applicant has undergone thus far in his career will give the interviewer insights into his degree of "trainability" with regard to future challenges.

Communicative Cultural Nuances

The "Nunchi Silence." Koreans engage in a form of "silent language", or *nunchi,* that is very similar to the Japanese *haragei,* or "belly language," in which a nonverbal *reading* of the other person's intentions is taking place. Through the silence much is mutually understood about where the conversation is leading, what is about to happen next. Koreans, as the Japanese, are quite comfortable with this, and the interviewer would do well to make use of *nunchi,* especially after the Korean applicant has finished responding to a question. In other words, the interviewer should allow for a three- to four-second silent gap to take place, remaining focused on the applicant and displaying a subtle pleasant smile.

Eye Contact. Unlike the Japanese who are uncomfortable with eye contact in normal social communication, let alone a job interview, the Koreans, especially those who have acculturated to western ways either in North America or Europe, or even in Korea itself, will tend to maintain a more steady eye contact with the interviewer with occasional breaks at more pensive moments during the conversation. The Koreans do have a tendency to *engage* the interviewer after only a short introduction as opposed to the Japanese, who may maintain a firm communicative distance throughout the meeting.

Animation.   Given the opportunity through interview questions that evoke motivational responses, Korean applicants will demonstrate animation in their communication through the use of hand gestures in particular, especially when emphasizing a point. They also show more emotion in their facial expressions than do the Japanese.

French

Accomplishments

"Please enumerate the important achievements you have accrued in your career to date that have come from your operating in a team."

Rationale.   There has been for a long time a commonly held perception of French as being individualists with a penchant for isolationism and not being particularly interested in team play as it is demonstrated in Asia. Thus it would be wise for the interviewer to elicit as many examples of *team interaction* from the applicant as possible. That is, a focus on *both individual* roles of allied team partners and *collective* roles as a supportive unit should be characterized by the applicant. Each example explained by the applicant should be represented as a *scenario of action,* since this is culturally for the French the manner in which they prefer to respond to such questions.

"Which of your outstanding accomplishments exemplified your preferred management (operating) style?"

Rationale.   The question structured this way allows the interviewer to derive two facets of information:

1. A characterization of the applicant's work behavioral style as either a team leader or team partner.
2. There is a good chance that the applicant will single out *one* chief accomplishment that will reflect his philosophy of managing himself and the work in a given situation.

Skills

"Which of your skills do you rely on the most to produce results?"

Rationale.   The French usually concern themselves with technical skills as the key vehicles for producing results and achieving objectives. They are of the opinion that one's technical abilities are the true measure of his worth to the organization. They pay close attention to detail and systematic processes in an operation, since they like to be in control of an event or situation at all times.

"Which of your skills do you employ the most consistently that demonstrate your ability as a leader?"

Rationale.   The French are known to be still influenced by the "Napoleonic Code," so to speak. That is, managers tend to adhere to a sociocultural norm of managing an operation through the eyes of a military general. They tend to be very pedantic and "senser-like" in the way they delegate work and monitor results. By "senser-like" we mean very "hands-on" and immediately reactive to what's going on. It is therefore important that the interviewer key into the applicant's response in order to detect the following:

1. The degree of enthusiasm and commitment he has toward his perceived role as a leader.
2. Any glaring, firmly stated rules or principles the applicant strongly adheres to vis a vis the socio-cultural "code" which may be the veritable navigator of his managership.

Points 1) and 2) should indeed be probed by the interviewer especially because it can affect the prospective manager's style fit within the company's culture.

Knowledge

"Describe the intensity and breadth of your formal education and how that prepared you to compete in this industry (business)."

Rationale.   The French are very keen on formal education and especially credentials—that is, degrees, titles, certificates, diplomas, and so on. From a sociocultural standpoint, these clearly represent achievement and preparedness to handle challenges. The applicant will probably speak at great length about certain academic courses, theses, projects, independent studies, and the like that reflected his industriousness and allowed him to stand out among his peers. He will sometimes go to great lenghts to impress the interviewer with the breadth and depth of his knowledge, and this helps the interviewing determine the following:

1. The applicant's degree of "learnability," that is, his ability to acquire new knowledge quickly and with motivation.
2. The amount of transferable, readily usable knowledge the applicant brings to the operation.

> "What method of training employees do you prefer, and how do you personally use that method with your immediate staff?"

Rationale.   The interviewer should try to focus on the one-to-one training modality, since this directly relates to the applicant's ability to coach his employees toward improved performance. The interviewer may be quite surprised to receive a response that does not really focus that much on a mentor reltionship between the applicant and his employees, since the French as managers tend not to be mentors when it comes to providing personal assistance to employee training.

The United Kingdom

Although we are considering here the British, the Scottish, and the Welsh as representative of the United Kingdom, the differences among them are not significant enough to be able to make definitive distinctions in the approach to the interview.

Accomplishments

> "Give three accomplishments that have produced results that had a direct influence on productivity outcomes for your company (business unit)."

Rationale.   The emphasis on results and productivity is characteristic of managers from the United Kingdom, although it has been argued that they tend to theorize more than they put words into action. By the applicant's answer, the depth and detail rendered, the interviewer can determine if the applicant is a doer with a drive toward results or merely an "armchair" manager. The British do, however, tend to be a bit more peripheral in their answers than their Welsh or Scottish counterparts. They may not get to the point as quickly.

> "Take me through, from beginning to end, an account of your role in a key project your unit (company) was involved in."

Rationale.   United Kingdom applicants tend to be visionaries or big-picture oriented, and they are at their best when describing a process or an event in vivid detail, finishing with an outcome that has clear future implications for the industry on a global scale.

Skills

"What particular set of skills have you employed toward the achievement of your goals as a manager?"

Rationale.   To get a wide-angle view of the applicant's array of skills used on a broad, long-term scale that is in keeping with the applicant's work-ethic purview.

"Which of your skills are you planning to further develop?"

Rationale.   Because of the influence of the social class system, especially in Great Britain, there exists a strong drive in professionals from that country to improve themselves toward a greater acceptance by peers and superiors. The applicant most probably will answer this question with a sense of purpose and enthusiasm. The interviewer will thus be able to get a clear reading of the applicant's self-motivation along with a prescribed set of ready skills.

Knowledge

"What aspect(s) of your job function do you know the most about?"
"How much do you know about the newest state-of-the-art technology influencing the industry?

Rationale.   Both questions are intended to elicit the kind of thorough comprehensive response the interviewer would expect from the applicant since U.K. applicants, by virtue of their educational culture, are very keen on being thoroughly knowledgeable about their fields of endeavor.

American

The approach to be taken with Americans is very similar to that for the British, but with a bit more of a "hands-on" focus in the questions, as follows.

Accomplishments

"Which of your accomplishments do you regard as the most meaningful from an immediate, direct-results orientation?"

Rationale.   Americans are accustomed to producing tangible outcomes with quick turnarounds. They prefer talking about major undertakings in which they took charge, met the objective, and maintained the impact on the environment. To elicit a "hands-on" response requires that the interviewer maintain a direct, declarative questioning style when discussing the applicant's accomplishments.

Skills

"Give me three or four of your most critical skills that you use consistently and that are recognized by others as excellent."

Rationale.   Because Americans are generally accustomed to an immediate application of skills to produce end results quickly, they are usually ready to enumerate the skills that have made them adept at the work they do. They usually rely on three or four key skills that they have honed and reinforced throughout the years via training and transferring to new jobs or new companies much more frequently than their British counterparts. The interviewer will be more successful in being able to probe the depth and use of each skill rendered in response to his asking the question as phrased above.

Knowledge

"Explain what you know about *X*" (where *X* might refer to (1) product knowledge, (2) a management process or method, or (3) a competitor's recent product, strategy, and so on).

Rationale.   This direct question cuts right through to the heart of the applicant's knowledge base, since it goes right to the specifics and allows for *direct probes* that may follow the applicant's response. Americans who are accustomed to keenly competing with peers in various business arenas are the ones likely to respond most accurately and with a good deal of depth. The interviewer should expect the applicant to even go so far as giving a mini-dissertation regarding his knowledge base.

II. Approaches to Performance Coaching on an International Basis

Particular attention must be paid to the performance maintenance and improvement of the intercultural team as a whole, especially where a critical team project is concerned. The aggregate performance of the team is the direct result of the individual behaviors of each of the team partners, and the end result of the team's performance output will be affected in terms of quality, quantity, and *efficiency* according to the behavioral work styles of the team partners, both in concert with other team partners and in terms of *individual* style preferences.

That is why a manager must tailor a performance coaching approach to each team partner according to that team partner's cultural paradigms encompassing the following:

1. Individual work style preference.
2. Sociocultural behaviors stemming from environmental conditioning in the home country.
3. The OCL (Operating Comfort Level) that is manifest in the team partner's work environment.
4. Influences by former bosses.

The methods of performance coaching that can be successfully used are:

1. Developmental Coaching
2. Corrective Coaching

Developmental Coaching is defined as the process used to get the individual to perform at a higher level, taking on new and different responsibilities and tasks of usually greater magnitude, depth, and diversity. The individual is coached in a way that allows him to "stretch" his capabilities to acquire new skills, add new knowledge, and accept a new paradigm of perceptions and behaviors regarding the operation as a whole.

Corrective Coaching, on the other hand, is the process by which remedial action is taken to adjust and modify a worker's performance that has fallen below expected standards of output or has incurred a behavior or behaviors that have detracted from the individual's overall job performance. The objective is to get the worker back on track to an acceptable level by prospective developmental coaching.

In both types of coaching the manager must establish a format or schema for the *coaching engagement,* which is defined as one-to-one communication modality with a predetermined set of objectives and a well thought out structure for obtaining the most positive results from the dialogue.

A suggested approach for the manager conducting a Developmental Coaching engagement might be the following:

1. Identify the target areas of prospective achievement desired for the worker to attain. List the precise performance objectives and the skills/knowledge factors required to reach this new level of performance.
2. Examine the worker's *current* track record of performance from previous evaluations.
3. *Thoroughly* review the worker's *cultural profile,* that is, communicative style and aptitude in the designated language spoken in the current

work environment. Also include a review of previous intercultural teams the worker has been a member of and the *specific role* he has played on that team.

4. Set aside at least one hour for the one-to-one engagement.
5. Prepare a list of specific questions to ask the worker along with a list of select motivational and reinforcing statements you will direct at the worker at the appropriate times during the meeting. The content, nature, and timing of these statements will vary according to the cultural background of the worker.
6. Structure and be prepared to explain the JPCU (Job Performance Check Up).

The manager has two roles in Developmental Coaching:

1. "Tell" role
2. "Helper" role

In the "Tell" role the manager acts as mentor/adviser who informs the worker of the details, purpose, and overall rationale of the plan to develop the worker's performance to an expanded level. Key facts are revealed to the worker to provide a clearer picture of his obligation to the proposal. The manager *fully explains* the "how's" and the "what's" of the new paradigm of performance objectives.

In the "Helper" role the manager provides *coaching* skills in assisting the worker (usually at the work site) to acquire new facets to his work style and to learn new skills. Here the manager does indeed serve as a *personal instructor* to the worker. Also, if the worker feels more comfortable in being coached in his native language and not in the work environment operational language, the manager can work with an interpreter (usually a co-worker of the employee) in tandem in the "Helper" role.

The Job Performance Check Up (JPCU)

The JPCU is a *weekly* meeting between the manager and the employee to review what has transpired since the previous coaching engagement. The JPCU is usually informal and lasts no longer than 15 to 20 minutes. The benefits of the JPCU are the following:

1. Tracks the worker's progress more closely.
2. Manager can give the worker updates on new events or objectives that might affect the worker's progress.
3. Maintains a tighter reporting relationship between manager and worker.
4. Allows for a timely intervention in the way of adjustments or "course corrections" that are necessary in the worker's development.

5. Acts as a *motivational device* to keep the worker's enthusiasm and energy high.

In consideration of cross-cultural factors affecting the success of Developmental Coaching, it is necessary to infuse CSDs (Cultural Densitivity Devices) into the process that take into account the worker's temperament and learning readiness for the engagement.

Here are some coaching suggestions when dealing with Japanese and Korean workers.

Coaching the Japanese

It is well known that Japanese tend to work well in teams, but each team partner has a dislike for being singled out to take on new tasks or responsibilities, since he does not want to appear to the others as "breaking the harmony (*wa*) of the team." If for example, a Japanese worker is suddenly given supervisory responsibility over his peers in the team's having to tackle a crisis or emergency, he will accept the responsibility but will be slow to take action and even may meet with each peer separately to give them the reason for his new post and to assure them that he will be fair. He may even go so far as to *apologize* to his peers for his sudden "move up" in the team and display *his* discomfort for having discomforted *them*. That is why the manager must try to gain the confidence of the Japanese worker during the "Tell" role phase of the engagement. The recommended procedure is as follows:

1. Indicate what it is you wish to teach or communicate.
   Explain in the form of an overview what you expect as an end result.
2. Provide concrete examples of what you are talking about. Use visuals, graphs, and physical displays if necessary.
3. Summarize what you have said or demonstrated.
4. Repeat the rationale behind your explanation.
5. Ask for feedback from the worker.
6. Assure the worker that you will be his mentor and guide throughout the event.
7. Schedule a follow-up engagement soon after the worker has had a chance to use the information you imparted. Japanese are usually reluctant to take the initiative to approach the manager soon after the engagement. They feel embarrassed to admit they are unclear about their directives.

Some typical reactions to notice and interpret during the engagement are the following:

1. The Japanese will listen very attentively to everything the manager is saying, but they are processing the information in separate mental boxes, or *kata,* and may not be integrating the information into a big

picture with enough vision to actually see themselves operating in a new paradigm.

2. The eyes looking downward during the manager's explanation of changes to which the worker will be expected to adjust.
3. A lengthier-than-usual silence or pause by the Japanese worker when asked to respond to the manager's remarks.
4. Sometimes the Japanese will respond with "I see" intermittently after several of the manager's consecutive statements. This does not necessarily indicate that the worker understands the content and rationale of the statements but is using the Japanese communicative culturism of *aizuchi,* which is the verbal reinforcement voiced to keep the speaker talking. This is used both as a means of politeness and deference to the speaker and for the purpose of "buying time" to determine how the listener really feels about what is being conveyed to him.
5. The Japanese worker may have no questions if asked or will ask a question pertaining to *when* the new duties will commence and *where* the location will be. In other words they usually focus on the "time" and "place" elements rather than the "how's" or process elements of the new paradigm.

Suggested Communicative Techniques When in the "Tell" Role

1. Explain the details in a sequential fashion from point A to point B to point C, and so on. Try not to loop back to previous statements at random or use appositives, since the Japanese process information in straight lines and tend to re-analyze only information immediately transmitted from the previous sentence.
2. Do not maintain steady eye contact with the Japanese worker, and be relaxed and deliberate in your communication delivery.
3. Ask the worker to summarize what you have explained to him.
4. Suggest that the worker take notes before you begin. Japanese usually prefer to write down important statements in their native language even though they are being communicated to in another language which they understand.
5. Assure the worker that you have every reason to believe that he will adapt very well to the changes and that you are confident in his abilities.

Typical Expressions Used in the "Tell" Role

1. "Before I explain the details of your role in this new project, Yoshi, I would like to say that this will be a valuable experience for your career in this organization."
2. "As I am explaining the new job point by point, please feel free to ask me a question at any time during my explanation. I want to be sure that we both understand the facts in the same way."

3. "At this time what assistance do you think you'll need to adjust to that new situation?"
4. "Kenzo-san, you can rely on me as your teacher to help you adjust to your new responsibilities. So, please, call me anytime."

Statement 4 may sound trite to the Westerner, but to the Japanese it is reminiscent of the zen master demonstrating his interest in the pupil so that the latter will develop and grow in the teaching.

Suggested Communicative Techniques When in the "Helper" Role

1. State the purpose of your intervening to help the worker adjust to the new situation. It is important to gain a clear understanding with the Japanese worker as to exactly *how* you as the coach/mentor are prepared to help him develop further. A typical introductory comment might be:

"I'd like to take time out now and again to see if I can assist you in your efforts. Before I suggest specific ways, do you have any wishes or ideas?"

If at this point, the worker responds negatively or indifferently, there may be a number of causes. Such behavior may occur with subordinates who possess limited verbal skills or with those who truly have not given much thought to their own growth or progress. If this occurs, the following comments may be successful with Japanese worker:

"I think it must be a little difficult for you to talk about this topic. I understand. We can talk later, all right."

"Please understand that it is perfectly all right with me if you prefer to continue on your own for a while. We will talk again in a couple of days, okay?"

"I understand how tricky the adjustment can be at first. I can remember when I was in that situation a few years ago. I'm here to help. We'll talk about it later."

Any one of the foregoing statements leaves the door open for the worker to mention what is making it difficult for him to adjust. These expressions are structured in a similar way to the zen master's approach to the pupil in encouraging him to come forward, on his own, when he has a problem that he cannot solve.

The manager will find that these expressions are very motivational to the Japanese worker. More direct and coercive expressions may alienate the worker immediately and trust on the part of the worker may dissipate quickly.

2. Invite self-appraisal. Although this is an important step in the process, it must be handled very carefully. Since Japanese do not like to self-analyze or compare themselves to others, the manager must take great care not to press the worker to step out of his "comfort zone" when asking for his opinion of his progress thus far. Also, the manager should be very careful not to probe too deeply into the Japanese worker's *kata* of his performance, that is, his perception of his self-esteem. This will be regarded as an attempt at penetrating his OCL (Operating Comfort Level) to the point of breaching his personal *wa* (harmony). He may reveal to the manager at this point only those areas of development he feels comfortable speaking about. That is why the manager must anticipate another follow-up meeting to cover those areas not brought up by the worker.

   Useful expressions are:

"Well, Kenji, how have you adjusted so far? What has been relatively easy for you to accommodate?"

"Kondo-san, this is our first follow-up meeting since my explaining the details of the new project and your new role. How have things been going so far? Feel free to tell me, in your own words, what some of the high points and low points have been."

Corrective Coaching. When the worker's performance has fallen off and is not meeting the agreed-to requirements of the job, the manager *must* intervene to take corrective action. The primary objectives of the intervention are to:

1. Cause the worker to be aware of the problem.
2. Identify the source of the problem—social or work related.
3. Come up with a prescription for change leading to reestablishment of the worker's performance at an acceptable level.

The manager has noticed negative behaviors in the worker's performance that the worker himself may not have detected. If this is the case, the manager should begin a coaching engagement as soon as possible. A good corrective coaching model is the following:

1. Get to the point. Explain the reason for the engagement and your perception of the problem.
2. Describe the situation or event(s) that have either resulted from or have been influenced by the worker's deficient performance levels or negative behavior.
3. Listen to the worker's response to determine if he is aware of the problem.
4. Identify and agree on the problem.

5. Identify and propose possible solutions to the problem and *include* the worker in the finding of the solution.
6. Have the worker sum up the agreed to course of action.
7. Set a follow-up date for another engagement (a JPCU).
8. Close the session by showing encouragement to the worker.

Numbers 5 and 6 are what constitute the "Action Plan Negotiation and Summary" of the corrective coaching engagement. The points of the plan are actually written down in prescription form and are *mutually* agreed to by both manager and worker. The worker is asked to review the plan privately and respond with questions before it is implemented.

A JPCU no more than seven to ten days later is conducted to determine the employee's comfort level with the plan.

With Japanese workers, corrective coaching engagements are difficult, especially for Western managers whose cultures are so divergent from the Japanese culture. Here are some helpful guidelines:

1. Never appear annoyed or angry with the worker during the engagement. Expressions of anger, either vocal or nonverbal, will demoralize the Japanese worker and defeat the purpose of the engagement.
2. Be sure to repeat the positive points you wish to make in the meeting while downplaying the negative ones.
3. Refrain from using the word "you" in your context, so as not to appear accusatory.
4. Do not unduly praise the worker at the start of the engagement and then suddenly switch to a more serious and penetrating communicative style.
5. Avoid phrases or comments like the following:

"Look, I'm not here to make you feel uncomfortable or to alienate you from the others, but . . ."
"Well, *you* seem to think that there is no problem here, but *I* do!"
"Akira-san, do you believe that you are performing in the way that is expected?"

Comments like these will cause an immediate breakdown in communication. The worker may even fail to respond at all, despite the fact that his communication skills in the operational language are excellent.

When faced with a worker who is reluctant to respond, the manager may want to revert to the "Five Action Steps," which may expedite the coaching process.

Five Action Steps

1. Focus immediately on the need for improvement in the worker's performance and *your* proposed prescription for positive change. Be positive and constructive in your comments.

2. Ask for the worker's feedback and for his cooperation in agreeing on a direction to take toward improvement. Be open to discussing the ideas you both have.
3. Come to agreement on and write down the steps each of you will take—the overall strategy.
4. Motivate the employee by expressing your confidence that he will succeed in his attempt to improve.
5. Set a follow-up date for a JPCU (within three days) to keep a closer check on the worker's attempt to correct the problem.

Coaching the Koreans

Unlike the Japanese, the Koreans expect a more *direct* approach to be taken in performance coaching, whether they be in the manager's role or in the role of the employee. What the western manager must understand when coaching Koreans is the concept of *han,* which seems to be an intrinsic aspect of the Korean's drive to succeed in overcoming all odds. *Han* is a state of mind that has as one of its precepts an "always going forward" motion toward completion of a task or goal. *Han* has been part of Korean culture for centuries and is responsible for their having overcome so many hardships in their past, their battles with and occupation by the Japanese in particular. One British manager remarked, when reflecting on his management of a small manufacturing company in Seoul in the mid-1980s, "Just tell the Korean what you would have him do, the manner in which it is to be done, a long list of details to be observed, and say this to him only once, and he will return with *exactly* your expected results and probably in record time!"

Therefore the "Tell" role is of paramount importance when coaching Koreans. The manager must be *clear* and *emphatic* when giving instructions and explaining the rationale behind the requirements for the job or task. Because Koreans tend to keep fairly direct eye contact when communicating (unlike the Japanese), the western manager should not be reticent about squarely facing the employee with good, steady eye contact when communicating. The Korean will not feel uncomfortable, provided that the manager has determined the employee's positive attitudinal state of mind, or *kibun,* as the Koreans call it. *Kibun* is a culturalism that can be defined as "good feeling" or "sense of well being," which is a strong self-motivating factor among Koreans in society. When their *kibun* is high, they are more likely to get the most out of the coaching session, whether it be developmental coaching or corrective coaching. In the absence of *kibun,* corrective coaching should be avoided by the manager, because the Korean will take even subtle reprimands very seriously and become demotivated. Koreans very much enjoy statements of praise or confidence coming from superiors. This elevates their *kibun* and spurs them on to greater achievement. The Korean employee has the boss as the center of attention. Unlike the

Japanese who centers his achievements around the company (*kaisha*) as being the prime entity, the Korean, because of Confucian precepts embedded in his psyche from both formal educational and family educational tenets of behavior in Korean society, is bound to obey the boss, give him undying fialty. The concept of "the company" is not as important.

The JPCU is a strong motivating factor to use when coaching Koreans because it demonstrates the manager's concern for the employee's performance, in that the manager is encouraging the employee to do a good job. This feeds into the employee's *kibun* and serves as a motivator in itself.

Useful Statements to Use in the JPCU

1. "Mr. Kim, you seem to be in control of things at this point. How do you feel about the new assignment after one week?"
2. "I will go to great lengths to help you, Mr. Park. Just call me when you feel you need to."
3. "Mr. Li, if there are other resources you may need, please do not hesitate to come to me."
4. "It's okay to express your thoughts freely about this assignment to me, Mr. Choi."
5. "Your efforts in adjusting to the new situation are greatly appreciated by me and other members of the team, Mr. Park."

Do not regard these statements as patronizing, as Western employees might interpret them. The Koreans take such statements at their face value, and they put a great deal of trust in the boss for expressing his sentiments.

The manager need not closely monitor the Korean's performance by walking about his work area and "inspecting" the work. Koreans are independent-minded and entrepreneurial and demonstrate a great degree of responsibility in the work they do. That is why it is usually not necessary to apply the "Helper" role in performance coaching with most Koreans.

Coaching the French

The French tend to be difficult to coach because of their tendency to take charge and run things their way. The Napoleonic Code indeed still has a strong influence on French business, and it is openly reflected in the way Frenchmen work.

In coaching French employees several caveats must be taken into account:

1. Be sure not to get to the point right away in addressing a performance deficiency. The French do not take criticism lightly, and they may

become very defensive—in fact, rather argumentative. Engage in small talk at first. Avoid discussing work issues at the outset.

2. When confronting a work issue that reflects performance deficiencies, the manager would do well to *preface* corrective remarks with statements like:

> I realize that at times we all experience intense pressure when faced with a difficult challenge, and we refrain from airing our concerns to others who might help, because we feel we alone can handle it. But *I* believe, Mr. Dufresne, that it is important to ask for assistance and advice when the situation becomes difficult to manage. I have noticed that on two recent occasions you have had some difficulty.

3. Keep direct eye contact and lean forward in the chair to fully engage with the employee. This will cause the employee to take you seriously because the French tend to adopt a relaxed sitting posture in one-to-one meetings which is accompanied by a casual attitude toward the issue.

4. Do not give the employee at this meeting a prescription for improvement. He may resent it. With the French, the manager has to use a "shaping" process for behavioral change. That is, he must present the plan for corrective action in small doses so that the employee will feel more comfortable with the process.

5. Do not enter into a debate with employee over details and minor issues. The French are accustomed to putting up long-winded arguments on minutia. At times the rationale behind their argument can be to the non-French quite convoluted and difficult to sort out.

6. In a Developmental Coaching modality try to avoid expressions like:

> Mr. Dumont, we feel that you're ready to take on a new responsibility.

The employee, not having had a chance to negotiate the issues, will probably feel pressured and will resent being dictated to. This may appear to be a curious reaction from the non-French manager's point of view, since the same Napoleonic tenets are now being directed *toward* the French employee, who will fell uncomfortable with the situation.

JPCU's should be handled judiciously, in that they should be very informal and arranged to allow the employee to *volunteer* feedback on his own accord.

Positive feedback to the employee is essential. The manager must reinforce any positive behavior the employee is responsible for. The French tend to see themselves as perfectionists who pay attention to detail in their work. They consider their work more an art form than an obligation or a series of mechanical score points. Hence, the manager must reinforce the employee with positive comments early in the engagement.

Coaching United Kingdom and American Employees

In recent years the American and British business cultures have come closer together in terms of communicative protocols, team alliances, partnerships, and so on. Many British businesspeople have been educated in and have done a considerable amount of business in the United States. Americans similarly have spent more time in the United Kingdom on business than ever before, and their interface with the British in both the United States and the United Kingdom has increased significantly since the mid-1970s. Experience therefore dictates that the developmental and corrective coaching techniques outlined in the beginning of this section are applicable with *little adjustment,* from a sociocultural point of view, when dealing with both British and American employees. As one would expect, both the British and the American manager have to take into account the socioeconomic standing and educational level of the employees being coached, but no significantly different approach or protocol need be taken or observed when coaching in either culture. One minor exception regarding the American manager coaching the British employee is that the American should realize class distinction is still a very observable reality in Great Britain. One still hears Brits talk about the class system as a determinant to one's getting ahead. In this regard, American managers should refrain from the use of words or phrases that might mark a clear distinction between classes of employees or cause a British professional to feel as if he is being treated on an equal footing with those below his social and professional station. This may very well result in his failure to cooperate with the manager during and after the coaching sessions.

III. Performance Evaluation: An Intercultural Approach

One of the most serious challenges facing managers is finding a performance evaluation approach, a system, fair to all employees of different cultural backgrounds, that will accurately evaluate their performance against standards set and explained during the selection process in the prehire interviews. Of the many systems tried in international companies, the MBO (management by objectives) performance evaluative approach, with its consistency in measuring, results in an *objective* way without undue concern for cultural differences as deterrent. Simply put, a set of agreed to (by the manager and employee jointly) work objectives with timelines for completing each objective is worked out by both parties. JPCUs are arranged in advance on a schedule so that the employee's performance can be monitored and coaching intervened, if necessary, to prepare the employee for the formal MBO review.

In a normal MBO review meeting, the manager covers each of the objectives that the employee should have completed by the time of the review. Each objective is examined as to its completeness, the quality of the end result, and the workstyle executed. Besides the objectives, a review of Actions Qualities (AQ) can be part of the evaluation. Action Qualities are performance behavioral characteristics demonstrated by the employee during the achievement of the objectives. What is taken into account are the degree and magnitude of the AQ and how they had a positive impact on the results. Some typical Action Qualities are the following:

1. Follow through
2. Leadership
3. Ingenuity
4. Delegation
5. Goal setting
6. Fact-finding
7. Persistence

The manager can apply the MBO approach using the Job Model as a standard. For example, he can take the Results Achievable section (Section I) and compare that to what the employee has actually accomplished since starting the job. In addition, the manager can set a weighted scale (1 to 5, "5" being the heaviest) to measure the magnitude of the AQs. Also, when considering an objective as having been completed, the manager may take into account the AQ connected with that objective and its influence on achieving the objective.

In the review meeting the manager must proceed step by step, covering each objective in an explanatory manner, allowing the employee ample feedback for each objective. The feedback should be in both oral and written form to minimize the perceptual disparity that can enter the picture in a performance review meeting. Perceptual disparity is most glaring when exhibited by individuals of diverse cultures. For example, an American manager may adopt a review style that is direct and somewhat admonishing in the meeting. If this attitude is directed toward an Asian employee—Chinese, Japanese, or Filipino, in particular—it will almost definitely demotivate and even demoralize that employee. Asians do not receive criticism or negative news very well.

The French employee, however, might take offense at this approach in the way of openly disagreeing or even debating with the manager; *and* he might very well "go his own way" and not adhere to the recommendations made by the manager. With the Koreans, it is okay for the western manager to be somewhat direct when discussing performance objectives, since it is well known that the Koreans are very objectives-oriented in their work performance, even more than the Japanese; and they will go to great lengths to succeed in meeting goals. They will not feel offended as much as their

Asian counterparts will when they are confronted directly. In fact, they are always eager to know exactly where they slipped and are ready to make an adjustment immediately. Koreans take their job performance seriously, and they expect feedback from their managers. The reason stems from a cultural factor originating from Confucianism. Like the father in a family, the immediate manager is the focal point, the most important figure in the company to the employee. It is to the boss one pays homage and shows respect, and to whom one goes for advice. The boss has the greatest influence on the Korean employee and is trusted implicitly. This may not always be the case with the Japanese manager/employee relationship, where the company, *kaisha,* is more important than the immediate boss. In fact, most Japanese employees are reluctant to approach their managers for help or coaching. Performance review meetings are conducted with plenty of indirect communication about performance objectives and results.

Both the British and the American employee can accommodate a more direct MBO format with tighter guidelines in the evaluation's structure. For example, the manager more easily reviews each objective in terms of measurable and specific details, which can call forth an explanation from the employee as to how and why he either did or did not meet the objectives and thereby justify a numerical weight assigned. One also will discover that both British and American employees are sensitive to the aforementioned seven Action Qualities. They take an aggressive stand with regard to measuring up to the comparative analysis the manager may set up as a standard reference point for employees at that particular peer level. Thus, the manager would do well to explore each AQ in an in-depth manner with the employee in *two* dimensions: (1) how the AQ affects his managing others, and (2) how the AQ affects the manager's managing himself (i.e. how has he become a better self-leader).

In considering the apparent contrasts in feedback when comparing Japanese, Korean, French, British, and American employees in terms of their respective performance records, it behooves the manager to establish a culturally contrastive categorical chart that will at a glance allow the manager to recognize areas of the evaluation he should avoid emphasizing and areas he should explore more deeply with each employee according to the employee's cultural background (see Table 1).

TABLE 1
Evaluative Areas

Culture	Planning	Managing People	Quantitative Problem Solving	Team Play
French	Tend to be pedantic; inconsistent; good at short range.	Inflexible; little feedback; expect accuracy, details.	Deep thinkers; excellent; cover all bases.	Inconsistent; prefer to be leaders; detach from team early.
Japanese	Good at long range *only*. Need guidance.	Good with own culture; Poor with non-Japanese.	Good; accurate; cover all bases.	Excellent; consistent, harmonious.
Korean	Good at both long and short range; act on plan quickly.	Direct, abrupt, too noncommunicative; poor with non-Koreans.	Top of the line; accurate, detailed.	Excellent; forward moving; tireless.
American	Good at short range, weak on long range, spends too much time on planning.	More subjective than objective, not enough book knowledge on human psychology.	Fair, not exemplary.	Good, but needs leadership; trouble with self-leading.
British	Visionary; lack implementation readiness; tend to philosophize too much.	On and off consistency; need role model; class distinction plays a key role.	Good	Can be good with proper leadership skills.

Intercultural Skills and Recommended Behaviors

The Psychological Perspective for Training Programs

Tomoko Yoshida   Director of Training, Japanese Programs, ITT
Sheraton Hawaii, Honolulu, Hawaii

Richard W. Brislin   Senior Fellow and Project Director, Program
on Education and Training, East-West Center,
Honolulu, Hawaii

Introduction: A Joint Venture

Jack Robinson is the regional manager of XY corporation, a joint venture between an American firm X and a Chinese firm Y. He has been working in Guangdong for the past two years. After initial difficulties, Jack now feels very much part of the ingroup. Jack has felt especially indebted to his subordinate, Mr. Wu, who has been an invaluable source of assistance and advice.

During the last meeting with their board of directors, however, Jack started to doubt Mr. Wu's allegiance to him. When Jack's proposal was attacked by Mr. Yang, a senior executive and the representative of the Chinese side of the venture, Mr. Wu remained silent and did not back Jack up. Because Jack had previously discussed the proposal with Mr. Wu and had received his full endorsement, he was puzzled by Mr. Wu's seemingly apathetic attitude. After the meeting, Jack confronted Mr. Wu about his lack of support during the meeting. Although Mr. Wu apologized profusely, he was unable to provide adequate reasons for his behavior and was therefore unable to dissipate Jack's disappointment, confusion, and anger.

112

Distressed by Jack's resentment toward him, Mr. Wu sought out Mr. Shi, a former classmate and a trusted friend, for advice. Below is an excerpt from their conversation.

S: You look very troubled Mr. Wu . . . how can I help you?
W: Thank you for coming, Mr. Shi. I have found myself in a very difficult situation at work. During our last meeting, Mr. Yang attacked Jack's proposal. As you know, I have been working under Jack for two years now, but previous to that I worked under Mr. Yang for ten years. Although I feel obligated to Jack, I cannot let down Mr. Yang either. Jack also doesn't seem to understand how inappropriate it would be for me to speak out against an older person at a public meeting like that. I know he feels betrayed but I am not sure what to do . . . he is my boss after all.

After extensive discussion regarding the conflict Mr. Wu was experiencing between his former Chinese manager and Jack, Mr. Shi agreed to talk to Jack about the matter. Although Jack felt that he understood better the predicament in which Mr. Wu found himself, he was still angry and confused as to why Mr. Wu did not talk to him directly. Did Mr. Wu perceive their relationship to be too fragile? Or was he simply being dishonest?

It is not uncommon to find very knowledgeable and culturally sensitive individuals in situations similar to that of Jack's because the issues involved are commonly experienced by overseas businesspeople. Chances are that if Jack read this critical incident as a third person, he would not have any problems pointing out some of the reasons underlying this conflict. He might argue that "Jack" should not have expected to override Mr. Yang's authority since seniority is a crucial factor to the Chinese. He might have also mentioned that "Jack" should have used to his advantage Mr. Wu's connection with Mr. Yang instead of putting Mr. Wu in a very awkward position. The use of an intermediary is often talked about but used too infrequently by businesspeople working in Asia. "Jack" could have asked Mr. Wu to talk to Mr. Yang *prior* to the meeting to elicit Yang's response and support.

Knowing and doing too often do not coincide. Many Westerners know that eating raw fish is perfectly normal for the Japanese, but they have a hard time eating *sashimi* themselves. Most behaviors that are culturally different from one's own tend to provoke strong gut-level reactions. Although Jack might be comfortable *knowing* that the Chinese use intermediaries frequently, if prompted to do so himself, he might feel a strong sense of guilt for being "manipulative and scheming." Learning to act in a culturally appropriate manner consists not only of awareness and knowledge that the behavior is important but also of overcoming the emotional reactions and actual practice of the skill.

In the following sections, we begin by proposing that there are four basic components of a good cross-cultural training program designed to prepare people for successful interactions in cultures other than their own (described more fully in Brislin & Yoshida, 1994b). These components are (1) awareness, (2) knowledge, (3) emotional challenges, and (4) skills/ behaviors. With the understanding that trainees should go through all four dimensions either on their own or during a workshop, we then turn our focus on one possible method trainers can use in teaching these skills as well as offering various examples of culture-specific behaviors that can be taught during training sessions.

Cross-Cultural Training: The Challenges

Cross-cultural training refers to the special efforts made in preparing people to deal effectively with culturally different others (Black & Mendenthall, 1990; Brislin & Yoshida, 1994a, 1994b; Gudykunst & Hammer, 1983). Training periods can range from hours, weeks, or even to months. Because of the practicalities of time and cost, however, businesses often opt for the shortest possible training package.

Although the importance of cross-cultural training has been acknowledged by more businesses in recent years, the general public's awareness leaves much to be desired. Consequently, many trainers find that a significant amount of their time is spent explaining to their clients and trainees the all-important role that cultural understanding takes in determining the success or failure of overseas business dealings. The unfortunate result is that too often trainees leave a short cross-cultural training workshop painfully aware of their past insensitivities without learning alternative behaviors that are more appropriate

In the same way that computer illiterate people must (1) recognize that there is a need to learn how to use a computer (*awareness*), (2) learn about the various components of the machine (*knowledge*), (3) deal with the stresses and frustrations (*emotional challenges*) that accompany learning something new, and (4) practice using the computer (*skills/behavior*), effective cross-cultural training should also ensure that trainees have covered all four stages. Without *awareness,* trainees will be less inclined or motivated to learn about effective cross-cultural communication strategies. On the other hand, a workshop that covers only *awareness* will result in a group of trainees who are very much aware of their cultural faux pas yet unable to correct them. Coverage of knowledge only is also incomplete. To reinforce this notion, take a moment to jot down a list of behaviors you know you should do or change and yet have not been able to implement. Some examples are eating less junk food, exercising more, being more patient with one's children, watching less TV, avoiding procrastination, and cutting down one's alcohol intake. If you are like the majority of us, you should not have any problem coming up with a substantial list.

The third component of a good cross-cultural training program is dealing with emotional challenges. Most people who have had fairly extensive contact with culturally different others admit that their experiences have been quite trying at times. When interacting with culturally different people who challenge our core values, many people feel their personal identities being questioned as well. As mentioned earlier, culturally different behaviors can also elicit gut-level reactions that we need to resolve (e.g., Jack and Mr. Wu's emotional reactions in the critical incident). An effective cross-cultural training program should, therefore, prepare trainees to face these challenges by helping them come up with realistic expectations as well as by providing them with effective methods to reduce stress.

The importance of creating realistic or even pessimistic expectations cannot be exaggerated. Often when we are disappointed by something, it is not so much the actual object or event that is disappointing but the *disparity* between our expectations and reality that we find so frustrating. For example many of us have, at some point or another, probably sat by the telephone in wild anticipation hoping for it to ring. When hours pass and the phone does not ring, disappointment, remorse, and possibly anger follow. If we had not been expecting the phone to ring in the first place, however, none of those feelings would result. It is, therefore, not the fact that the phone did not ring but the reality that there was a gap between our expectations and what actually happened that created the undue stress. Helping trainees come up with a realistic picture of what to expect during cross-cultural interaction is, therefore, a critical training technique. Although it is tempting to overlook "emotions" as a dimension when faced with a tight time frame, trainers should keep in mind that the most common reason for the premature return of expatriate businesspeople and their families stems from stress and other psychological reasons (Adler, 1991).

Because of scarcity of time, some trainers skip the first three steps and plunge into the skills/behavior component. The problem that this creates is that trainees may either be uninterested in learning since they do not understand the significance of the behaviors, *or* they may use the behaviors inappropriately. An example is teaching a group of businesspeople how to bow properly toward their Japanese counterparts. Two possible problems are likely to arise. Some resistant trainees might exclaim, "Why should *we* be the ones who need to change!" On the other hand, extremely enthusiastic trainees can also find themselves in trouble if they bow indiscriminately without understanding the various rules that surround this gesture.

Another problem that conscientious trainers face is that if they try to cover the three preceding stages during a short training program, they will be barely able to touch on the actual practice of the behaviors or skills. Using the analogy presented earlier, sending trainees out without enough coverage of the skills/behavior component is similar to sending computer trainees out of the classroom before they have actually touched a keyboard, much less used the keyboard to command the computer to carry out a variety of tasks. Although some trainees will be able to teach themselves by carefully consulting a manual, this tedious process is likely to discourage many others.

The ideal, of course, is that businesses be willing to buy training packages that are at least two weeks long. Without that luxury, however, trainers can often effectively shorten their programs by conducting a good needs assessment because the main concern for trainers is that participants have covered all four stages, whether it be during the workshop or not. In many cases, trainers may be pleasantly surprised by a group who are already past the awareness, or even the knowledge, stage.

The other alternative is to provide trainees with field exercises they can work on outside of the training setting (examples can be found in Brislin & Yoshida, 1994a). In the same way that socialization is a lifelong process, resocialization must also be approached with a long-term perspective. Training sessions should, therefore, not be seen as ends in themselves but should be perceived as a means to an end. Instead of drilling specific information into trainees' minds, trainers should focus on teaching them how to learn on their own.

Awareness

I don't believe that people from other countries are that different from us. I feel that as long as we treat them with respect and genuine interest, true understanding is possible.

This remark can often be heard from well-intentioned individuals who believe in commonalities among people while ignoring the differences that exist among cultures. Although the statement may be quite true in essence, what it misses is that the *manner* in which "respect and genuine interest" are shown can vary across cultures. A well-intentioned American's casual posture and use of first names can be interpreted as rude by the British, whereas British formality may, in turn, be interpreted as being aloof by the Americans.

Culture provides guidance as to what is considered "good or bad," "right or wrong," "desirable or undesirable." Culture also provides us with what is considered "common sense" and what is "normal." Furthermore, culture provides us with the specific manner in which the various messages are relayed (Brislin, 1993). For example, does one look into the other person's eyes to show respect or does one avoid them? Does a soft voice mean politeness or lack of confidence? Is the ability to say "no" considered an asset or a liability?

Looking back at the critical incident that was used to introduce this chapter, it is obvious that neither Jack nor Mr. Wu was *intentionally* creating this dilemma. What it reveals is that what Jack considered as the "proper way" for Mr. Wu to behave in a meeting differed from Mr. Wu's. Jack expected Mr. Wu to verbally support his proposal at the meeting, whereas Mr. Wu felt it inappropriate to do so. What both parties need to recognize is that the *intentions* were good. What they also need to recognize is that for culturally different others to receive the intended message we sometimes need to change our behaviors.

To help trainees realize that good intentions alone do not facilitate effective communication, various strategies are often used. One effective strategy is to trigger discussions by using critical incidents similar to that found at the beginning of this chapter. A useful resource is Brislin et al.'s 1986 book *Intercultural Interactions: A Practical Guide,* which contains a hundred critical incidents. Interesting discussion can also emerge from the viewing of certain movies readily available in video rental stores such as *Dances with Wolves, Mr. Baseball, Witness,* and *Hester Street,* among others.

Another time-consuming but effective strategy that is often used involves simulations. Many of the simulations used in cross-cultural training attempt to create a "culture shock experience" for trainees. In these exercises some of the trainees are "socialized" into becoming members of an artificial culture with specific cultural rules that govern them. They are then instructed to interact with other trainees who have been "socialized" by different, often clashing, cultural values. Because trainees are assigned a task to accomplish during their interaction, cultural differences can be seen by them as formidable barriers that create tension and frustration. Through these simulations trainees can experience on the emotional level the trials and tribulations of interacting with culturally different others. Simulations can help trainees come up with more realistic expectations while providing them with a safe environment in which to deal with the emotional issues that may arise. (More information on simulations, also referred to frequently as "role playing," can be found in Gudykunst & Hammer, 1983, and Brislin & Yoshida, 1994a; 1994b). Once trainees have attained a *general* understanding that culture is integral in determining a person's behavior, they then have the task of acquiring culture-specific awareness. Trainees who plan to conduct a significant amount of business with Koreans, for example, need to identify *specific* behaviors that differ from their own.

Knowledge

Once trainees are aware that specific behaviors may have to be modified, their next task is to understand why, where, when, to whom, and how these behaviors are displayed. Without knowledge of *why* a group of people choose to act in a certain way, it is hard for most people to accept a set of behaviors different from their own. For example, if a group of businesspeople are told that in China they should always keep their hands on the table rather than placing them on their lap during a meal, they will most likely forget and revert to their old habits during an actual dinner. On the other hand, if they are told that keeping their hands under the table will make their Chinese counterparts *very* uncomfortable wondering *what* the Westerner is doing with the hand that is under the table, trainees will most likely remember and try their best to change their behaviors.

Any behavior is accompanied by a multitude of contextual rules that determine its applicability. Take the act of shaking hands as an example. Imagine the following scenarios.

1. Diedra is introduced to Mark at a cocktail party. She shakes his hand for a few minutes and continues to hold onto it until Mark uncomfortably withdraws his.
2. Sally walks into the restaurant to meet her boyfriend Frank for an intimate dinner. As she reaches the table where Frank is, she walks up to him and shakes his hand.
3. Shawn is at the same cocktail party as Diedra and is introduced to her. Shawn does not shake hands with Diedra at that moment. Ten minutes later, however, she approaches Diedra and takes her hand to shake it.
4. Pat walks into an executive meeting 30 minutes late. As he sits down he, realizes that the person who is sitting next to him is unknown to him. Even though one of the managers is in the middle of his presentation, Pat immediately shakes hands with the new person and introduces himself.

Most people socialized in the United States should find all the foregoing scenarios inappropriate for some reason or another. The point is that even a socially desirable skill such as shaking hands can create a very bad impression if used without understanding the contextual rules that surround it.

Although the task of trying to understand these contextual rules may seem overwhelming, it can be done systematically and with relative ease with the aid of effective "cultural informants." In the same way that as children we observed, questioned, listened, and learned from parents, teachers, siblings, and the media, we can do the same when placed in a new country or society. Americans living in Japan, for example, might choose several cultural informants. They might be Japanese colleagues at work, Americans who have lived in Japan for a long time, a friendly grocer or banker, and characters from TV shows and movies.

Choosing a cultural informant, however, must be done carefully. It is not uncommon to find host country nationals who are simply bad role models or expatriates who have never learned to act in a culturally appropriate manner. It is, therefore, advised that you observe and choose very carefully those behaviors you would most like to adopt. It is also suggested that several informants be chosen. The criteria that we suggest are the following:

1. Choose someone whom you perceive to be socially adept.

2. Choose someone who is similar to you in terms of: age, gender, and social position.
3. Choose someone else who is much older than you who can provide a more traditional perspective.
4. If possible, choose someone who has lived in another culture and consequently knows about cultural differences in appropriate behaviors.

Once informants are chosen, trainees should learn from them through observing and taking notes on the "five Ws" that many people are familiar with from journalism classes:

1. *What* is the behavior?
2. *Why* is this behavior considered desirable?
3. At *whom* is the behavior aimed?
4. *Where* is this behavior most often seen?
5. *How* is this behavior delivered? What are the exact words used? How loud is the voice? What sort of facial expressions are present? Are any other types of gestures involved?

Television dramas and movies are easily accessible and handy resources that trainees can use in understanding a new and different culture. Trainees can ask the same five W questions when watching the shows. Instead of dismissing TV dramas and movies as being fictional, we recommend that trainees watch them skeptically but carefully and later continue their analyses by bringing up some of the observed behaviors during discussions with their cultural informants.

An important part of understanding culture-specific behaviors is knowing that these rules are simply generalizations that *most* people in that culture accept as common practice. Whether a person actually behaves according to the generalization depends on the individual's preferences. For example, a Japanese mother may know that it is the norm in her culture to speak with humility regarding her children's accomplishments and yet dismiss this rule and, instead, speak with pride about her children when talking to other mothers. Does this mean that the rule is not valid? We think not. A behavior becomes a cultural norm when a large percentage of the people *either* ascribe to it *or* break it while acknowledging it as a norm in which they do not believe.

Emotions

Once behaviors have been identified and trainees understand why, where, when, to whom, and how to implement them, what prevents them from putting their thoughts into action? Trying out something new often takes a lot of courage. Even when we can form an intellectually sound argument to change our behaviors, a gut-level message often manages to dissuade us. For example, people on a diet may be thoroughly convinced that eating junk food is taboo yet cannot resist listening to that inner voice that says "eat it, eat it"!

To make matters even more complex, some behaviors that are considered favorable in one culture may very well be frowned upon by another. If we reflect again on the critical incident that introduced this chapter, Jack could have asked Mr. Wu to play the intermediary for him prior to the meeting so that he could find out Mr. Yang's viewpoint ahead of time and negotiate behind the curtains. This concept, however, does not sit well with many people socialized in the United States. The gut-level reaction is that it is underhanded, manipulative, and unfair. Jack is, therefore, listening to the voice that has guided him throughout his life, the voice that has taught him how to be a "good American." To go against this voice takes a lot of conviction.

Expecting this gut-level reaction and understanding it as being normal is a first step. As we discussed earlier, creating realistic expectations is crucial in preparing oneself for changes. Another strategy that is often used is role playing. Role playing, which will be described in more detail later, is a strategy that is often used in training that allows participants to practice new behaviors in a safe and nonthreatening environment.

Almost all people who interact extensively in other cultures have many strong emotional experiences. These frequent emotional challenges to the familiar behaviors from their own culture, behaviors that no longer are useful in the other culture, are a major contributor to the phenomenon known as "culture shock." As a result of emotional confrontations, people often become the victims of stress. Dealing with stress, then, becomes an important part of cross-cultural training (Walton, 1990). Various methods have been suggested. One is to remember what methods have been successful in reducing stress in one's own culture and to try them in the other culture. These methods can include muscle relaxation, physical exercise, moving from one's work to one's enjoyable hobby, interacting with others experiencing similar stress and participating in the mutual display of sympathy, and so forth. In general, building a support system is good advice for long-term success in other cultures. The people in one's system can include co-workers, cultural informants (as already discussed), fellow countrymen also on assignment in the other country, people who share a hobby, host nationals interested in interactions so that *they* can build their foreign language skills, people met through planned activities for one's children (sports, drama groups, crafts), and so forth. Barna (1983) discusses the use of various stress innoculation procedures in which people are encouraged to think about emotional events in their lives in less threatening terms. For example, people might learn to use such general thoughts as, "This seems stressful, but perhaps I'm overinterpreting. I should check this with my cultural informant." Another generally helpful thought is, "This may seem emotional now [e.g., the events in the incident that introduced this chapter], but perhaps I'll learn a lot about this other culture if I learn to interpret the events from the *viewpoint of people in the host culture.*"

Skill Streaming: An Approach to Learning Culture-Specific Behaviors

We have thus far argued that learning a new behavior is no easy task. We have also stated that learning a behavior that contradicts our own cultural values presents an even greater challenge. As trainers, how can we help facilitate this process? One useful approach is the "Skill Streaming or Structured Learning" approach developed by Goldstein (1988). Although this method was originally developed for the purpose of educating long-term skill-deficient patients in mental hospitals and was then adopted for use with noninstitutionalized aggressive individuals, the underlying argument is the same—to teach skills that are considered prosocial by a specific society. Goldstein argues that many of these individuals act in antisocial ways not because they *choose* to avoid prosocial behaviors but because they *do not know* how to act appropriately. Most of these individuals have grown up observing and learning from negative role models. His curriculum is a step-by-step method covering various prosocial skills such as how to: apologize, introduce oneself, thank someone, ask a favor, say "no," as well as many others.

Perhaps the greatest difference between Goldstein's agenda and ours is that our target audience consists of people who can effectively communicate *within their own cultures*. Instead of *replacing* their old skills we seek to teach them *additional* ones they can use when placed in a specific context, that is, another culture. The commonalty our group has with Goldstein's is that they, too, have missed out on the "normal" socialization process that effective communicators from the target culture have undergone. The advantage of using the skill streaming curriculum is that it can be used in teaching very basic social skills that would otherwise be too fundamental or embarrassing for adults to ask and learn. Goldstein's method tries to duplicate the natural learning processes with which most people are familiar—that is: (1) modeling, (2) role playing, (3) performance feedback, and (4) transfer of training (Burke & Day, 1986; McGinnis et al., 1984). For example, children who are learning how to play the piano will watch the instructors place their hands over the keyboard *(modeling)*, will then imitate the same behavior *(role playing)*, and will receive *feedback regarding* their performance before actually playing in front of an audience *(transfer of learning)*. The skill streaming approach takes trainees through all these stages in a safe, nonthreatening environment, using as many positive reinforcements as needed. The more general approach to training, of which skill streaming is an example, is known as behavioral modeling, and studies have shown it to be an effective approach for managerial training (Burke & Day, 1986).

In the next few paragraphs we describe briefly how the skill streaming approach can be adopted for use in cross-cultural training programs. However, we strongly encourage those who plan to use it in an actual workshop to consult directly either *Skill-Streaming the Elementary School Child* (McGinnis et al., 1984), or *The Prepare Curriculum* (Goldstein, 1988).

Let us now develop a program aimed at teaching Jack how to use an intermediary properly using the skill streaming formula.

Modeling

Trainers must first go over the step-by-step instructions (see Table 1 for an example) and should then entertain trainee questions and concerns. It is crucial that trainees find the steps logical and acceptable *before* trainers

TABLE 1
Using an Intermediary

Steps to Follow	*Trainer Notes*
Step 1—Decide if you need to use an intermediary.	Discuss why the use of an intermediary is considered important in many Asian cultures. Explain that using an intermediary is favored over direct contact since it helps maintain "face" instead of embarrassing anyone with direct confrontation.
Step 2—Decide who you would like to use as an intermediary and why.	Not everyone is a good intermediary. Trainees may want to consider the following: (1) how trustworthy is this person? (2) how well does this person know both parties? (3) will I be putting this person in an uncomfortable situation by asking him or her to be an intermediary?
Step 3—Think about how you want to approach the person and what you plan to say.	Discuss how directly you want to ask the favor. Do you want to do it directly, indirectly, or hint at it slightly. Discuss the advantages and disadvantages of the three choices.
Step 4—Choose a good time and place.	Discuss how to choose a good time. Do you want to talk to the person at work, or is it better to do it after work in an informal setting. Talk about the pros and cons of after-work socializing.
Step 5—Carry out your best choice in a sincere way.	Discuss the body language and facial expression associated with sincerity.

embark on demonstrating the actual behavior. While demonstrating the behavior, trainers should say the steps out loud, making sure that they are following them in order. The trainer notes that accompany the steps are useful in explaining the five Ws described in the "Knowledge" section. To contextualize the behavior, trainers need to create and describe a scenario to go with the behavior. In our case, trainers need to describe to the group Jack's situation and why he needs to use Mr. Wu as an intermediary. They should then assign a co-trainer or a participant to play Mr. Wu's role. When possible, trainers should bring in a resource person from the target culture as a co-trainer. The trainer will need to explain to "Mr. Wu" how to act and what to say. To make the role play more realistic the use of simple costumes and props can be helpful. To ensure success, trainers should practice the role play in advance with the co-trainer or participant, making sure that it is clear and simple and that irrelevant information is eliminated. Trainers should make sure that the role play ends with a successful outcome, since positive reinforcement is crucial. It is also important to remember that when teaching several behaviors, it is always better to start out with the easiest one because success is an effective positive reinforcer.

Role Playing

It is now the participants' turn to practice the behavior. *ALL* trainees should be the "main character" of the role-play at least once. For the more difficult skills, it is recommended that all trainees go through the primary role at least twice. To increase the chances of transfer, it is recommended that trainees work with a real situation from their lives. Trainees can either use past events (lower risk) or work on a current situation (higher risk, as discussed in Brislin & Yoishida, 1994a, 1994b). The participants are encouraged to make the role play seem more "real" by choosing actors and actresses who resemble, as much as possible, the people they are trying to depict. These actors and actresses should then be coached regarding how they should act, what they should say, how to say it, what types of body movements they should make, and so forth. As mentioned earlier, for cross-cultural training purposes, it is often helpful to bring in at least one resource person from the target culture.

Performance Feedback

To reinforce effective behavior and correct those that should be changed, immediate feedback is necessary. To ensure success, Goldstein (1988) postulates the following rules:

1. Co-actors are the first to comment on the trainee's performance.
2. Prior to the role play, some of the trainees are assigned the task of observing a particular step to pay attention to.

3. Those observers are the next to comment.
4. The remaining observers are then asked to comment and give suggestions on how the trainee can improve his or her performance further.
5. Trainers should then comment.
6. Then the target trainee should comment.

Trainees should be encouraged to ask questions, make comments, or share any concerns they might have at this point.

Transfer of Training

The ultimate test of the effectiveness of a training program aimed at the development of new behaviors and skills is whether trainees are able to exhibit the behaviors in their everyday interactions. To facilitate transfer, trainees are assigned to practice the skill outside of the training environment in between sessions. Trainees are given a form to fill out regarding their performance and outcomes. During the next session, trainees report to each other, receive feedback, give support, and share their thoughts and concerns regarding the skill they are practicing.

Culture-Specific Behaviors: Examples

What sorts of behaviors can businesspeople learn that will improve their performance in other cultures? Obviously, there are many competencies that can be acquired. One's choice will be affected by a host of different factors such as the type of contact one has with culturally different others, one's personality, and so on. To give readers a better idea of the type of behaviors that can be singled out and targeted, we have compiled Tables 2 through 9 which include not only behaviors from various cultures but also some information that trainers can use when introducing them. We have chosen the following set of examples because they can occur for all businesspeople on *either short or long assignments* in the specific countries identified in each discussion.

TABLE 2
How to Take Clients Out in Japan

Behavior: Taking your client out to a business lunch or dinner

---

Why?   Since Japanese society places a very high value on human relationships, establishing trust with one's business partners is considered to be crucial. Instead of plunging into business discussions and negotiations immediately after meeting prospective business partners, the Japanese often spend a considerable amount of time getting to know them by taking them out to dinners and other meals (Nishiyama, 1989). Also, according to Hall and Hall (1990 pp. 118–120), meals have a similar function for the French as well.

How?   Find out what type of food your client likes best and choose an expensive restaurant. Insist on opening the door for them and letting them walk ahead. Since you are taking them out make sure that you offer them the most important seat, the *kamiza* (see Figure 1 for specific seating arrangements). Since you are the host, you should initiate by making suggestions on what they should order. Make sure that you are offering the most expensive items from the menu. Often they will want you to decide for them. If that happens, order the *omakase ryoori* or some other set dinner (Nishiyama, 1989, pp. 125–126).

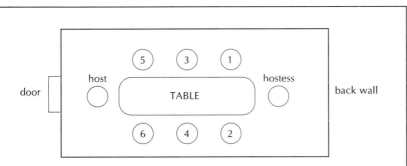

FIGURE 1
Seating Order

Chair number one is considered the most prestigious, and chair number 6 is considered the least desirable. As a rule, the highest ranking guest should sit in seat number one while members of the host's party should sit in the seats closer to the door. The general rule is that the seat far away from the entrance and from any sort of traffic is more pleasant and is, therefore, preferred. Another rule is that seats on the right side (when facing the door) are considered slightly higher in rank than those on the left side.

Special Concerns: For many Americans time is money. Business trips are often very brief with little time for social niceties. What they need to be reminded of is that, for the Japanese, entertaining is not a social nicety but an important part of doing business. Another potential problem many American trainees may experience when discussing the specifics of this behavior is the importance placed on the amount of money spent and the little details about who walks in front of whom and who sits where. The importance placed on status and the deference shown to those with high status directly conflict with the egalitarian belief many Americans idealize. In addition, the importance placed on "going to an expensive place" rather than a "place that serves good food" also clashes with American pragmatism. To elaborate on these two points, trainers may want to include Hofstede's (1980; 1991) discussion on high vs. low power distance countries as well as Hijirida & Yoshikawa's (1987) discussion of Japan as a "culture of form."

TABLE 3
How to Use Apologies as a Social Lubricant in Japan

Behavior: Using apologies as a social lubricant

Why?   Because human relationships are at the core of the Japanese culture and society, the ability to create and maintain good feelings between people is considered an important skill socially adept adults should have. The Japanese apology is not an admittance of guilt but is more of an expression of remorse for the unfortunate incident. In other words, when the Japanese say "I am sorry" they usually mean "I am sorry this had to happen between us," *not* "I am sorry, I am guilty." (Naotsuka & Sakamoto, 1981).

How?   The Japanese apologize directly without unnecessary excuses or explanations. They apologize often *regardless* of personal responsibility. For example, a front desk clerk at a hotel would not hesitate to apologize for a mistake someone in housekeeping made.

Special Concerns: Apologies often mean an admission of guilt to Americans. It is, therefore, very difficult for them to apologize for someone else's mistake without inserting, somewhere in their apology, the fact that **they were not** the ones who made the mistake. Trainees should be reminded that Japanese do **not** assume that the person who apologized is responsible. If they are still uncomfortable, they might want to use the full sentence "I am sorry this had to happen to you."

TABLE 4
How to Address Korean Colleagues properly

Behavior: Addressing Korean colleagues appropriately

Why?:   Since there are relatively few last names and since first names are used only by family and close friends, it is better not to use names unless necessary. This is because Korea is more status oriented and formal compared to the United States.

How?:   Use their title, position, trade, profession, or some other honorific title such as teacher (or professor) instead of their names. "Good morning" is better than "good morning, Mr. Kim." The president of South Korea is referred to by high officials as "excellency" even in his absence, because it is considered too familiar to use such a high person's name in conversation (Moran & Stripp, 1991).

Barrier: Because the American culture believes that the use of first names creates familiarity and shows sincerity, it can be difficult to convince many Americans how important it is *not* to do so. Another problem is that Koreans will often feel insulted when called by their first name but will not directly let their American counterparts know of their feelings.

TABLE 5
How to Be Convincing in Egypt

Behavior: Appearing convincing to Egyptian business partners

Why?   According to Shouby (1970), in the Arabic language it is not uncommon to find many similes and metaphors as well as long series of adjectives used to modify a single word. In the same way that an assertion made by a Japanese might seem too indirect and wishy-washy to Americans, an American version of assertiveness often goes by unnoticed by their Egyptian counterparts.

How?   Use exaggeration and hyperbole.

Barrier: People who are not used to exaggeration and hyperbole may feel a very strong gut-level reaction when using it.

TABLE 6
How to Advertise in Germany

Behavior: Advertising mainly through printed materials

Why?   Because store hours are very short in Germany, the people have little time to comparison shop. If advertisements are very detailed, including price, specific features, and so on, people are able to do the comparison *before* entering the stores. Also, advertisements on the television are extremely limited and controlled by the government, so most companies use printed materials instead (Hall & Hall, 1990).

How?   Products are described and analyzed in detail. Advertisements often provide prices as well as exact locations of where the products can be purchased. Comparative advertising is banned by the government. Instead of playing on atmosphere, emotions, or novelty, German advertisements stress quality, performance, and durability of the products. The primary purpose of advertisements is to provide accurate information (Hall & Hall, 1990).

TABLE 7
How to Negotiate with Germans

Behavior: Negotiating effectively with Germans

Why?   Hofstede (1980; 1991) reports that Germans rank high in uncertainty avoidance. In the same way that Germans require specific details in their advertisements, they require a large amount of quantifiable data before they are willing to make a business decision.

How?   During negotiations, Germans tend to be detailed and to ask for everything to be documented and/or quantified. In addition, they often want everything confirmed in writing (Neumann, 1992). It is important to be organized and present a logical argument. Always end your argument with a summary that includes all your major points. Give your German counterparts "all the information you have, and then more" (Hall & Hall, 1990, p. 50). Trust and respect are earned by providing them with a multitude of written materials that include the specific details of every possible aspect of the business proposal.

TABLE 8
How to Communicate with the French

Behavior: Communicating with the French—be formal, polite, and respectful
---

Why?   The French are more formal than Americans and look down upon casual behaviors such as slouching, sprawling out, joking around, and first-name calling.

How?   Dress properly and address your colleagues with their title followed by their last names. Avoid joking, teasing, or backslapping (perceived as phony chumminess), and especially avoid off-color jokes. Although superiors may engage in informalities such as joke telling, subordinates should refrain from such behavior (Hall & Hall, 1990).

Barrier: Americans often take pride in being straightforward and informal with everyone. Informality is perceived by Americans as a sign of trustworthiness and sincerity. This is a potential pitfall when interacting with people from many other cultures who prefer a more formal approach to business.

TABLE 9
How to Protect "Face" in China

Behavior: Protecting the other person's "face"

Why?   Interpersonal relationships are perceived as being all-important in China (as is in many other Asian countries). Saving someone from public embarrassment is considered "saving face," and is treated as a basic social courtesy. "It is well to remember that the Chinese concept of sincerity is the stark opposite of the American concept, in that the Chinese believe that they can manifest sincerity only by adhering carefully to prescribed etiquette. In a sense they are saying, "I will show my sincerity in my relations with you by going to the trouble of being absolutely correct toward you so that you will be happily untroubled about any matters of face." (Pye, 1982, p. 89)

How?   (1) Be *very* indirect (use hints) when making requests, responding to requests, or when giving advice or criticism. (2) Avoid pointing fingers at anyone and if necessary bend the truth a little. (3) If you have to choose between a statement that will make the other person feel good and one that is closer to the truth, choose the former. (4) If one must confront someone, do it through an intermediary (Macleod, 1988, p. 71).

Barriers: Those who are not used to the custom of "saving face" often find it tedious and unnecessary. They do not realize that interpersonal events such as pleasant encounters, "saving face," and a sense or trust can make or break a business relationship in China as well as in many other Asian countries.

Conclusion

As mentioned earlier in the chapter, one of the major dilemmas cross-cultural trainers face is the lack of time and funds to perform an adequate program that covers awareness, knowledge, emotions, *and* skills. Too often, trainees are *either* exposed to skills without adequate coverage of the preceding three stages *or* are not taught any skills at all. Although there is no easy solution, trainers can often shorten programs by performing a good needs assessment and by assigning fieldwork exercises to trainees. Furthermore, trainers using the skill streaming curriculum introduced in this chapter are able to cover both knowledge as well as skills at the same time. In other words, trainers are able to cut down the stages to three—(1) awareness, (2) knowledge & skills, and (3) emotions—instead of four.

The approach we introduced in this chapter is effective not only as a training tool but as a guideline for trainees to use *outside* of the classroom to enable self-initiated learning. It can be summarized as follows:

1. *Identify.* Become aware of which skills one needs to acquire to be able to function well in the target culture.
2. *Understand.* Know why, where, when, to whom, and how the behavior is appropriately used.
3. *Use cultural informants to understand specifics.* Always observe and consult people from the target culture to make sure you are using the behaviors in the proper context and are delivering them appropriately.
4. *Practice, practice, and practice!* Knowing and doing are two different things. It is only through practice that we can gain proficiency in a new skill.
5. *Deal with emotions.* Trainees should anticipate strong emotional reactions to cultural differences, as well as to the new behaviors they will be using, and should be prepared to face them.

Throughout this chapter, we have emphasized that success in cross-cultural business dealings involves the identification of behaviors considered appropriate in other cultures. People must consider modifying behaviors *learned in their own* culture so that they will have a greater chance of successful business dealings. There is not a universal way of doing business such that one set of behaviors are appropriate everywhere. Nor is there one country whose economy is so dominant (e.g., United States, Germany, Japan) that its citizens can expect their natural behaviors to be acceptable, given the desire of others to engage in transactions with businesspeople from a powerful country. Rather, the current and future status of a global economy means that there will be many countries whose businesses will be attractive to outsiders. The citizens of any one country will be appreciative of overseas businesspeople who are knowledgeable about and sensitive to culture and to cultural differences. Cross-cultural training programs have an important role to play in the successful movement of businesspeople who are seeking opportunities in this global economy.

References

Adler, N. (1991). *International dimensions of organizational behavior* (2nd ed.). Boston: PWS Kent.

Barna, L. (1983). The stress factor in intercultural relations. In D. Landis & R. Brislin (Eds.), *Handbook of intercultural training, vol. 2: Issues in training methodology* (pp. 19–49). Elmsford, NY: Pergamon.

Black, J. & Mendenhall, M. (1990). Cross-cultural training effectiveness: A review and a theoretical framework for future research. *Academy of Management Review*, 15, 113–136.

Brislin, R. (1993) *Understanding culture's influence on behavior*. Fort Worth, TX: Harcourt.

Brislin, R., & Yoshida, T. (Eds.), (1994a). *Improving intercultural interactions: Modules for cross-cultural training programs*. Thousand Oaks, CA: SAGE.

Brislin, R., & Yoshida, T. (1994b). *Intercultural communication training: An introduction*. Thousand Oaks, CA: SAGE.

Brislin, R., Cushner, K., Cherrie, C., and Yong, M. (1986). *Intercultural interactions: A practical guide*. Beverly Hills, CA: Sage Publications.

Burke, M., & Day, R. (1986). A cumulative study of the effectiveness of managerial training. *Journal of Applied Psychology*, 71, 232–245.

Goldstein, A.P. (1988). *The prepare curriculum: Teaching prosocial competencies*. Champaign, IL: Research Press.

Gudykunst, W., & Hammer, M. (1983). Basic training design: Approaches to intercultural training. In D. Landis & R. Brislin (Eds.), *Handbook of intercultural training, vol. 1: Issues in theory and design* (pp. 118–154). Elmsford, NY: Pergamon.

Hall, E.T., & Hall, M.R. (1990). *Understanding cultural differences*. Yarmouth, ME: Intercultural Press.

Hijirida, K., & Yoshikawa, M. (1987). *Japanese language and culture for business and travel*. Honolulu: University of Hawaii Press.

Hofstede, G. (1980). *Culture's consequences: International differences in work-related values*. Beverly Hills: Sage Publications.

Hofstede, G. (1991). *Cultures and organizations: Software of the mind*. London: McGraw-Hill.

Macleod, R. (1988). *China, Inc.: How to do business with the Chinese*. New York: Bantam Books.

McGinnis, E., Goldstein, A.P., Sprafkin, R.P., & Gershaw, N.J. (1984). *Skillstreaming the elementary school child*. Champaign, IL: Research Press.

Moran, R.T., & Stripp, W.G. (1991). *Successful international business negotiations*. Houston, TX: Gulf Publishing Co.

Naotsuka, R., & Sakamoto, N. (1981). *Mutual understanding of different cultures*. Tokyo: Taishukan.

Neumann, I. (1992). German for negotiation. *Language and intercultural training,* *13*(1), 4–6.

Nishiyama, K. (1989). *Strategies of marketing to Japanese visitors.* Massachusetts: Ginn Press.

Pye, L.W. (1982). *Chinese commercial negotiating style.* Cambridge, Massachusetts: Oelgeschlager, Gunn & Hain, Publishers.

Shouby, E. (1970). The influence of the Arabic language on the psychology of the Arabs. In A.M. Lutfiyya & C.E. Churchill (Eds.), *Readings in Arab Middle Eastern societies and cultures.* The Hague: Mouton.

Walton, S. (1990) Stress management training for overseas effectiveness. *International Journal of Intercultural Relations,* 14, 507–527.

Training and Development of Expatriates and Home Country Nationals

Alan M. Barratt Alan M. Barratt & Associates

Introduction

This chapter deals with practical and strategic issues that make or break the success of doing business in a different culture.

I wish to start with a mini-case, which is true and happened to me on a trip back from the Middle East. As a part, and a significant part, of the world market, many organizations have either submitted proposals for business or taken a sales/marketing trip to the Middle East in order to tap this profitable marketplace. Many corporations have succeeded whereas many others have failed. What makes the difference?

On a flight from the Middle East to Europe, my window seat neighbor, immediately after takeoff, ordered a large drink that was quickly followed by a second and third. During the second, I struck up the usual passenger conversations: How was your trip? How long have you been out? What business are you in? Was the trip successful? And in response to the last question it was clear his trip had not met expectations—hence, the two to three or even four rapidly consumed drinks. In our subsequent conversation, it became clear that his lack of success was due to his insensitive behavior toward the potential new clients in a culture that was relatively new to him and his corporation. Now many of you will say it was the individual's (he was the sales director) fault for not doing his homework. But you could also argue that his company's human resource group, knowing that new business areas were being explored, should have identified management development and cultural issues that needed action to achieve success. Regardless of where the blame should be placed, the fact remains that this company "blew it." This was all related to *being sensitive* to different cultures. It is inadequate to obtain the visa, the various medical "shots" needed, and the airline ticket. A proactive and well-informed approach to equipping executives who will be making overseas trips to foreign parts is absolutely crucial to successful business. Take no chances and be prepared; the responsibility for educating expatriate employees rests with the human resource or international personnel groups. I don't place blame; I just hope that organizations, large and small, become more attuned to the *cultural sensitivities* that are key in all cultures around the world.

Preparing Expatriates for Overseas Assignments

Key Strategic Questions

Some of the strategic questions that companies need to ask to achieve this level of *cultural sensitivities* follow:

1. How much do I know about the host country's culture?
2. How much do I know about the host country's values?
3. How much do I know about my own culture and its values, and how they are viewed by host country nationals?
4. How will I or my organization deal with the differences and potential conflicts that could exist?
5. Do I and my organization believe it important to be sensitive to the host nation's culture and values?
6. Are we prepared to make an effort to learn or train ourselves in the culture and its values and sensitivities?
7. Do we believe the cultural issues *do not* have a significant impact upon doing business successfully?
8. Do I expect hostility and rigidity from my new potential clients? If so, how do I plan to get around these traits?
9. Am I (are we) prepared to change our behavior toward our new clients?

If you and your organization attempt to address some of those strategic questions, you may find some clear direction emerges that could mean training, cultural briefing, sending an individual on a course, or just giving the individual a reading list. If successful, these actions would eliminate the situation given in my mini case.

Cultural Factors

I published a paper in 1989 titled "Doing Business in a Different Culture." It appeared in the *Journal of European Industrial Training,* and I reference this paper throughout this chapter. For example, I refer to one of the strategic questions previously asked, namely, "How really important are the cultural issues of the country being visited to the potential business success?" If your product or service is good and the price is competitive but you *offend* the culture of your host country or organization, your trip or visit may be unfruitful, and your management may challenge your personal effectiveness.

It is clear that with the globalization of business, the increasing ease of travel (not all international travelers agree with that), the importance of being successful internationally will be a key factor in success and profitability through to the end of the century. Cultural awareness is similar to perception. There are no rights and wrongs; it is a set of established values that are often different from our own.

International businesspeople who have had considerable success in this area show they are concerned for the interpersonal impact they make on others, a key management competence. They also behave in a *proactive* way to help open up the relationship and show that they wish to understand the local customs and culture, indicate their tolerance, and provide evidence that they do not wish to offend through their own personal ignorance.

It is clear that the organizations that are doing business and wish to compete in the international business scene must review the preparation and skills needed to cope with the cultural issues. To me, it is just as important as obtaining one's airline ticket or visas that are needed to ensure that the trip takes place.

How do you go about planning and structuring relevant actions to provide you and your employees with an appropriate cultural awareness? We have suggested to many clients a short but effective orientation session lasting a couple of days but focusing on the *key issues* that help to reduce the anxiety and to protect the individual from any cultural *faux pas*. You need to look on this kind of preparation as an insurance policy to protect the organization's image and reputation.

These actions can take the form of skill development in a one-to-one briefing session, or if sufficient numbers are involved, a classroom type of seminar may be justified.

Further Strategic Questions

Experience suggests that an orientation of some form is *vital* and that some key questions should be reviewed. The organization should ask the following questions:

- Do we have enough cultural experience and knowledge to do business in that part of the world?
- Are we rushing too fast into business here?
- What is our strategy for building long-lasting relationships in this culture?

- In any particular cultural environment, do we know enough and respect the way they do things?
- Are we prepared to be open-minded and learn from others?
- Do we share our experiences sufficiently with others on adapting to cultural change, particularly on unanticipated issues?

Many myths and generalizations develop among the business community about specific cultures. Obviously, *open communications and good personal relationships* are the keys to success in all cultural environments. Let us push some of these myths aside and look at the example of an Arab executive. Muna (1980) made a number of key points about Arab executives, such as the following:

- There is a close relationship between the Arab executive and his environment. The Arab executive is looked on as a community and family leader. There are numerous social pressures on him as a result of this role. He is consulted on all types of problems, even those far removed from his position. These demands are very time consuming.
- With regard to decision making, the Arab executive is likely to consult with his subordinates, but he will take responsibility for his decision himself rather than arriving at it through consensus.
- The Arab executive is likely to try to avoid conflict. If there is an issue that he favors but that is opposed by his subordinates, he tends to impose his authority. If it is an issue favored by the subordinates but opposed by the executive, he is likely to let the matter drop without taking action.
- The Arab executive's style is very personal. He values loyalty over efficiency. Though some executives find the open-door tradition consumes a great deal of time, they do not feel that the situation can be changed. Many executives tend to look on their employees as family and will allow them to bypass the hierarchy in order to meet them.
- The Arab executive, contrary to popular belief, puts considerable value on the use of time. One of the things he admires most about Western or expatriate executives is the use of their time. He would like to encourage his own employees to make more productive use of time.

Muna also points out the difficulties facing the manager, including the following:

- The inadequacies of the economic and organizational infrastructure—that is, a bureaucracy that causes innumerable delays.
- The social pressures.
- The low level of delegation. The interpersonal style of the managers requires a great deal of time to be spent on other than business matters.

Furthermore, Muna takes exception to the myth that Arabs are completely fatalistic. He points out that the Arab executive does plan ahead and places emphasis on preventative maintenance. There are situations, however, that the Arab executive feels are beyond his control. These include political and economic issues, government rules and regulations, and labor shortages, for example.

My observations over the past fourteen years of working in the Middle East on a regular basis support Muna's comments. However, it is also important to be aware of the *cultural variations* in Arab countries. The variations among countries and provinces are often more dramatic than what we experience in the West.

For anyone planning to visit a new culture with the objective of conducting new business in the area, the best practical advice is to brainstorm a list of cultural factors to consider, and seek expertise and understanding of the actions needed to address those factors.

Implications for Management Development

It has been clearly established by many consultants and management developers that some special adaptations and design features should be built into training and OD interventions. El Gazzar Elwy (1988) refers to factors that enhance the fit of organizational development and the Arabian Gulf cultural environment. However, it is clear that adaptation is needed to be successful in developing managers in a different culture.

A number of managerial skills should be emphasized, including the following:

- Conceptual skills, which encourage the executive to see the whole picture.
- Delegation, which enables the executive to save his time and to train and motivate his employees.
- Conflict management, which encourages opposition (i.e., voicing their opinion) from subordinates.
- Management of time to provide skills to balance the needs of the job with those of the executive's role in society.
- Change agent skills. The executive has the responsibility for introducing change into his environment. He needs skills for introducing the change, managing resistance to change, and understanding the process of change and its consequences.

These skills should be built into management development programs or action learning events dealing with the real organizational issues and opportunities.

Perhaps the major implication for management development is ensuring that the organization's representatives, from board directors to technicians, are aware and equipped to deal with the cultural differences. There are many different ways of "skinning this cat," but the key point is that some action and briefing should take place before an employee visits a new culture to conduct business. An example of this is a two-day, hands-on orientation program for Westerners doing business in Saudi Arabia (Mobil Oil, 1982).

An Orientation Outline (For Expatriates Visiting the Middle East)

Religion

1. Declaration of Faith. There is one and only one god—Allah—and Mohammed was his messenger (prophet).
2. Prayer. Rigorous observance of prayer five times a day at a mosque or if not able to attend a mosque, pray at home or at workplace.
3. Zakat. Practice of giving alms to the poor. Amount donated should be a nominal percentage of a person's income.
4. Ramadan. Strict fasting during the holy month of Ramadan. From sunrise to sunset, one cannot eat food, drink liquids, or smoke. The dates of Ramadan change each year based on the lunar (Hegira) calendar.
5. Hajj. The pilgrimage to Mecca prescribed as a religious duty for Moslems. Moslems are duty-bound to make the pilgrimage to Mecca once in their lifetime during the month of Dhu Al Haijjah.

Family

Roots come from tribal regional societies. There are very strong family orientations and ties. Family name and honor are extremely important. Although formerly nomadic, Saudis now make up a less mobile society; families tend to live in the same town, village, or city for generations and establish a strong family reputation. It is important to preserve family honor and good standing in the community. Social activity tends to focus around families and relatives. Respect for parents and elders is important.

However, to outsiders (Westerners), the family is considered by the Arabs to be private and not usually discussed in casual conversations. The wife is considered very private and needs to be protected by the husband. It would be considered an intrusion of privacy or even insulting if you asked a Saudi, "How is your wife?" If you knew the Saudi well, it would be correct to enquire, "How is your family?" Wives do not go outside the home unaccompanied. They are usually veiled in public and are not permitted to drive in Saudi Arabia. Usually, the property around homes is completely walled in on all four sides for privacy.

Courtesy and Hospitality

Saudis place great emphasis on hospitality and courtesy. They are polite, friendly, and generous in their hospitality when entertaining socially. It would be considered impolite to drink coffee in their presence and not offer them a cup. Also, it would be discourteous to greet one Saudi in a room (meeting) and not greet others present. When they do entertain socially, it is not uncommon for men and women to be separated and gather together in different rooms in the house, maintaining privacy between men and women.

Time

Time is not as important in the Middle East as it is in the Western world. Saudis are not driven by the clock and may not always rigidly adhere to exact schedules. They may be late for meetings and for social occasions but do not consider that to be impolite. There is a concept of *En Shallah:* If God wills it, it will happen.

Food and Beverages

Saudis do not eat pork or pork by-products (lard). Their religion does not permit the drinking of alcoholic beverages. Most will not be offended if you drink alcohol in their presence, but it would be a serious affront to include a pork dish as part of a menu for dinner. If you entertain Saudis, be sure to have juice as a beverage, since this is a common and preferred drink in the Middle East. Soda is also an appropriate beverage.

Honor

Saudis do not like to be criticized in the presence of other people; this is considered a loss of honor or loss of face. Of course, no one likes criticism (including Westerners), but Saudis tend to react more strongly since it is a matter of honor to them. They may not express their reaction to you but will suffer with their humiliation privately. If there is a need for constructive criticism, be sure to do it in private.

Authority

As in the case of most societies, Saudis respect authority and the long-established folkways and mores of their culture. However, in the kingdom

(Saudi Arabia), an ordinary citizen has the right to have his grievance heard by the king.

Entertainment

There are no entertainment activities in Saudi Arabia similar to those we have in the western world. For example, there are no movie theatres, bowling alleys, opera houses, ballet companies, Broadway plays, night clubs, dance halls, circuses, ice shows, and so on. Entertainment is usually a family affair and may involve a family picnic with close relatives or listening to music or watching TV. Because the east and west coasts of Saudi Arabia are on the Arabian Gulf and the Red Sea, respectively, a family outing to the shore is not uncommon during the weekends (Thursday and Friday).

Sports

Saudi Arabia does not have mass spectator sports like baseball, football, basketball, and the like. However, they do play soccer, which is very popular in the kingdom, and their national team has competed in the Olympics. When a large group of Saudis go to the United States for a long-term training assignment, they have on occasion organised teams for recreation. Also, Saudis visiting the United States seem to enjoy the sport of wrestling and will attend wrestling exhibitions.

Women

Women hold a different position in the Middle East from that in the West. Some examples are the following:

* Women are not permitted to drive in Saudi Arabia.
* Girls attend schools separate from boys.
* For the most part, women are not part of the work force, except as teachers, doctors, or nurses.
* At most social events, the women stay in groups separate from the men.

Dating

There is no dating between young adults in Saudi Arabia as is the custom in the West. Young girls may not be in the company of boys unless they are chaperoned with an appropriate mature adult woman. Marriages tend to be arranged by the parents (with the consent of the boy and the girl), and girls usually marry at an early age (16 to 18). A marriage contract is negotiated and agreed on between the two families. This document formalizes the agreement and indicates the dowry that the bride's parents are to provide.

Justice

Law and justice are based on *Shariah* law, which stems from the Koran. Justice can be swift and severe for those who are criminally inclined. For capital offenses, which rarely occur in Saudi Arabia, punishment may include execution by beheading in the public square. Because the machinery of justice is swift and severe, Saudi Arabia has almost no crime.

The foregoing discussion is a typical cultural outline for the briefing of Westerners due to visit Saudi Arabia.

Given good educational design on this program, participants may be provided with a clear perception of the do's and don'ts. This training, at least, may save them from making some serious cultural *faux pas* that would affect the progress of conducting business.

Training and Developing Host Country Nationals

The question to ask before developing host country nationals is "How significant is it to the host country (government) and also the individual company?" For example in the Middle East, Saudization, Qatarization, Emiratization, Omanization are not only key but vital national objectives. Some would say the *only* objective.

It seems to me, as a practitioner, that three issues are critical in developing host country nationals, as follows:

1. Their training have depth, comprehensiveness, and effectiveness and be cost efficient.
2. Organizations doing business in a host country are ambassadors to and "coaches" of the host country trainees.
3. The final issue is to really understand people. This general issue clearly is superimposed on the cultural issues and is based on the work of Jung adapted by Margerison and McCann (1990) in their team management system.

Obviously, it would be foolish of me not to mention the speed and style of learning that will have an impact on any organization trying to do business in a different culture. However, considerable data on this subject are available from sources in the United States and Europe. It is vitally crucial to adapt the training of local nationals to address the following critical factors:

- Ability and speed in assimilating ideas, knowledge, data, and concepts.
- Particular style of learning that best suits.
- The basic language capability.

- The methodology of the training materials and training delivery system.
- The sensitivities of the instructors or trainers.
- Degree of one-to-one instruction.
- Timing and scheduling of the actual hours per day are significant. For example, prayer times must be considered.

Making Training of Nationals Effective

Building executive success is vital to organizational success, national success, and global success as well as the benefits it brings to the individual and families. As individuals we often leave our personal growth, training, and development plans to *others* to manage. It is of key importance that we take charge of our own development for total success. Some of you are responsible for career development and professional growth programs of nationals. What is needed is some depth of understanding about developing successful individuals but *empowering* all executives and trainers to take control of their own career growth and development.

Two key concepts are cornerstones of building individual success. The first concept deals with the *depth of view* that individuals, organizations, and nations should take in analyzing the impact of individual performance. My own published *BARRIMP* (Improving Management Performance) (Barratt, 1984) model addresses this concept in depth. The second concept relates to how *Jungian theory* can help us all to be successful by understanding ourselves and understanding how to effectively interface with others. In other words, it is the *key* to interpersonal success.

First Concept: Depth of View

The management development model (see Figure 1) was created several years ago to help clients understand that to develop managers in any culture, comprehensively, it is necessary to look at the whole picture of development. We often concentrate on skills and knowledge (abilities), which has been the practice in the past. For example, a *job vision* as well as a job description is needed to clarify a person's role. It is vital to raise questions related to each part of this model if you intend to specifically pinpoint training and development needs for greater performance. Let me explain what each of the boxes shown in the model represents.

Abilities.   What is the level of your abilities in the current job?

Do you have the appropriate level of skills to do the current job?

Do you have the necessary relevant job knowledge to perform to the maximum level?

Do you have the needed qualifications or formal credentials to do this job?

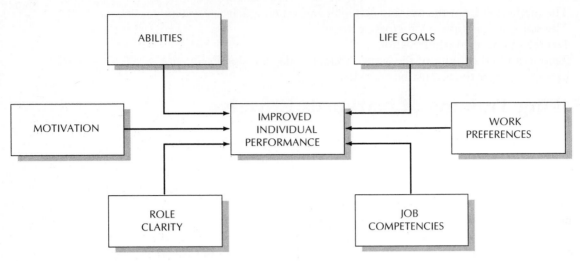

FIGURE 1
The Management Development Model

Do you have the relevant work experience appropriate for this job's demands?

Motivation.   Are you motivated to give your best? If not, why not?

Do you have the drive to perform?
Are you a self-starter?
Are you a team player?
Do you inspire others?

Role Clarity.   This has nothing to do with job descriptions! This concept relates to an individual's *vision* of what is expected in terms of job clarity in achieving high performance. If we had a job-mapping technology, my job might be seen by me as X and by my boss as Y. (See Figure 2.) Whose perception is right? (Answer: *both*.) Whose perception matters the most?

FIGURE 2
A Job's Perception Plot

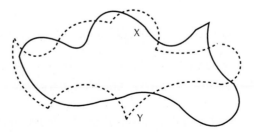

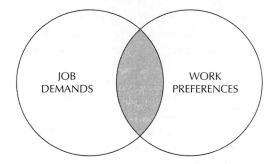

FIGURE 3
Job Demands versus
Work Preferences

(Answer: *the boss's.*) The discrepancy means you need to role-negotiate the boundaries of your role on a regular basis with your boss.

Life Goal Planning.   A practical approach to life goals could include asking some of the following questions:

What specifically do you want out of working life?

What goals do you hope to achieve before you retire?

How do you plan to achieve them?

What risks and changes are you prepared to take?

How do your work and business goals integrate into your family goals?

What price are you prepared to pay to achieve your life goals?

Job Competencies.   In the last decade, Tom Peters, in his book *In Search of Excellence* (1982), raised the issue of job competencies. What this term means is that the *best* performers in any specific field of activity do something different from their average peers. That difference can be termed "practices of excellence." Thus, average and good performers can learn to be the *Best,* which will clearly have an impact on performance.

Work Preferences.   Those types of work that give each of us the maximum satisfaction are called work preferences. The closer we can align our preferences with our job, the higher the level of performance and job satisfaction we can achieve. (See Figure 3.)

Second Concept: Understanding Each Other for a Successful Partnership

Margerison and McCann (1990) have taken the work of Carl Jung and developed a practical system for understanding fellow employees. This process is achieved by understanding and recognizing the work preferences of others with whom you work closely. This provides an excellent mechanism to talk about people's differences and a springboard to coach, train, and develop the local work force at all levels, from supervisors upward to top executives.

What Determines Work Preferences?   Different executives demonstrate varying preferences for the type of work they engage in, but how do these differences come about? To answer this question, the writings of C. J. Jung (1923) were utilized. More than sixty years ago, Jung suggested that several key factors might explain many of the differences among people. An examination of his ideas found a clear relevance to the work of managers and his early concepts in explaining individual work preferences could be adapted in a way similar to that adopted by Myers-Briggs (1976).

Four Key Work Questions.   In my work with executives, four key issues analogous to the ones Jung had previously identified began to emerge (see Figure 4).

1.   How do people prefer to relate with others?
2.   How do people prefer to gather and use information?
3.   How do people prefer to make decisions?
4.   How do people prefer to organize themselves and others?

Each day at work these four questions were addressed. The first question is all about *relationships*. Some people are outgoing and sociable in their relationships and relate to others in an extroverted way, whereas others are qui-

FIGURE 4
Key Issues in Work
Preferences

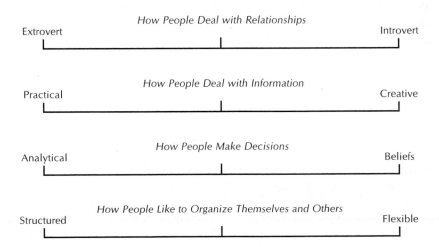

eter and do not have a high need to be with people (i.e., they tend to relate in an introverted way). This clearly affects their work in a team, and this distinction was built into the assessment method.

The second question relates to *information management*. When people gather and use information, they often have a preference to be either practical or creative. Practical people prefer to work with tested ideas and to pay attention to facts and detail, whereas creative people tend to challenge the status quo and come up with new ideas.

The third area relates to *decision making*. When decisions are made, they are normally done so either in an analytical way or according to an individual's beliefs. Analytical people set up objective decision criteria and choose the decision that maximizes the payoff, whereas beliefs-oriented people tend to make decisions that accord with their own personal principles and values.

Finally, the fourth question relates to *organizational issues*. Managers seem to organize themselves and others in a structured or flexible way. Structured people are action-oriented and like to conclude or resolve issues, whereas flexible people prefer to spend time diagnosing a situation and tend to put off "concluding" and "resolving" it until they have gathered all the information possible.

I thus presented *two* key concepts, my BARRIMP model and Jungian theory, as practical tools for building executive success. When systematically used, these concepts can enrich one's plans for personal growth and success in all cultures.

Conclusion

We hear management theorists arguing that the way to go is with the "global manager." That is easy to say, but if it is not accompanied with the cultural awareness and sensitivity support by the necessary training and human resource planning needed, the mission will be ineffective.

Tickets and visas are not enough! The message is clear. If organizations wish to exploit the vast opportunities of international markets, they should invest the little resources needed, particularly time, to prepare their management to manage the cultural differences.

It has been noted by Muna (1980) and others that despite the continual fluctuation in oil prices in the Middle East, the next decade will continue to focus on training and development. Add to this the onslaught of technology change and the worldwide information explosion, and businesses will have to take cultural considerations more seriously when conducting business abroad. Increasing awareness of culture is like taking out insurance; it reduces anxiety and provides a comfort level that lets you concentrate fully on the business at hand.

Management developers should be proactive in influencing their top management in dealing with other cultural issues effectively. It has an impact on the occasional traveler just as much as the manager being assigned for a couple of years to the country in question. "It is better to light one cultural candle than to curse the darkness of ignorance."

I wish to finish with a story conveyed to me by an Arab during the Gulf War in Iraq and Kuwait. The U.S. troops were an epitome of U.S. ambassadors. I was in Saudi Arabia no less than five times during the Iraqi–Kuwaiti conflict, and the U.S. service people I met in the Al Khobar Souk (market) in Dhahran were well mannered and well behaved. However, my Saudi friend said that one of the most talked-about points regarding the U.S. troops in Saudi was that they were excellently behaved in a strange environment but that their cultural training included "Do not look an Arab in the eye." Those of us who are frequent visitors know clearly that the opposite is true. Eye contact in the Middle East is much more highly valued than in the West. It became an interesting issue of debate within the Saudi Kingdom.

Developing and training expats and host country nationals require a very complex, sophisticated business strategy. Those who think it is less than that do so at their peril. However, with good planning, good counsel, and building excellent rapport, success is possible.

References

Barratt, A. M. (19XX). *Management development in the next decade.* London: 84' World OD/MD Congress.

El Gazzar Elwy, M. (1988). "Organisational development: An assessment of its applicability to Arabian Gulf countries." *Organisational Development Journal,* Summer.

Jung, C. J. (1923). *Psychological types.* London: Routledge & Kegan Paul.

Margerison, C., & McCann, R. (1990). *Team management.* Mercury Books.

Mobil Oil. (1982). Internal document.

Muna, F. A. (1980). *The Arab executive.* New York: St. Martin's Press.

Myers-Brigg, J. (1976). *The Myers-Brigg type indicator.* London: Consulting Psychologist's Press.

Peters, T. & Waterman, R. H., Jr. (1982). *In search of excellence.* New York: Harper & Row.

International Compensation

Elaine K. Bailey University of Hawaii-Manoa

How do you reward a Canadian citizen who works in a Japanese corporation in Indonesia? When this person relocates how are adjustments made to ensure continuity and equity? According to Lawrence Watson, a managing director in the Hay Group's European headquarters in Brussels, multicountry scenarios similar to this one will become more and more common. "Getting to the top will require two to three countries on your curriculum vitae," he says. "And the concept of having a 'home base' to return to—the foundation of most current expatriate pay programs—will no longer be the norm. For many, there will be no real home base" (Payson & Rosen, 1993).

Tremendous change is occurring in all areas of domestic and international compensation—from flexible compensation programs adapted to regional norms to creative results-sharing programs based on individual and group performance. As companies become increasingly global in their operations, compensation strategies must be shared across borders, throughout industries and between organizations. As regional trade agreements are signed, more companies are establishing operations in other signatory countries.

An excellent example of the implications for compensation is the European Economic Community (EEC) single market, which is challenging corporate compensation programs on all issues.

Manfred Fiedler, a human resource vice president at Honeywell, Inc., Germany (Overman, 1993) stated:

> At no previous time have goods, money and people crossed national borders so rapidly, in such high volume with so far-reaching impact as today. Training and moving people around can no longer be a matter of lavish luxury, but will be an absolute necessity and an integral part of business to support competitiveness through flexibility. Pay, working hours, vacation, fringe benefits, retirement and other HR systems have to be harmonized so as to be transferable on an international as well as organizational basis.

147

As people move from business to business, market to market, and country to country, organizations will increasingly be tested by the need to bring multinational and multicultural perspectives and practices to the human resource management function of employee compensation.

Compensation programs implemented in global organizations will not mirror an organization's domestic plan because of differences in legally mandated benefits, tax laws, cultures, and employee expectations based on local practices. The additional challenge in compensation design is the requirement that excessive costs be avoided and at the same time employee morale be maintained at high levels. Compensation practices frequently act as a lightning rod, attracting scrutiny from any direction at any time, without warning. If business conditions warrant atypical and irregular compensation programs or practices, they must be justified when challenged by the multiple stakeholders.

Compensation as a Strategic Tool

The challenge for global corporations is to design compensation programs that span the globe and support the organization's strategic objectives. Compensation plans that are directly linked to the strategic planning process of the organization can assist in driving that change and supporting the corporate culture, or they can seriously hinder the process. "Compensation plays a significant role in encouraging the shape and direction of the corporate culture," said Alastair Morton, chairman and group chief executive of the binational Eurotunnel Group (Overman, 1993).

An example of the interrelationship between strategic planning, national culture, corporate culture, and compensation is the Du Pont Shares Program. The program's objective is to convey and reinforce the new vision of Du Pont to become a great global company through people. When Ed Woolard became Du Pont's chairman and CEO in 1989, the company was reorganized by eliminating multiple levels of management and by increasing employee responsibility. An extremely successful global stock option program was initiated to align employees with shareholders and reinforce the new Du Pont vision (Harrison, 1992). This innovative global compensation practice is proof that compensation strategies aligned with corporate strategies and corporate culture can meet the challenge of crossing national and cultural boundaries.

The challenge to communicate stock options effectively across groups of employees both within the United States and other countries was not without its difficulties, the obvious problems being barriers to language, differing monetary and investment systems, and different tax implications. The unexpected problem areas, for example, were interacting with individuals who were not literate in their own country's language, communicating the desired linkage between compensation and productivity, and at times dealing with employees who did not even know they were working for a United States–based company. However, eventually ". . . most employees understood that the options would not only promote a growth culture but would also create value for them personally over time" (Harrison, 1992). The corporate perception was that employees outside of the United States were excited to be recognized as part of the corporation. The basic Du Pont Shares Program enrolled the maximum number of eligible employees (136,000) worldwide. The same number of shares were sent to each employee, with the intended message being that "each person is a member of the team" and of equal value to the organization (Harrison, 1992).

The Du Pont program was designed and managed at the corporate headquarters and operationally implemented on a regional and national level. The program provides an excellent example and reinforces the results of a Towers Perrin and British Institute of Management study of thirty large British companies in which a significant correlation was found between the level of centralization of management structure, style, and control and the coordination of pay and benefits arrangements (Brown, 1993). Nestlé and Unilever are also excellent examples of organizations that combine highly decentralized operations with unifying global themes and very strong corporate cultures. Foreign compensation packages designed on an individual basis are a luxury of the past. Global corporate strategies force organizations to develop compensation policies and plans that guarantee consistency across borders, equity and transferability throughout the entire work life of the new mobile work force. At the same time, companies must continue to strive to achieve maximum effectiveness from typically limited and closely monitored compensation budgets.

Compensation programs are always under close scrutiny from multiple stakeholders ranging from consumer groups to shareholders to politicians. This scrutiny is expanded as compensation packages go international. Companies must often explain the interrelationship between their compensation package and the strategy and objectives of the organization to all stakeholders. In an effort to align pay with various stakeholder interests, organizations with international operations as well as domestic operations are decreasing the proportion of base pay in a package and increasing the portion linked to long-term performance. In addition, the relationship between the strategy and structure of the organization to the compensation package is continuously shifting in response to changes in the external environment and internal organizational environments (Brown, 1993).

Organizations have a distinct competitive advantage in the global marketplace, where a match exists between global strategy and appropriate reward systems. As reward systems define and reinforce the expectations and relationships between the organization and employees, the systems become powerful tools by which to implement strategy and to reinforce corporate culture. The traditional definition of compensation to include all forms of financial returns and tangible services and benefits that employees receive as part of an employment relationship (Milkovich & Newman, 1993) will provide the parameters for the topics included in this chapter.

Pay for Performance Designs

Corporate goals and company definitions of performance must be established to restructure measurement and reward systems to improve pay for performance linkages. Surveys indicate that approximately 80 percent of U.S. employees find no link between their job performance and their compensation. This same study reports that only 13 percent of U.S. workers believe they personally benefit from improved organizational performance. On the other hand, 93 percent of Japanese workers feel that they benefit from improved organizational performance (Rich, 1992, p. 28).

Performance-based reward systems will need to refocus on compensation for improved results, employee identification of their evolving responsibilities, and upgrading of skills on a continuous basis to more effectively meet customer needs and productivity goals. General Electric's "Work Out" process illustrates the parameters for such endeavors. CEO Jack Welch has encouraged teams to "relentlessly challenge" the way they perform their job and make improvements (Rich, 1992).

Compensation based on increased worker competence on the job in critical skill areas is evident in major companies around the globe. Major Japanese corporations have used for many years broad categories for employee development as well as compensation, providing a model for firms around the world to emulate. Japanese companies also changed job titles to match this broad-band approach to "technicians" at Nissan, "team workers" at Mazda and Toyota, and "associates" at Honda (Perry, 1988). General Electric, following this example, created broad-band management categories based on management competencies through which their managers progress (Rich, 1992). In the early 1990s, Motorola eliminated 106 job descriptions by condensing more than 100 job classifications into five broad categories. Work force compensation is then based on the demonstrated job competency and ability to perform multiple tasks.

> The most important benefit of competency pay will be that the focus of discussion about employee salary increases will shift from "How can I load up my job description to get a higher grade classification?" to "How can I develop my competencies or skills to earn more money?" All the unproductive employee, staff, and line management time previously devoted to describing and evaluating jobs will be replaced by discussions of how employees can develop their competencies. (Rich, 1992, p. 28)

Some of the vehicles international companies are incorporating into their reward programs include gainsharing, profit-sharing (exclusive of retirement programs), group incentives, lump-sum payments, key contributor programs, suggestion/proposal programs, and variable pay programs. A highly visible global approach is the practice of innovative compensation pay for teams within companies that have a fundamental commitment to more team-oriented work environments. On the other hand, organizations that were previously only team oriented are now maximizing individual, unit, and organizational competencies and developing pay systems that reward all three levels (Gross, 1993). Volvo Corporation is a good illustration of this integrated reward strategy with their departure from the previous team-only approach.

The impact of culture on the organization of work and compensation for work has rarely been discussed. Research in international compensation has been restricted to country-specific or issue-specific analysis with almost no comparative analysis. However, recent research indicates that culture has a significant effect upon pay practices and that culture is a predominant factor that influences certain compensation patterns (Hodgetts & Luthans, 1993; Townsend, Scott, & Markham, 1990).

The cost of available labor and pricing requirements for goods and services have an impact on the total compensation package as macroenvironmental issues. Considering that compensation is a primary organizational recruitment, motivational, and retention device, it could also be considered an element of the macroenvironment. The new mobile work force will create an extremely competitive marketplace with varying sets of exceptions. Organizations best able to predict these expectations through the design of compensation packages will be the most successful in staffing their organizations. Using a cultural analysis method such as the national cluster model developed by Ronen and Shenkar (1985) provides the predictive potential to assist managers in the design of compensation packages to coincide with employee expectations (Townsend, Scott, & Markham, 1990).

Developing compensation packages for local management and workers across countries and regions creates a unique new challenge for human resource managers. Compensation research has been directed toward remuneration of the expatriate manager and the corporate strategic relationship. Country differences have been viewed from microperspectives and issue differences, some of which are identified later in this chapter. However, management of complex compensation systems across numerous regions and countries tends to be treated as "unique and isolated" decision-making processes. One of the critical challenges becomes the development of equitable, fair, and culturally sensitive compensation for the entire corporate work force to include local country personnel.

The national clusters model previously mentioned delineates similarities between nine groups of countries based on individual attitudes toward work as reflected in work values and goals. These divisions can provide managers with cultural values and attitudinal differences that can be used as a means of differentiation and distinction in developing country- or region-specific compensation packages. The national clusters model is particularly significant because eight empirical studies using attitudinal data were reviewed to establish the country clusters. Another significant dimension of this model is that the variables were used to group countries or nations rather than cultures (Ronen & Shenkar, 1985). Therefore, as variables are identified that explain differences in work values, goals, and attitudes, adjustments can be made in the compensation package to accommodate these issues. The national analysis is compatible with other differences such as national and local legal requirements, monetary structures, and taxation systems, which also require analysis on the national level. The unit of analysis thus becomes a constant at the national level. The cluster model also can assist the human resource manager by providing a vehicle by which to generalize application of compensation practices from one country to others in the same cluster.

Bonuses

Bonuses are a significant element in the total compensation package in many countries. The amount and variety of bonuses is as variable as all other forms of compensation. In Japan, South Korea, and Malaysia, for example, bonuses are expected two times a year and are significant supplements to employee income. Approximately 25 percent of Japanese workers' compensation is in the form of bonuses as measured against 1 percent in the United States (Perry, 1988). In many socialist and previously communist countries, such as the former Soviet Union, Poland, Hungary, and even in parts of China at various times since 1949, managerial bonuses are given when economic planning targets are met or surpassed.

Cost-of-Living and Hardship Adjustments

Typically the cost-of-living adjustment for expatriate and third country employees is used to prevent an erosion of an employee's compensation level. Historically, firms have adjusted compensation upward due to the increase in replication of lifestyle in a new setting. This cost-of-living increase is also referred to as goods-and-services differential, because the cost of services and goods in many developing countries is actually lower than in the home country. However, organizations seldom adjust salaries downward in these instances because of probable morale and recruitment problems. Most compensation departments rely on various countries' cost-of-living indexes and government surveys. However, as a result of rapid and often drastic changes in exchange rates, inflation indexes and survey differences may become obsolete during an assignment. This information must be current and up-to-date to be of value in determining cost-of-living differentials.

Knowledge of a country's culture as well as of the availability, cost, and purchasing practices that have a direct impact on cost of living is necessary.

In regions where individuals are expected to bargain or where store prices are significantly higher than market shopping, individuals will also incur greater costs. The suggested solution to this situation is that the differential be adjusted on the basis of the length of time in the assignment, or as familiarity and acculturation take place. This adjustment allows for an understanding of local purchasing habits and the acquisition of taste for local foods that take place over time (Daniels & Radebaugh, 1992). An example of compensation differentials is provided in Table 1. Buying power represents what net pay will purchase in reference to a "basket" of commonly required goods and services. The amount excludes any and all housing costs, either short-term or long-term.

Hardship adjustments apply to family members as well as employees. Schooling for children is often affected by relocation as well as employment and career opportunities for other family members. Educational assistance for dependents varies on the basis of conditions in the foreign country and where the family is geographically situated within the country. Typically, assistance is not given if local schooling is determined to be satisfactory. Where substandard or other unacceptable conditions exist, educational expenses, including board and room and all related schooling costs, are paid in the country of choice. In some instances, organizations or groups of organizations may operate a school in the foreign country.

The general living conditions in specific geographic regions that are a result of climatic conditions can create an additional inconvenience. Political instability, health conditions, and terrorism place an additional burden on

TABLE 1
Pay for Production Department Head

City	Gross Pay	Net Pay	Buying Power
Hong Kong	$33,399	$27,901	$38,861
Geneva	67,200	45,300	35,789
New York	58,199	35,500	35,500
Copenhagen	77,099	41,199	32,259
Sydney	39,001	23,800	28,437
Tokyo	73,000	54,599	27,645
Singapore	30,600	20,600	24,752
Paris	29,100	22,401	23,717
Madrid	11,800	9,400	9,717

Source: *Financial Times,* November 23, 1988, p. 13.

companies as well as employees. Deteriorating economic conditions, increases in inflationary rates, actions that result in a declining standard of living, poverty, and unstable political conditions often prompt these actions. Other conditions, such as controversy over causes of pollution or health hazards, also create potentially dangerous situations. Legal suits on the grounds of corporate neglect have been filed against companies on behalf of victims and their families. Because of kidnappings, such as those at Kodak and Ford, some companies are purchasing ransom insurance at a very high premium (Daniels & Radebaugh, 1992).

Among countries in which such acts have occurred in the past are Mexico, Ethiopia, Columbia, West Germany, Argentina, and Iran. A dangerous situation occurred in Guatemala, for example, when a union attempted to organize Coca-Cola employees. The violent dispute resulted in the deaths of several individuals, and employees took possession of the plant. Eventually Coca-Cola U.S. forced the franchise owner to sell the franchise. One way for an organization to combat terrorism is to become a valued employer with loyal employees through equitable and fair compensation practices.

In some extremely remote areas and countries with extreme cultural differences, corporations have created national enclaves to support the lifestyle and safety of employees and their families. Japanese corporations have established enclaves with support school systems, food shops, clothing, cleaning, and many other services. Lockheed Aircraft established its own color television broadcasting station in Saudi Arabia, and INCO built a golf course and yacht club in Indonesia ("Mind over Matter," 1987).

Housing Assistance

Housing allowances are often part of the compensation packages of expatriate as well as regular employees within countries. For example, in Japanese companies, most single Japanese females are expected to live in dormitories or with their parents. Housing expenses are an expected portion of compensation, and upon marriage there is a significant increase in the amount. This benefit is extended to foreign employees within Japanese corporations in Japan but not necessarily ventures located abroad. Another approach is a housing allowance that is the difference in housing costs between two countries or that is based upon a percentage of the base salary. Some companies provide housing assistance that is free through company-owned housing.

Stock Options

Stock options become less attractive as a vehicle for compensation when companies are required to charge the value of stock options against earnings. Even those companies that favor stock options increasingly agree that the options should be related to specific goals and not be merely a giveaway (Keische, 1993). An example is the the Du Pont Shares Program, which encountered numerous regulations, customs, and laws that presented obstacles. Private citizens in some countries could not own stock, and in some countries they still cannot. In other countries, options are taxed as of the date they are granted instead of when they are exercised. This is an obvious disincentive, for the programs become a cost to employees before they gain any value. The acquired rights legislation in other countries, such as Malaysia, posed a problem because once a particular compensation benefit is awarded it becomes an entitlement and must continue. There is also the problem of inflation and fluctuating currency exchanges, especially in the high inflation countries of Latin America (e.g., Brazil, and Argentina). This could result in significant individual income disparity over time. In countries where options were impossible to administer, even after working extensively with the government, Du Pont introduced a stock appreciation rights program. However, for legal or cultural reasons it was necessary to withdraw from some countries, and the program has yet to be implemented in these countries (Harrison, 1992).

The implementation phase of the Du Pont program had some particularly interesting dimensions. Corporate practices had kept certificates in conservative colors, but regional businesses wanted bright colors. There was the additional concern about stock certificates looking too official for fear they would be traded as currency. This was solved by printing in large letters on the back that the certificate had no monetary value. Because slang and humor do not translate, brochures were written in a succinct and direct manner. Also multiple versions of the materials were required to accommodate country and regional language differences. Each employee's name was printed in an alphabet familiar to that employee, on each certificate to personalize it and to make everyone feel comfortable with the certificates (Harrison, 1992).

Taxation

Responsibility for counseling and providing information on compensation structure and benefits relative to tax equity issues falls to the compensation specialist. This area of compensation is one of the quasi-legal financial areas and is extremely complex and challenging, and it differs from country to country and even among regions within countries. Tax equalization can be extremely expensive for the organization, and the greater advantage to the employee as well as the corporation must be weighed. For example, an executive in Belgium earning $100,000 could cost almost $1 million in taxes over a five- to seven-year period (Dowling & Schuler, 1990).

Often salaries will be split between local and home country currency to maximize the benefits to both parties relative to tax systems and exchange markets. The demands of national tax codes require flexibility based on country differences.

Benefits

The cost and design of organizational benefits poses another incredible challenge to the management of international compensation. The issues, requirements, and expectations of employees vary tremendously between countries, within various regions of countries, and between types of workers within any given work force. Right-sizing of organizations has led to reduced hierarchical levels, which means managers must find new ways by which to reward employees, other than traditional promotions and pay schemes. The increasing cost of benefits creates another critical problem area for organizations: the need to require employee contribution to benefits that were previously provided by the organization. The percentages of benefits range from approximately 35 percent in the United States, to 45 percent in Germany, to 70 percent in France, to as high as 92 percent in Italy (Ball & McCullouch, 1990).

Providing employee benefits across national boundaries requires an analysis of the country's legally mandated requirements, local provisions, and the cultural expectations of all categories of employees within the work force (Morgenstern, 1993). An excellent illustration of the variety of legal benefits is France, which requires companies to provide profit-sharing, bonuses, typical medical, vacation and holiday benefits, paternal leave when children are born, severance pay, death, retirement, disability, plus allowances for housing, moving, and children. Examples of more unusual benefits are the requirement in Brazil that a grant be paid to dependents of a worker sent to prison and in Mexico where up to three scholarships must be provided for workers' children (Ball & McCulloch, 1990).

Characteristics that differentiate benefits in Western Europe from those in the United States typically involve nonwage benefits. U.S. employees receive significantly more benefits from their employers, and Western European employees receive more Social Security benefits, adding significantly to labor costs. Western European governments have granted important concessions on costly social benefits to encourage employment practices that support national priorities (Springer, 1989). The critical concerns for organizations then become the maintaining of benefit standards in terms of quality, the price for the service provided, and how to maintain controls—all from a distance.

Paid Time Off (Vacations, Holidays)

In the past, significant compensation trends and practices began in the United States. However, currently new trends are emerging in Western

Europe, Japan and, from regional trade alliances. For example, traditional overtime rules are in the process of changing in Western Europe. In France, based on a recent law, employers may use compensatory time off to compensate for overtime and only for hours worked in excess of forty-four (Springer, 1989). Historically, Western European firms have required a paid vacation of four to six weeks with actual plant closings forcing individuals to take vacation time when it is allocated.

A natural assumption is made that all legal and cultural holidays must be observed because organizations operate across national boundaries. However, the differences in cultural practices and length of time required away from work may vary from as much as a few days to several weeks. For example, in many Pacific Island countries funeral leave as well as Christmas holidays may amount to two to three weeks in duration.

Home leave of four to six weeks every year or every other year is usually granted to expatriate employees and their families. This leave typically includes paid round-trip air fare for the entire family. Third country employees may also negotiate or expect this benefit from organizations for themselves as well as their families.

Retirement Plans and Social Insurance

Diversity in country laws and practices continue to be evident in the area of retirement and pension legislation. The social security, pension and non-pension benefit practices and standards of countries require close examination and critical comparison. In Hungary, for example, laws are being introduced in the field of insurance that are similar to those of Western practice. Under the previous system, all social protection was the responsibility of the State. The new legislation reduces retirement pensions because the entire income of an individual is no longer used in the calculation of the pension base. Social insurance provisions have also been reduced in health care benefits. This legislation also determines the health services provided free of charge and which services must be paid for by the individual. Conditions do not yet exist for private insurers to undertake a greater role, because contribution payment obligation plans make self-provision almost impossible (Meeus & Karcsay, 1993).

Global organizations may have multiple pension plans in effect in numerous countries covering multiple nationals. Knowing where plans exist, how they are funded, how they are invested, what restrictions apply, and what local regulations are in effect is an incredible responsibility. An excellent illustration is Johnson & Johnson's pension plan, which covers 20,000 participants and has $1.2 billion in assets in the United States, and its fifteen international plans, with 15,000 participants and $700 million in assets. Johnson & Johnson found that the most effective way to deal with this complex area was to form a committee, because pension management includes disciplines such as law, tax, and accounting as well as benefits and compensation.

Funding pension plans in some countries such as Germany is not feasible because there is a disincentive to do so that is based on government social security benefit regulations. In the United Kingdom, in addition to pension reserves, a new regulation requires a surplus to accommodate automatic cost-of-living adjustments to pensions paid after retirement. The basic questions to ask should be if it is advisable to fund a pension in a given country of operation from an economic and noneconomic viewpoint, from a legal perspective, and from the employee relations point of view. The Johnson & Johnson pension plans vary from country to country and within countries including two country plans that have defined benefits but remain unfunded (Di Leonardi, 1992).

In October 1992, the Italian parliament approved a law requiring reform of pensions paid from the primary social security authority in Italy. The retirement age was increased, and there was a reduction in the amount of pension payable to young workers who retire at the middle management level and above. The law also included a mandate to increase regulation of private pensions plans. The purpose of the law is to encourage higher levels of retirement benefits and to base regulation on the criteria of fiscal efficiency, flexibility, and diversification of benefits for participants. The regulation also requires separate and autonomous funding of retirement plans and the capitalization of benefits (Canafax & Pinna, 1993).

The French pension system, established following World War II, was based on the principle of directly linking contributions and benefits without necessarily establishing reserves. Because demographic and economic pressures have increased, as in many other countries, the existing system will require some type of reform. A new coalition has been established by manifesto that is committed to guaranteeing a balanced system (Kamienieck & Leon-Marinolli, 1993).

A similar situation exists in Japan where companies with 500 or more participants are converting their lump-sum retirement allowance into partial payment pension plans. A record 118 Employee Pension Funds (EPFs) were formed in fiscal 1990 alone. The massive retirement of the baby-boom generation is driving this change, as in many other countries around the world. Sharp Corporation has initiated a new system it calls the " Gold Plan," which enables retiring employees to collect a monthly pension of ¥500,000, which at the exchange rate of ¥110, amounts to about $4,500. An EPF has the advantage of being integrated into the national system; thus they are highly desired by the new generation of workers. An additional company advantage is the ability of companies to be able to invest contributions in their EPFs of up to one-third of the total assets, at their own discretion.

International social security agreements or totalization agreements eliminate dual social security taxation and provide additional benefit protection for workers employed in more than one country. Without these agreements people who work outside their country of origin may find themselves contributing to, and covered under, the systems of two countries simultaneously. The objective of U.S. totalization agreements is to eliminate dual social security coverage and taxation while maintaining the coverage of as many workers as possible under the system of the country to which they are most likely to retire (Powell, 1993).

Severance Compensation

Many countries require organizations to provide severance pay to permanent employees when they are terminated. The amount paid has no relation to the length of employment. In Mexico, for example, employees who have been employed for only one day require an amount equivalent to three months pay; whereas Peru requires that an employee work for three years to qualify for severance compensation. In Italy, there is a legally mandated severance obligation, but no vehicle by which to fund the requirement.

Flexible Compensation Programs

Factors that influenced the growth of flexible programs in the United States, such as the need to control benefit costs, budget restrictions and limitations, changes in work force demographics, and the expectation and demand for enhanced employee benefits, are also present in other countries. Canada has sixty-five flexible programs, and Europe and Australia are following this lead (Cook, 1993).

Flexibility in adapting to the new work force is evidenced by the fact that more than half of the industrial firms surveyed by the EEC in Western Europe are experimenting with more flexible working hours. More organizations are using part-time employees and fixed-term work contracts. Firms in Germany and France have adopted work teams and the four-day work week. Volkswagen has just recently converted its work force to the four-day work week and has realized significant increases in productivity. Probationary time frames have been extended, and regulations concerning layoffs have been moderated. Organizations have gained more control over compensation in many countries by the curtailment of national policies that tied wages to the inflation rate (Springer, 1989).

Executive Compensation

The most controversial area of compensation in recent years has been CEO pay, especially in American companies. The results of multiple studies range from finding CEOs underpaid to contributing to 70 percent of the gross national product. Global comparisons of executive compensation become even more complex and varied. Executive compensation in Japanese companies is continuously measured against other countries, especially the United States. However, generous perquisites, which are not taxable and not required to be reported, constitute a major percentage of Japanese executive compensation. Perquisites within American companies are usually much lower in value and require disclosure. This is only one example of how cross-national compensation comparisons can be misleading.

Two dimensions of compensation management predominate reward structures in executive compensation today. One is the compensation committee, and the second is the issue of pay for performance. Successful performance-based reward systems need to be measured by the kind of performance and the time period involved in each measure of performance. Properly designed performance measures must provide a large enough stake in the business to result in a level of performance for value creation. In 1992, Ernst & Young and the American Quality Foundation released the International Quality Study, which examines a variety of management practices at more than 500 major corporations in Canada, Germany, Japan, and the United States. The survey indicates that, between 1993 and 1996, a dramatic rise will occur in the number of companies that plan to introduce compensation programs for senior management that are linked to quality performance (Willett, 1993).

Compensation committees with external compensation consultants as advisors have the capability to assure equitable compensation. Especially critical is the unproved claim that management and directors might overcompensate each other when they are responsible for determining each other's pay and benefit increases (Roberts, 1993). Committees can also assure that executive compensation is in line with the company's and shareholders' rewards. Measures such as return on investment, return on equity, dividend, and share price can be used as benchmark measures. The ethics of pay not linked to performance could imply that the corporate governance process is neglecting to provide management accountability.

Supplemental executive benefits are most often provided in the following areas: health care, disability income, death benefits, vacation, capital accumulation, and retirement income. Special supplemental benefits for executives are provided for a variety of reasons, such as restoration of limits, recognition of unique compensation, tax shelters, executive mobility, uniformity of benefits, attractive compensation, and executive retention. Trends in executive benefits are expected to change in the following manner: There will be a decrease in medical benefits and an increase in nonqualified retirement and capital accumulation plans. Executive concern for security will no doubt increase, and a separate specialty devoted to international and executive benefits may develop in the HR field (Sugar, 1991).

Inflation as well as fluctuations in monetary valuation increase the costs of executive lifestyles abroad. For companies coming to Mexico City, for example, the cost is high and continues to climb. Similarly, Mexican companies that want to hire and retain their foreign executives must find competitive compensation packages. Employees at lower levels in the organization or those who come to Mexico seeking work must absorb the extra costs. Shipment of household goods, trips outside Mexico City, automobiles, and housing must be paid by those who come to Mexico to seek employment and international business experience (Cohen, 1993).

Performance Appraisal and Compensation

The processes of performance appraisal and compensation are closely linked through the management control function. When transferred into the international arena, the appraisal process must be adjusted to the categories of employees and consideration must given to cultural appropriateness of the methods and techniques. For example, in collective cultures such as Japan, the contribution to the group, group harmony, and group success is a very critical dimension of performance. On the other hand, many of the performance appraisal methods and techniques used globally were developed in the United States and focus on individual contributions and performance. In group-oriented cultures and work organizations, these performance measurement systems must be adapted to fit the existing expectations and requirements of the work force.

In Japan the major aspect of performance evaluation is that employees continue to make efforts to improve themselves and help others improve. One's efforts are a significant expression of their sincerity to their group. As long as the effort is made, the evaluation tends to be positive. The manner in which evaluation is expressed also varies across cultures. Continuing the comparison with Japan, if the performance is substandard the evaluation may be less positive but never negative. By adopting a positive and motivational approach, it is expected that the employee will continue to make an effort to improve. Appraisal is primarily used for motivational and developmental purposes. The actual appraisal process in most all Japanese companies has no feedback loop whereby appraisal results are discussed with the employee. This is to prevent embarrassment or antagonism, and the HRM/Personnel department makes adjustments to eliminate or narrow differences in evaluation that make a true dialogue between the direct assessor and assessee difficult. The long-term significance of the more frequent informal evaluation interaction demands attention as well as the structured formal system. The relationship between evaluator and employee has the greatest impact on the adopting of values and expectations of performance on the part of the work force. An awareness of cultural differences and expectations are critical in this emotional and intense interpersonal interaction.

Conclusion

All company as well as country environments are unique, and each must determine the compensation mix that best meets it needs. However, the inclusion of some of the following basic concepts will assist in the development of a defensible, competitive, and motivational international compensation program.

Salary Comparisons

Salary comparisons need to include the total compensation package: salary, bonuses, and long-term awards. The types and levels of pensions, welfare, and fringe benefits that are offered by domestic and other international corporations that would attract the same or similar work force need to be considered.

Link Between Performance and Compensation

Another area of concern is the link between performance and compensation, and the cultural and national expectations regarding that link. The level of training and education required needs to be measured against the nature, extent, and scope of duties and responsibilities of the work force. The number of hours and the nature of the effort involved in performing the categories of tasks and responsibilities at the level expected must be identified and quantified.

Operating Environment

The environment in which the organization operates is also a consideration, for it is necessary to determine the prevailing global economic conditions. The economic and financial state of the organization as well as the industry measured against the financial condition of the organization after payment of compensation are the components of a critical assessment (Morgenstern, 1993). The primary consideration is the rationale used for the total compensation package compared to operating measures before and after deducting pay awarded.

The essence of the corporate compensation philosophy is how the organization positions its total pay against the appropriate marketplace and how it can use the three foregoing broad categories to defend against unreasonable compensation packages. A global compensation philosophy needs to be developed with strategies that address long-term objectives and that make the organization responsive to local variations as well as to future changes and competitive pressures.

References

Ball, D. A., & McCullouch, W. H., Jr. (1990). *International business: Introduction and essentials,* 4th ed. Boston, MA: BPI Irwin.

Brown, D. (1993, Sept./Oct.). Centralized control or decentralized diversity?: A guide for matching compensation with company strategy and structure. *Compensation and Benefits Review,* 25(5), 47–52.

Canafax, L., & Pinna, C. (1993, July/Aug.). The first effort at promoting private pensions plans in Italy. *Benefits and Compensation International,* 23(1), 42–48.

Cohen, J. A. (1993, July). The high costs of executive living: The myth of economical Mexico. *Business Mexico,* 3(7), 38–40.

Cook. M. (1993). *Human resource management handbook, 1993–1994.* Englewood Cliffs, NJ: Prentice-Hall.

Daniels, J. D., & Radebaugh, L. H. (1992). *International business: environments and operations,* 6th ed. Reading, MA: Addison-Wesley.

DiLeonardi, F. A. (1993). International pensions—Money makes the world go 'round. In M. F. Cook (ed.), *The human resources yearbook: 1992–1993.* Englewood Cliffs, NJ: Prentice-Hall.

Dowling, P. J., & Schuler, R. S. (1990). *International dimensions of human resource management.* Boston, MA: PWS-Kent Publishing.

Gross, S. F. (1993, July/Aug.). Trends in compensation. *Benefits and Compensation International,* 23(1), 11–15.

Harrison, S. A. (1992). *Rethinking corporate compensation plans.* Conference Board, Report no. 1015.

Hodgetts, R. M., & Luthans, F. (1993, Mar/Apr.). U.S. multinationals' compensation strategies for local management: Cross-cultural implications. *Compensation and Benefits Review,* 25(2), 42–48.

Kamieniecki, J. A., and Leon-Marinolli, J. (1993, June). The French pensions debate takes a few new turns. *Benefits and Compensation International,* 22(10), 2–4.

Keische, E. S. (1993, June 30). Executive compensation. *Chemical Week,* 152(25), 22–31.

Meeus, T., & Karcsay, M. (1993, July/Aug.). Possibilities for private insurance plans. *Benefits and Compensation International,* 23(1), 54–57.

Milkovich, G. T., & Newman J. M. (1993). *Compensation,* 4th ed. Homewood, IL: Irwin.

Mind over matter. (1987). *Wall Street Journal,* A6.

Morgenstern, M. L. (1993, Jan./Feb.). Compensation and benefits challenges for the 1990s: The board speaks out. *Benefits and Compensation Review,* 25(1), 22–26.

Overman, S. (1993, Mar.). European Community's single market challenges HR managers. *Human Resource News,* A2.

Payson, M. F., & Rosen, P. B. (1993). Playing by fair rules. In M. F. Cook (ed.), *The human resources yearbook: 1992–1993.* Englewood Cliffs, NJ: Prentice-Hall.

Perry, N. J. (1988, Dec. 19). Here come richer, riskier pay plans. *Fortune,* 50–58.

Powell, B. L. (1993, June). U.S. international Social Security agreements. *Benefits and Compensation International,* 22(10), 6–10.

Rich, J. T. (1992, July/Aug.). Meeting the global challenge: A measurement and reward program for the future. *Compensation and Benefits Review,* 24(4), 26–29.

Roberts, S. (1993, Aug. 30). Poor profits, shareholder scrutiny limit CEO raises. *Business Insurance,* 27(36), 1, 72.

Ronen, S., & Shenkar, O. (1985). Clustering countries on attitudinal dimensions: A review and synthesis. *Academy of Management Review,* 10, 435–54.

Springer, B. J. (1989, July/Aug.). 1992: The impact on compensation and benefits in the European Community. *Compensation and Benefits Review,* 21(4), 20–27.

Sugar, D. M. (1991, Sept./Oct.). Why are executive benefits needed? *Benefits and Compensation International, 23*(1), 16–19.

Townnsend, A. M., Scott, D. K., & Markhan, S. E. (1990). An examination of country and culture-based differences in compensation practices. *Journal of International Business Studies, 21*(4), 667–678.

Trucks Inc. vs. *United States.* (1984). 588F. Supp. 638 (D.C. Nebraska).

Willett, D. (1993, Autumn). Promoting quality through compensation. *Business Quarterly, 58*(1), 107–111.

Women Managers[1]

Moving Up and Across Borders

Nancy J. Adler McGill University

Dafna N. Izraeli Bar-Ilan University

*The best reason for believing that more women will be in charge
before long is that in a ferociously competitive global economy, no
company can afford to waste valuable brainpower simply
because it's wearing a skirt. (Fisher, 1992:56)*

World business has become intensely competitive. Top-quality people allow corporations to compete. Yet, although outstanding human resource systems provide competitive advantages, companies worldwide draw from a restricted pool of potential managers. Although women represent over 50 percent of the world population, in no country do women represent half, or even close to half, of the corporate managers. Even in the United States, where many believe the proportion of female executives to be outstanding, reality belies the belief: Whereas 46 percent of the American work force is female, women constitute only 5 percent of the expatriate managers (Moran, Stahl, & Boyer, 1988), 3 percent of the senior executives (Ball, 1991; Segal & Zellner, 1992), and less than half of 1 percent of the highest paid officers and directors (Fierman, 1990).

Cross-National Comparisons

Until the late 1970s, women were virtually invisible as managers, and their absence was generally considered a nonissue (Antal & Izraeli, 1993). Since then, women managers have become increasingly visible in many countries

Dr. Adler would like to thank the Social Sciences and Humanities Research Council of Canada for its research funding of her work on transnational human resource management strategies and women in international management.

where broad societal forces during recent decades resulted in more women entering lower-level managerial positions.

In the economically developing and recently industrialized countries, a shift took place between the 1950s and early 1970s from agrarian toward manufacturing economies. This shift, along with the development of labor-intensive industries, primarily by multinational corporations, created a demand for cheap labor that brought many women into the urban labor force. Governments saw increasing women's participation in the labor force as essential for national economic growth and development, and therefore encouraged women's economic activity. These governments, however, had no special interest in women's promotion into management. Moreover, the traditional male ethos associated with manufacturing industries made industrial firms less friendly toward women managers than would be the next wave of service sector firms.

In both the industrialized and industrializing worlds, the expansion of the public and service sectors, along with the increased importance of staff positions, became major factors promoting women's initial breakthrough into management. The expansion of banking and other financial services opened opportunities for women in lower- and middle-level management positions. In most countries in the 1970s and 1980s, the growing public sector also absorbed the growing population of educated women into lower-level managerial positions. As new jobs were created, women moved into management and men moved up the hierarchy. Reference to positive stereotypes—such as recognizing Asian women's traditional experience managing family finances and regarding women as more honest and trust-worthy than men—helped employers rationalize women's presence in what had previously been a male domain (see Chan & Lee, 1994; Cheng & Liao, 1994; Siengthai & Leelakulthanit, 1994; and Steinhoff & Tanaka, 1994, among others).

In both the industrialized and industrializing worlds, economic growth and increasing global competition heightened the demand for top-quality managers. Economic enterprises began to take advantage of the growing availability of qualified women to fill the new positions. In each country, however, the specific processes used to bring about change differed.

In the United States, powerful women's groups used the political process and the courts to help establish regulations that held employers responsible for implementing equal opportunity within their organizations (see Fagenson & Jackson, 1994). Such political and legal changes made it in organizations' self-interest to open their doors to women for lower-level managerial positions. However, neither the political nor the legal changes were sufficiently powerful to counter resistance to women entering the most senior levels.

In France, legislation passed in the 1980s gave unions responsibility for negotiating equal opportunity on behalf of women. Progress, however, was very limited. The French unions appear to have lacked sufficient motivation to effect the previously legislated societal changes. Many French observers believe that the union leaders, most of whom are men, share management's prejudicial attitudes against women (Serdjenian, 1994).

In Hong Kong, where government intervention in commerce has been purposefully minimal and sex discrimination in employment continues to be legal, the proportion of women among corporate managers remains negligible (see de Leon & Ho, 1994).

In the social welfare states of Western Europe and Israel, social democratic parties created large public service bureaucracies that became the major employers of women and therefore provided a major channel for women moving into management. Not surprisingly in these countries, gender segregation emerged along sectorial lines, with women managers concentrated in the public sector and men in the private sector (see, for example, Hanninen-Salmelin & Petajaniemi, 1994; and Izraeli, 1994).

Under communist rule, Eastern European countries and the former Soviet Union set quotas for women in local-level management. However, women remained highly under represented in more senior and national positions. In the former Yugoslavia, for example, opportunities for women managers depended on the political interests of the Communist Party (see Kavcic, 1994). Women's chances for promotion were best during periods of economic growth and political calm. However, during the times when political unrest was greatest, the proportion of women promoted into and within management dropped. At those times, the Communist Party allocated positions either to men known to be loyal to the Party or to men whose loyalty it needed to secure. In Poland, since women rarely filled managerial positions in state enterprises, few now have sufficient experience to draw upon for managing in the new market-oriented economy (see Siemienska, 1994). The large women's organizations in certain former communist countries, such as Poland and Russia, operated essentially as extensions of the Communist Party. As such, they served primarily a social control function for the Party, rather than an advocacy role for women (see Puffer, 1994; and Siemienska, 1994).

Countries recently freed from communist rule appear to be experiencing a backlash against many of the policies that were supportive of women's employment, professional advancement, and general freedoms (Moghadam, 1992). For example, high unemployment has increased competition, including for managerial positions, most often to women's detriment. In addition, due to a lack of funds, most former communist countries have chosen to severely reduce the extensive network of childcare services, thus further increasing unemployment among women managers forced to quit working because too few acceptable childcare options remain available. Moreover, the belief that a woman's place is in the home is replacing the quota system that guaranteed women's representation in lower- and middle-level management in most former communist countries. For example, under pressure from the Catholic Church, the Polish parliament recently passed a severely limiting antiabortion law. In Russia, Poland, Eastern Germany, and parts of former Yugoslavia, women face a difficult struggle ahead to maintain or regain their previous representation in the economy (see Antal & Krebsbach-Gnath, 1994; Kavcic, 1994; Puffer, 1994; Siemienska, 1994). Only now are women in these transitional economies beginning to organize to advance their professional and political status and interests (Moghadam, 1992).

Other countries, such as Singapore, Malaysia, Indonesia, and Zimbabwe, have only recently emerged from extended periods of colonial rule. Colonialism's impact on women differed in important ways from its the impact on men. For example, in colonial Indonesia, the Dutch recruited upper class men for roles in the civil service and reinforced women's exclusion from public life (see Wright & Crockett-Tellei, 1994). Moreover, the Dutch in Indonesia did not develop an educational system for the local people. In contrast, the Americans introduced universal education in the Philippines, thus giving Philippine women a decided advantage in urban labor markets compared with women from many other post-colonial countries. In Zimbabwe, where white men control the private business sector and black men control family life, black women continue to face a double challenge both as women and as black women (Muller, 1994; also see Erwee, 1994, for similar patterns in South Africa).

In most post-colonial countries, women participated in the struggle for liberation. A number of them later became members of their country's new government, thus providing role models for other women. However, because they were brought into government positions only by these unusual circumstances, the token women leaders did not necessarily become harbingers for succeeding women's continued involvement in the centers of economic or political power. More commonly, they emerged as exceptions to a pattern that generally continues to exclude women from power (see Muller, 1994). This exclusion has most frequently reasserted itself with the passing of the original leadership.

To date, there is no systematic research on the few executive women of almost every nationality who have succeeded in assuming very senior positions; however, they appear to come from the same societal groups as do male executives. For example, in cultures in which executives are drawn primarily from the upper classes, such as from the Javanese Priyayi in Indonesia, the few female executives, like their male counterparts, are most likely to come from elite families in which family connections smooth the way for business success (Wright & Crockett-Tellei, 1994). Similarly, in cultures such as Hong Kong in which the dominant enterprise structure is the family business, senior women, like their male counterparts, are most likely to run their family's business (de Leon & Ho, 1994). In such cultures, executives generally view themselves as working in the service of their family. However, for a woman, being an executive in a family business is not necessarily recognized as qualifying her to assume an executive position in a nonfamily enterprise. For example, in the Malaysian province of Kelantin, where women have traditionally dominated both business activity and family finances while men worked primarily in agriculture, the proportion of women who have been promoted into upper-level managerial positions in nonfamily enterprises and government organizations remains negligible (Mansor, 1994).

Women as Senior Executives and Expatriate Managers

Until recently, a single theme dominated questions about women managers worldwide: the concern for understanding their under-representation, under-utilization, and skewed distribution among the levels of domestic and international management. Only in the 1990s has the question of global competitiveness and transnational efficacy begun to transform and complement these equity-based concerns.

Although the proportion of women managers has increased significantly in recent years in all countries for which data are available, the anticipated breakthrough into the centers of organizational power seems even less likely today than it did twenty years ago when the groundbreaking book *Breakthrough: Women into Management* noted: "It's when and how, not if women move up. The groundwork has been laid" (Loring & Wells, 1972:15).

This optimism was reflected in many of the countries described in our earlier book, *Women in Management Worldwide* (1988), the first to provide a multinational perspective on women in management. We were cautioned, however, that we must analyze the gains carefully to separate myth from reality (Keller Brown, 1988).

Whereas the optimism about women's movement into management appears to have been well grounded, the optimism about women moving into the international arena or up into the executive suite now appears to have been premature. Conditions that we, like other observers, expected would remove the barriers to women's progress throughout the profession of management, left most women well below the glass ceiling, where they could glimpse the executive suite but not quite enter it. Similarly, it left most women in the domestic positions while power was shifting to the global market (Calas & Smirich, 1993). Women's increased investment in higher education and greater commitment to management as a career, as well as new equal opportunity legislation and the shortage (or anticipated shortage) of high-quality managers, did not result in a significant breakthrough either into international management or into the executive suite. Regardless of the proportion of women managers at lower levels, women in every country remain only a tiny fraction of those sent on international assignments and those who make it to senior positions (Segal & Zellner, 1992). According to *Business Week*, "at the current rates it will be 475 years before women reach equality in the executive suite" (Spillar, 1992:76).

Our earlier work as well as that of others had failed to appreciate the important distinction between entry into management and upward mobility within management (Izraeli & Adler, 1994). We implicitly assumed that women managers moving up into the executive level and across domestic borders involved dynamics similar to those facilitating women's initial entry into management. We were perhaps overly impressed with the thin trickle of extraordinary women, operating under exceptional circumstances in each country, who had succeeded in breaking through the glass ceiling and, in a very limited number of cases, assuming senior executive positions and increasingly important international assignments. The mass media heightened public exposure to their presence. In all countries, articles and feature stories in women's magazines and some mainstream business journals made these exceptional women highly visible. Visibility had the benefit of increasing the female executives' impact as role models, along with the unfortunate consequence of reinforcing the illusion that substantial numbers of women had and could make it to the top (Izraeli, 1988). The reality, however, is that the executive suite and the international arena have remained highly resistant to women's entry.

Clearly, the situation facing women executives as well as women international managers has not been the same as that facing lower- and middle-level managers in domestic positions. A fuller understanding of the barriers that have limited women's access both to international management and to the executive suite—as well as the differences between "moving into" and "moving up within" management—will better equip organizations to select more effective policies: Such policies are capable of both increasing organizational effectiveness and remedying the current inequality. New approaches free them from remaining trapped within their prior, self-limiting perspectives. The following sections examine women's under-representation both in international management and in the executive suite. The ways managers commonly think about women as managers is contrasted with the reality of women's experience as managers. We begin with three beliefs about women's unsuitability for international assignments that although widely held to be true are not supported by the facts of the case. Because they are held to be true, however, they become true in their consequences and serve to limit women's opportunities in international management.

Three Myths About Women Managing Across Borders

As cross-border business becomes more widespread and more firms become multinational and transnational, international assignments form an increasingly important component of the new definition of managerial roles (see

Adler & Bartholomew, 1992), and women as expatriate managers becomes a more important issue (see, for example, Izraeli & Zeira, 1993). Given the historical scarcity of local women managers in most countries, most firms have questioned if women can succeed in cross-border managerial assignments. They have believed that the relative absence of local women managers formed a basis for accurately predicting the potential for success, or lack thereof, of expatriate women. To predict what women's roles in management will be in the 1990s and the twenty-first century, it is important to understand the underlying assumptions that firms make in each country about the role of women in management.

Given the importance of these questions to future business success, Adler conducted a multipart study on the role of women as expatriate managers. Research revealed a set of assumptions that managers and executives make about how foreigners would treat expatriate women, based on their beliefs about how foreign firms treat their own local women. The problem with the story is that the assumptions have proven to be false. Moreover, because the assumptions fail to accurately reflect reality, they are inadvertently causing executives to make decisions that are neither effective nor equitable.

The study addressed three commonly held "myths" about women in international management:

Myth 1:   Women do not want to be international managers.

Myth 2:   Companies refuse to send women abroad.

Myth 3:   Foreigners' prejudice against women renders women ineffective, even when interested in foreign assignments and successful in being sent.

These beliefs were labeled "myths" because, although widely held by both men and women, their accuracy had never been tested.

Myth 1: Women Do Not Want to Be International Managers

Is the problem that women are less interested than men in pursuing international careers? The study tested this myth by surveying more than a thousand graduating MBAs from seven top management schools in the United States, Canada, and Europe (see Adler 1984b & 1986). The results revealed an overwhelming case of no significant difference: Female and male MBAs display equal interest, or disinterest, in pursuing international careers. More than four out of five MBAs—both women and men—want an international assignment at some time during their career. Both female and male MBAs, however, agree that firms offer fewer opportunities to women than to men, and significantly fewer opportunities to women pursuing international careers than to those pursuing domestic careers.

Although there may have been a difference in the past, women and men today are equally interested in international management, including expatriate assignments. The first myth—that women do not want to be international managers—is false; it is, in fact, a myth.

Myth 2: Companies Refuse to Send Women Abroad

If the problem is not women's disinterest, is it that companies refuse to select women for international assignments? To test if the myth of corporate resistance was true, human resource vice-presidents and managers from sixty of the largest North American multinationals were surveyed (see Adler, 1984a). Over half of the companies reported that they hesitate to send women abroad. Almost four times as many reported being reluctant to select women for international assignments as for domestic management positions. When asked why they hesitate, almost three-quarters reported believing that foreigners were so prejudiced against women that the female managers could not succeed even if sent. Similarly, 70 percent believed that dual-career issues were insurmountable. In addition, some human resource executives expressed concern about the women's physical safety, the hazards involved in traveling in underdeveloped countries, and, especially in the case of single women, the isolation and loneliness.

Many of the women who succeeded in being sent abroad as expatriate managers report having confronted some form of corporate resistance before being sent abroad. For example:

> *Malaysia.*   "Management assumed that women didn't have the physical stamina to survive in the tropics. They claimed I couldn't hack it [in Malaysia]."
>
> *Thailand.*   "My company didn't want to send a woman to that 'horrible part of the world.' They think Bangkok is an excellent place to send single men, but not a woman. They said they would have trouble getting a work permit for me, which wasn't true."
>
> *Japan and Korea.*   "Everyone was more or less curious if it would work. My American boss tried to advise me, 'Don't be upset if it's difficult in Japan and Korea.' The American male manager in Tokyo was also hesitant. Finally the Chinese boss in Hong Kong said, 'We have to try!' Then they sent me."

A few women experienced severe resistance from their companies to sending any female managers abroad. Their firms seemed to offer them an expatriate position only after all potential male candidates had turned it down. For example:

> *Thailand.*   "Every advance in responsibility is because the Americans had no choice. I've never been chosen over someone else."

Japan.   "They never would have considered me. But then the financial manager in Tokyo had a heart attack, and they had to send someone. So they sent me, on a month's notice, as a temporary until they could find a man to fill the permanent position. It worked out, and I stayed."

Although most of the women are sent in the same capacity as their male expatriate colleagues, some companies demonstrate their hesitation by offering temporary or travel assignments rather than regular expatriate positions. For instance:

Hong Kong.   "After offering me the job, they hesitated: 'Could a woman work with the Chinese?' So my job was defined as temporary, a one-year position to train a Chinese man to replace me. I succeeded and became permanent."

These findings concur with those of 100 top line managers in Fortune 500 firms; the majority of whom believe that women face overwhelming resistance when seeking managerial positions in international divisions of U.S. firms (Thal & Cateora, 1979). Similarly, 80 percent of U.S. firms report believing that women would face disadvantages if sent abroad (Moran et al, 1988). Thus, the second myth is, in fact, true: Firms are hesitant, if not outright resistant, to sending female managers abroad.

Myth 3: Foreigners' "Prejudice" Against Female Expatriate Managers

Is it true that foreigners are so prejudiced against women that the women could not succeed as international managers? Would sending a female manager abroad be neither fair to the woman nor effective for the company? Is the treatment of local women the best predictor of expatriate women's potential to succeed? The fundamental question was, and remains: Is the historic discrimination against local women worldwide a valid basis for predicting expatriate women's success as international managers?

To investigate this third myth—that foreigners' prejudice against women renders them ineffective as international managers—over 100 women managers from major North American firms who were on expatriate assignments around the world were surveyed. Fifty-two were interviewed while in Asia or after having returned from countries around the world to North America (Adler, 1987; Jelinek & Adler, 1988). Since most of the women held regional responsibility, their experience represents multiple countries rather than just their country of foreign residence.

Who Are the Female Expatriate Managers?   The women were very well educated and quite internationally experienced. Almost all held graduate degrees, the MBA being the most common. Over three-quarters had

had extensive international interests and experience prior to being sent abroad by their present company. On average, the women spoke two or three languages, with some fluently speaking as many as six. In addition, they had excellent social skills. Nearly two-thirds were single, and only three had children.

Firms using transnational strategies sent more women than did those using other strategies, with financial institutions leading all other industries. On average, the expatriate assignments lasted two-and-a-half years, with a range from six months to six years. The women supervised from zero to twenty-five subordinates, with the average falling just below five. Their titles and levels within their firms varied: Some held very junior positions—assistant account manager—whereas others held quite senior positions, including one regional vice-president. In no firm did a female expatriate hold her company's number one position in the region or in any country.

The women were considerably younger than the typical male expatriate. Their ages ranged from twenty-three to forty-one years, with the average age just under thirty. This reflects the relatively high proportion of women sent by financial institutions—an industry that sends fairly junior managers on international assignments—and the relatively low proportion sent by manufacturing firms, which select quite senior managers for expatriate positions (such as country or regional director).

The Decision to Go.   For most firms, the female expatriates were "firsts": Only 10 percent followed another woman into her international position. Of the 90 percent who were "firsts," almost a quarter represented the first female manager the firm had ever sent abroad. Others were the first women sent to the region, the first sent to the particular country, or the first to fill the specific expatriate position. Clearly, neither the women nor the companies had the luxury of role models or of following previously established patterns. Except for several major financial institutions, both the women and the companies found themselves experimenting in hope of uncertain success.

Most women described themselves as needing to encourage their companies to consider the possibility of assigning international positions to women in general and to themselves in particular. In more than four out of five cases, the woman initially suggested the idea of an international assignment to her boss and company. For only six women did the company first suggest the assignment.

Since most firms had never considered sending a female manager abroad, the women used a number of strategies to introduce the idea and to position their careers internationally. Many explored the possibility of an international assignment during their original job interview and eliminated companies from consideration that were totally against the idea. Other women informally introduced the idea to their boss and continued to mention it at appropriate moments until the company ultimately decided to offer them an expatriate position. A few women formally applied for a number of international assignments prior to actually being selected and sent.

Many women attempted to be in the right place at the right time. For example, one woman who predicted that Hong Kong would be her firm's next major business center arranged to assume responsibility for the Hong Kong desk in New York, leaving the rest of Asia to a male colleague. The strategy paid off: Within a year, the company elevated their Hong Kong operations to a regional center and sent her to Asia as their first female expatriate manager.

Most women claimed that their companies had failed to recognize the possibility of selecting women for international assignments, rather than having thoroughly considered the idea and then having rejected it. For the majority of the women, the obstacle appeared to be the company's naivete, not malice. For many women, the most difficult hurdle in their international career involved getting sent abroad in the first place, not—as most had anticipated—gaining the respect of foreigners and succeeding once sent.

Did it Work? The Impact of Being Female

Almost all the female expatriate managers (97%) reported that their international assignments were successful. This success rate is considerably higher than that reported for North American male expatriates. Although the women's assessments are subjective, objective indicators support the fact that most assignments, in fact, succeeded. For example, the majority of the firms—after experimenting with their first female expatriate manager—decided to send more women abroad. In addition, most companies promoted the women on the basis of their foreign performance and/or offered them other international assignments following completion of the first one.

Advantages

Given the third myth, the women would have been expected to experience a series of difficulties caused by their being female and, perhaps, to create a corresponding set of solutions designed to overcome each difficulty. This was not the case. Almost half of the expatriates (42%) reported that being female served as more of an advantage than a disadvantage; 16 percent found it to be both positive and negative; 22 percent saw it as being either irrelevant or neutral; and only 20 percent found it to be primarily negative.

The women reported numerous professional advantages to being female. Most frequently, they described the advantage of being highly visible. Foreign clients were curious about them, wanted to meet them, and remembered them after the first encounter. The women therefore found it easier for them than for their male colleagues to gain access to foreign clients' time and attention. The women gave examples of this high visibility, accessibility, and memorability, such as:

Japan.   "It's the visibility as an expat, and even more as a woman. I stick in their minds. I know I've gotten more business than my two male colleagues. . . . [My clients] are extra interested in me."

Thailand.   "Being a woman is never a detriment. They remembered me better. Fantastic for a marketing position. It's better working with Asians than with the Dutch, British, or Americans."

India and Pakistan.   "In India and Pakistan, being a woman helps in marketing and client contact. I got in to see customers because they had never seen a female banker before. . . . Having a female banker adds value to the client."

Again contrary to the third myth, the female managers discovered a number of advantages based on their interpersonal skills, including that the local men could talk more easily about a wider range of topics with them than with their male counterparts. For example:

Japan.   "Women are better at putting people at ease. It's easier for a woman to convince a man. . . . The traditional woman's role . . . inspires confidence and trust, less suspicion, not threatening."

Indonesia.   "I often take advantage of being a woman. I'm more supportive than my male colleagues. . . . [Clients] relax and talk more. And 50 percent of my effectiveness is based on volunteered information."

Korea.   "Women are better at treating men sensitively, and they just like you. One of my Korean clients told me, 'I really enjoyed . . . working with you.'"

Many women also described the high social status accorded local women and found that such status was not denied them as foreign women. The women often received special treatment that their male counterparts did not receive. Clearly, it was always salient that they were women, but being a woman was not antithetical to succeeding as a manager.

Hong Kong.   "Single female expats travel easier and are treated better. Never hassled. No safety issues. Local offices take better care of you. They meet you, take you through customs, . . . It's the combination of treating you like a lady and a professional."

Japan.   "It's an advantage that attracts attention. They are interested in meeting a *gaijin*, a foreign woman. Women attract more clients. On calls to clients, they elevate me, give me more rank. If anything, the problem, for men and women, is youth, not gender."

In addition, most of the women described benefiting from a "halo effect." The majority of the women's foreign colleagues and clients had never met or previously worked with a female expatriate manager. Similarly, the local community was highly aware of how unusual it was for North American multinationals to send female managers abroad. Hence, the local managers assumed that the women would not have been sent unless they were "the best," and therefore expected them to be "very, very good".

> *Indonesia.* "It's easier being a woman here than in any place in the world, including New York City. . . . I never get the comments I got in New York, like 'What is a nice woman like you doing in this job?'"
> *Japan.* "They assumed I must be good if I was sent. They became friends."

Some women found being female to have no impact whatsoever on their professional life. Many of these women worked primarily with the Chinese:

> *Hong Kong.* "There are many expat and foreign women in top positions here. If you are good at what you do, they accept you. One Chinese woman told me, 'Americans are always watching you. One mistake and you are done. Chinese take a while to accept you and then stop testing you.'"
> *Asia.* "There's no difference. They respect professionalism . . . including in Japan. There is no problem in Asia."

Disadvantages

The women also experienced a number of disadvantages in being female expatriate managers. Interestingly enough, the majority of the disadvantages involved the women's relationship with their home companies, not with their foreign colleagues and clients. As noted earlier, a major problem involved the women's difficulty in obtaining an international position in the first place.

Another problem involved home companies initially limiting the duration of the women's assignments to six months or a year, rather than offering the more standard two to three years. While temporary assignments may appear to offer companies a logically cautious strategy, in reality they create an unfortunate self-fulfilling prophecy. When the home company is not convinced that a woman can succeed (and therefore offers her a temporary rather than a permanent position), it communicates the company's lack of confidence to foreign colleagues and clients as a lack of commitment. The foreigners then mirror the home company's behavior by also failing to take the woman manager seriously. Assignments become very difficult, or can fail altogether, when companies demonstrate a lack of initial confidence and commitment. As one expatriate woman working in Indonesia described, "It is very important to clients that I am permanent. It increases trust, and that's critical."

A subsequent problem involved the home company limiting the woman's professional opportunities and job scope once she was abroad. More than half of the female expatriates experienced difficulties in persuading their home companies to give them latitude equivalent to that given to their male counterparts, especially initially. For example, some companies, out of supposed concern for the woman's safety, limited her travel (and thus the regional scope of her responsibility), thus excluding very remote, rural, and underdeveloped areas. Other companies, as mentioned previously, initially limited the duration of the woman's assignment to six months or a year, rather than the more standard two to three years. For example:

> *Japan.*   "My problem is overwhelmingly with Americans. They identify it as a male market . . . geisha girls. . . ."
> *Thailand (petroleum company).*   "The Americans wouldn't let me on the drilling rigs, because they said there were no accommodations for a woman. Everyone blames it on something else. They gave me different work. They had me on the sidelines, not planning and communicating with drilling people. It's the expat Americans, not the Thais, who'll go to someone else before they come to me."

A few companies limited the women to working only internally with company employees, rather than externally with clients. These companies often implicitly assumed that their own employees were somehow less prejudiced than were outsiders. In reality, the women often found the opposite to be true. They faced more problems from home country nationals within their own organizations than externally from local clients and colleagues. As one woman described:

> *Hong Kong.*   "It was somewhat difficult internally. They feel threatened, hesitant to do what I say, resentful. They assume I don't have the credibility a man would have. Perhaps it's harder internally than externally, because client relationships are one-on-one and internally it's more of a group; or perhaps it's harder because they have to live with it longer internally; or perhaps it's because they fear that I'm setting a precedent or because they fear criticism from their peers."

Managing foreign clients' and colleagues' initial expectations was one area that proved difficult for many women. Some found initial meetings to be "tricky," especially when a male colleague from their own company was present. Since most local managers had never previously met a North American expatriate woman who held a managerial position, there was considerable ambiguity as to who she was, her status, her level of expertise, authority, and responsibility, and therefore the appropriate form of address and demeanor toward her.

> *People's Republic of China.*   "I speak Chinese, which is a plus. But they'd talk to the men, not to me. They'd assume that I, as a woman, had no authority. The Chinese want to deal with top, top, top level people, and there is always a man at a higher level."

Asia. "It took extra time to establish credibility with the Japanese and Chinese. One Japanese manager said to me, 'When I first met you, I thought you would not be any good because you were a woman.'"

Since most of the North American women whom local managers had ever met previously were expatriates' wives or secretaries, they naturally assumed that the new woman was not a manager. Hence, they often directed initial conversations to male colleagues, not to the newly arrived female manager. Senior male colleagues, particularly those from the head office, became very important in redirecting the focus of early discussions back toward the women. When this was done, old patterns were quickly broken and smooth, ongoing work relationships were established. When the pattern was ignored or poorly managed, the challenges to credibility, authority, and responsibility became chronic and undermined the women's effectiveness.

As mentioned earlier, many women described the most difficult aspect of the foreign assignment as getting sent abroad in the first place. Overcoming resistance from the North American home company frequently proved more challenging than gaining local clients' and colleagues' respect and acceptance. In most cases, assumptions about foreigners' prejudice against female expatriate managers appear to have been exaggerated: The anticipated prejudice and the reality did not match. It appears that foreigners are not as prejudiced as many North American managers had assumed.

The *Gaijin* Syndrome

One pattern is particularly clear: First and foremost, foreigners are seen as foreigners. Like their male colleagues, female expatriates are seen as foreigners, not as local people. A woman who is a foreigner (a *gaijin*) is not expected to act like the local women. Therefore, the societal and cultural rules governing the behavior of local women that limit their access to managerial positions and responsibility do not apply to foreign women. Although women are considered the "culture bearers" in all societies, foreign women are not expected to assume the cultural roles that societies have traditionally reserved for their own women. As one female expatriate in Japan described:

> The Japanese are very smart: they can tell that I am not Japanese, and they do not expect me to act as a Japanese woman. They will allow and condone behavior in foreign women that would be absolutely unacceptable in their own women.

Similarly a Tokyo-based personnel vice-president for a major international bank explained (Morgenthaler, 1978: 1, 27):

Being a foreigner is so weird to the Japanese that the marginal impact of being a woman is nothing. If I were a Japanese woman, I couldn't be doing what I'm doing here. But they know perfectly well that I'm not.

Many of the female expatriates related similar examples of their unique status as "foreign women" rather than as "women" *per se*. For example:

Japan and Korea.   "Japan and Korea are the hardest, but they know that I'm an American woman, and they don't expect me to be like a Japanese or Korean woman. It's possible to be effective even in Japan and Korea if you send a senior woman with at least three or four years of experience, especially if she's fluent in Japanese."

Asia.   "It's the novelty, especially in Japan, Korea, and Pakistan. All of the general managers met with me. . . . It was much easier for me, especially in Osaka. They were charming. They didn't want me to feel bad. They thought I would come back if they gave me business. You see, they could separate me from the local women."

Pakistan.   "Will I have problems? No! There is a double standard between expats and local women. The Pakistanis test you, but you enter as a respected person."

Japan.   "I don't think the Japanese could work for a Japanese woman . . . but they just block it out for foreigners."

Hong Kong.   "Hong Kong is very cosmopolitan. I'm seen as an expat, not as an Asian, even though I am an Asian American."

It seems that we have confused an adjective, *foreign,* with a noun, *woman,* in predicting foreigners' reactions to expatriate women. We expected the most salient characteristic of a female expatriate manager to be that she is a *woman* and predicted her success on the basis of the success of the local women in each country. In fact, the most salient characteristic is that expatriates are *foreign,* and the best predictor of their success is the success of other foreigners (in this case, other North Americans) in the particular country. *Local managers see female expatriates as foreigners who happen to be women, not as women who happen to be foreigners.* The difference is crucial. Given the uncertainty involved in sending women managers to all areas of the world, our assumptions about the greater salience of gender (female or male) over nationality (foreign or local) have caused us to make false predictions concerning women's potential to succeed as executives and managers in foreign countries.

The third myth—that foreigners' prejudice precludes women's effectiveness as international managers—is false; it is, in fact, a myth. Of the three myths, only the second myth proved to be true. The first myth proved false: Women *are* interested in working internationally. The third myth proved false: Women do succeed internationally, once sent. However, the second myth proved to be true: Companies are hesitant, if not completely unwilling, to send women managers abroad. Given that the problem is caused primarily by the home companies' assumptions and decisions, the solutions are also largely within their control.

Why do companies hesitate? The following section attempts to move beyond surface explanations (for a review see Izraeli and Zeira, 1993) to the underlying factors that maintain the current situation of women's under-representation both in international management and locally within each country worldwide.

Four Perspectives on Women in Management

While the specific explanations offered for women's under-representation, under-utilization, and skewed distribution among the levels of management worldwide have varied, they reflect four essentially different perspectives. The first perspective emphasizes differences between women and men; the second perspective focuses on organizational context; the third analyzes institutionalized discrimination; and the fourth underlines the power dynamics that limit women's access to executive positions. We consider each in turn.

Perspective 1: Gender Differences—Why Can't Women Be More Like Men?

The most widely held explanation by managers and, until recently, by scholars for the paucity of women in management is perceived personality and behavioral differences between women and men. Taking men's characteristics and behaviors as the norm for effective managerial performance, many proponents of this perspective presumed that women's actual or perceived divergence from male norms explained women's limited representation in the managerial ranks. Perceived differences between women's and men's managerial behavior were usually attributed either to differences in women's and men's early socialization or to innate biological predispositions.

This perspective had the advantage of not assuming that women are identical to men. However, taken alone, it had three serious shortcomings in explaining women's under-representation in management. First, as will be highlighted in the second perspective, most studies that compared women and men managers in similar jobs found negligible differences (Chusmir, 1988; Nieva & Gutek, 1981; Powell, 1988; Ragins, 1991). Second, the contemporary emphasis on the manager as a "team-player and coach," especially in today's increasingly knowledge-intensive industries (see, for example, Peters & Waterman, 1982), suggested that a more people-oriented leadership style might render women more qualified than men for modern management positions. Similarly, the increasing emphasis on international and transnational management, and with it the heightened importance of relationship-building skills, again put a premium on the very characteristics that have been thought to be women's strengths. Third, focusing on the individual ignored and concealed the importance of organizational factors affecting women's managerial careers.

Perspective 2: An Emphasis on Organizational Context

According to the organizational context perspective, characteristics of organizations—such as the under-representation of women in management, the uneven distribution of women and men in various roles, as well as the greater opportunities organizations provide for men than for women to gain access to power, prestige, and monetary rewards—shape attitudes and behavior much more than do individual personality traits. For example, research suggested that opportunities for promotion, more than gender-related individual differences, influenced women's and men's ambition. Specifically, women's concentration in low-ceiling positions and in career tracks that limited their opportunities for promotion helped to explain women's lower level of ambition in relation to their job, career, and organization. Tokenism, for example, helped to explain the dynamics associated with being the only woman in a senior management position—such as higher visibility and more stereotypical responses from colleagues. These dynamics both increased the performance pressures on women and reduced their prospects for success. Proponents of the organizational context perspective argued that these and other difficulties associated with tokenism would disappear when women represented a substantially greater proportion of the managers in an organization, since colleagues would then respond to them primarily as individuals and not as stereotypical representatives of a group (see Kanter, 1977).

A limitation of the organizational context perspective was its implicit assumption that organizations are essentially gender-neutral (Acker, 1990; Calas, 1988); that is, that our culturally based ideas about women and men do not inherently influence our organizational concepts and practices. Essentially, organizational context explanations implicitly assumed that organizations treat women and men the same. Unfortunately, viewing organizations as gender-neutral allowed managers and scholars to ignore the gender specificity of organizational choices and responses. For example, according to organizational context explanations, being a token in a group creates strong performance pressure on the token person (Kanter, 1977). Moreover, the presence of a token in a team, whether female or male, heightens team members' awareness of their own gender identity as well as of the differences between themselves and the token. Given this heightened awareness of gender differences, the second perspective explained that the organization would be more likely to treat the token in a stereotypical manner: that is, as a representative of a group rather than as an individual. While true, what this argument concealed was that societal stereotypes of women and men differ and that therefore tokenism has very different consequences for token female managers than for token male managers (Izraeli, 1983). Specifically, organizations frequently derail token female managers to less powerful, more peripheral jobs, while they often promote token male managers up the glass escalator (Williams, 1992). An easily visible example of the latter in many countries is the rapid rate at which banks promote token male tellers into supervisory and managerial positions compared with the negligible promotion rates of their equally qualified female colleagues. Consequently, although problematic for women, being a token often works to the advantage of a man. By inaccurately equating the experiences of female and male tokens, organizational context explanations obscured masculinity's connections with power and privilege, connections that are embedded in the broader society as well as in organizations.

A second limitation of the organizational context perspective was its assumption that power negates the influence of gender (Kanter, 1977). According to this assumption, once a female manager achieves a certain level of power, her status as a woman becomes irrelevant. However, what actually happens is that women who attain positions of power become more likely, rather than less likely, to experience a backlash against them (Faludi, 1991). Thus, in reality, rather than eliminating the significance of gender, power often heightens it.

Third, organizational context alone inadequately explained the persistence and replication of the gender-based division of authority and power. Even in organizations in which women managers held a sizeable proportion of lower- and middle-level managerial positions, men continued to dominate the top positions. Theories that suggested that organizations and bureaucracy were gender neutral did not adequately account for this continued structuring based on gender (Acker, 1990).

Perspective 3: The Unveiling of Institutionalized Discrimination

The third perspective rejected the view that organizations were gender-neutral. Rather, it argued that established, taken-for-granted understandings about organizations have built-in assumptions about gender and that these assumptions explained women's persistent under-representation, under-utilization, and especially their skewed distribution in management (Acker, 1990; Calas, 1988; Calas & Smircich, 1992). This third perspective demonstrated that organizations were neither objective nor gender-neutral. Fundamentally, it argued that gender discrimination was embedded in managers' basic assumptions about society and organizational life.

> To say that an organization . . . is gendered means that advantage and disadvantage, exploitation and control, action and emotion, meaning and identity are patterned through and in terms of a distinction between male and female, [between] masculine and feminine (Acker, 1990:146).

From this third perspective, the significance of gender was seen to permeate all aspects of the organization. For example, the third perspective did not view management as simply a gender-neutral set of technical, human, and conceptual skills associated with various management positions. Rather, it viewed management as an occupation in which the assumptions about who was suitable to be a manager, including which social and personal characteristics were required, were based on societal assumptions about women and men. For example, common managerial beliefs were shown to support the lifestyle that societies most frequently reserve for men. Beliefs such as that successful managers must prove their worth by their early thirties, that career breaks to care for family members indicate a lack of organizational commitment, and that being the last person to leave at night demonstrates exemplary organizational commitment, all advantage a lifestyle more easily pursued by men than by women. Definitions of appropriate experience eliminate women from consideration for senior corporate positions. For example, the requirement of many British firms that candidates for board member positions must have had prior board experience in a public company—which few women have had—has eliminated most British women from consideration and explains, in part, the paucity of women board members (Hammond & Holton, 1994).

Most societies expect women to act subserviently to men and therefore assume that men—but not women—will exercise authority over other people, especially over other men. These societal expectations form part of the everyday taken-for-granted reality of organizations. Organizations only marginally violate such expectations when they promote highly qualified women into lower-level managerial positions, since these women frequently supervise other women. However, organizations generally perceive women as neither natural nor acceptable in positions of real power and authority, and consequently they overlook them for higher-level positions. When this happens, it rarely occurs to anyone that it should be otherwise.

In Western countries, research found that both women and men managers perceived the characteristics of the ideal manager to be those they associated with the typical man but not with the typical woman (Schein, 1973; 1975). A more recent study found that by the late 1980s, these perceptions were still held by men, but no longer by women (Brenner, Tomkiewicz, & Schein, 1989). Similar studies from other cultures, such as Hong Kong, also found that male managers held more prejudicial attitudes against women than did female managers (de Leon & Ho, 1994). The widely supported belief by male managers that typical masculine characteristics are requisites for effective management revealed the close coupling of management with masculinity. "A 'masculine ethic' of rationality . . . [has given] the managerial role in the West its defining image for most of the 20th century" (Kanter, 1977:22; see also Hearn & Parkin, 1988:20–21):

> This "masculine ethic" elevates the traits assumed to belong to some men to necessities for effective management: a tough-minded approach to problems; analytic ability to abstract and plan; a capacity to set aside personal emotional considerations in the interests of task accomplishment and a cognitive superiority in problem-solving and decision-making.

The specific image of an ideal manager varies across cultures, yet everywhere it privileges those characteristics that the culture associates primarily with masculinity.

According to this third perspective, three implicit and explicit processes produced and reproduced discrimination against women managers. These processes explained the persistence of institutionalized patterns of gender discrimination in organizations.

First, organizations emphasized gender differences by using deceptively circular logic. The circular logic begins by organizations presuming that women and men have different personality predispositions, abilities, and occupational interests, even when such managerially relevant differences have yet to be proven to exist. On the basis of such presumed differences, organizations then assign women to jobs different from those assigned to men, with those jobs assigned to women incorporating less prestigious tasks, lower rewards, and fewer opportunities for advancement. The organization then uses the contrasting patterns of jobs held by women versus men to reinforce its belief that differences between women and men are inherent, rather than in fact being constructed by the organization itself (West & Zimmerman, 1983). For example, when organizations assume that men have a tougher-minded approach to problem solving than do women, they tend to hire mostly men for managerial positions that they believe require such tough-mindedness. They then interpret women's absence from such positions as evidence of an inherent shortcoming among women; namely, that women lack a sufficiently tough-minded approach to problem solving. Neither women's actual tough-mindedness nor the assumption that such a characteristic is the best way to achieve desired results is questioned or tested. Once such a pattern is established, organizations then use women's absence from the initial managerial categories to justify women's continued exclusion from both the initial and similar managerial positions. Thus, the first process reproducing institutionalized discrimination was organizations' assignment of women and men to different categories of jobs.

The second process reproducing institutionalized discrimination was managers' tendency to promote people who most resembled themselves, those "who shared their own backgrounds, lifestyles, prejudices, politics and goals" (Martin, Harrison, & Dinitto, 1983:25). Some observers used the nature of managerial work to explain this pattern. They stated that since managerial work is highly indeterminate, full of uncertainty, and fraught with difficulty in discerning the direct consequences of actions and decisions, managers want to work with people they feel they can trust (Kanter, 1977; Mintzberg, 1975). Moreover, since ambiguity precludes any form of direct assessment and control, only similarity can form a basis for trusting new managers, rather than any form of more precise performance measurement. Because senior male executives perceived women as being different, and therefore as not being completely like *them,* they tended not to select women for senior management positions. Selecting new managers on the basis of similarity secured the status quo regarding the distribution of rights, privileges, and rewards for the current, primarily male, cohort of managers and executives (Offe, 1976).

According to this perspective, the third process reproducing institutionalized discrimination stemmed from the hierarchical interactions taking place daily between women and men in organizations. Hierarchies structure interaction into patterns of dominance and subordination, most commonly between senior men and junior women, including between male bosses and female secretaries. Such male-dominated hierarchical interactions create and reinforce power and positional distinctions between women and men and make them appear natural. When such gender distinctions form part of the organization's taken-for-granted reality, managers rarely question them. Moreover, individuals who are aware of such organizational discrimination often have difficulty obtaining sufficient support for their views to change the patterns. Thus, by hierarchical gender relationships becoming a part of the taken-for-granted reality of organizational life, organizations sustained women's absence from the centers of power.

The case of the Israeli military, where compulsory service applies to women and men, is an example of the processes that reproduce discrimination against women as managers and contribute to the persistence of institutionalized patterns of gender discrimination in Israel. First, gender is the basis for determining length of service and the assignment of recruits to training and career tracks. Women are excluded from the more prestigious activities and from the career tracks that lead to the more senior ranks and provide experiences that firms consider crucial for managing complex organizations.

Women's lack of experience then becomes evidence of lack of leadership ability and competence for senior level positions both within the military and civilian life. In addition, their very limited access to senior military positions prevents women from developing links to social networks that are crucial for gaining access to positions of power in the civilian economy (Izraeli, 1994). The informal ties among men are extended and reenforced through annual reserve military service not required of women. Once in positions of authority, former army officers tend to hire other former army officers, thus reproducing women's marginality from positions of power.

An important contribution of this approach has been that it challenged taken-for-granted definitions of reality and revealed many of them to be reflections of the pro-male bias embedded in society and organizations, rather than of objective, rational definitions of the best, or most effective, approaches to management. While the institutionalized discrimination perspective was highly instructive for understanding the persistence of discrimination, its primary shortcoming was that it failed to explain why, despite existing discrimination, women have nonetheless moved into lower- and even middle-management positions. A greater appreciation of power and of the interests of those in power to preserve it for other men was needed to understand the role of senior management in monitoring women managers' promotion into the executive suite.

Perspective 4: Revealing Power's Influence in the Organization

From the fourth perspective, societal and organizational institutions that give men privilege have persisted because individuals and groups with a vested interest in their persistence have had the power to preempt change. From this perspective, one reason current managers limit the number of women managers has been simply that they do not want more competition. Managers at each level in the hierarchy have not differed in their desire to limit competition but rather in their ability to do so. Only those at the top, most of whom are men, have had the power and authority to determine an organization's rules, including determining the criteria for promotion close to and into their own ranks. Senior executives are more able than lower-level managers to protect their sphere of influence from outsiders—including from the entrance of both women and all but selected other men.

In all countries surveyed, the proportion of women among lower-level managers increased significantly when a rising demand for managers created a shortage of equally qualified men (Reskin & Roos, 1990). During times of rising demand, it has been in organizations' interest to hire and promote the highest quality female and male managers available. The women hired did not replace male managers so much as they filled newly created positions. Senior executives remained largely unaffected by this dynamic because, given the limited number of executive positions, there has yet to be a scarcity in any country of interested and qualified male candidates. Moreover, because societies generously reward senior executives, firms are unlikely to suffer from a serious shortage.

In the United States, pressures to comply with affirmative action regulations and to establish the firm's image as an equal opportunity employer, have encouraged senior executives to create incentives for lower- and middle-level managers to promote women (see Fagenson & Jackson, 1994). Legislated affirmative action, a policy unique to the United States, was ostensibly intended for senior as well as lower-level management. In reality, however, it successfully opened up entry level positions to women but not to the executive suite.

Not only have senior executives been protected from such affirmative action pressures but they have also been exposed to pressures to exclude women from the most senior ranks. Managers who promoted women to senior positions could rarely do so without social support. For example, Ralph Ablon, chairman of American Ogden Corp., number 74 on Fortune's list of the 100 largest diversified service companies, recently appointed a woman as Ogden's chief financial officer. Ablon explained, "When I became CEO 29 years ago, I don't believe I could have been as liberal, and I couldn't have gotten away with appointing a woman as CFO. Today I could" (Fierman, 1990:42). Why was Ablon able to do today what he was unable to do in the past? Perhaps because societal norms in the United States have changed. Ablon implicitly explained his (and his colleagues') past choices not to select a woman to be the CFO, as emanating in part from his assessment of the potential cost to himself and to his company had he done so. Due to societal pressure, discrimination against women has often actually been rational from the perspective of individual senior executives, since behaving otherwise has usually elicited criticism from their peers (Larwood, Gutek, & Gattiker, 1984:341).

Adding the dynamic of power to the institutional discrimination perspective helps explain why some patterns have changed while others have not. It helps explain why, despite management's masculine image, women have succeeded in entering the lower levels of management, but once in, have failed to move up into the senior-most ranks.

Conclusion

Global competition and the need for top-quality managers are making women's promotion into senior management a business issue, rather than strictly an issue of equity. Global competition is, and will continue to be, intense in the 1990s (Adler & Jelinek, 1986). Can corporations risk not choosing the best person just because her gender does not fit the traditional managerial profile? Needs for competitive advantage, not an all-consuming social conscience, may answer the question, if not in fact define it. Successful companies will select both women and men to manage their domestic and cross-border operations. The option of limiting senior or international management to one gender has become an archaic "luxury" that no company can afford. The only remaining question is how quickly and effectively each company will increase the number and use of women in their worldwide managerial work force. Some observers already argue that the "number of qualified women will soon be so great that ignoring them will be bad business" (Segal & Zellner, 1992:76). Although this may well be true, those in power need to recognize the broader economic and competitive advantages of sharing the executive ranks with more women.

The power perspective emphasizes the need for executives to understand that it is in their own and their companies' best interest to welcome more women into the executive suite. The intensification of global competition has become a major influence compelling executives to view women managers as a competitive advantage rather than as a legislated necessity. Global competition challenges corporations to maximize the effectiveness of their human resources. The successful performance of growing numbers of women managers offers firms an opportunity to outperform their more prejudiced competitors by better using women's talents. A number of leading transnational firms have already accepted this reality and begun to act accordingly (see Adler, 1994, 1987).

Note

1. This chapter is based on Nancy J. Adler and Dafna N. Izraeli's book, *Competitive Frontiers: Women Managers in a Global Economy* Cambridge, Mass: Blackwell Publishing, 1994). Authors names are listed in alphabetical order.

References

Acker, Joan. (1990). "Hierarchies, jobs, bodies: A theory of gendered organizations," *Gender & Society,* 4(2): 139–158.

Adler, Nancy J. (1994). "Competitive frontiers: Women managers in the triad." *International Studies of Management and Organization,* 23(2), 3–23.

Adler, Nancy J. (1986). "Do MBAs want international careers?" *International Journal of Intercultural Relations,* 10(3), 277–300.

Adler, Nancy J. (1987). "Pacific Basin managers: A gaijin, not a woman," *Human Resource Management,* 26(2), 169–191.

Adler, Nancy J. (1984a). "Expecting international success: Female managers overseas," *Columbia Journal of World Business,* 19(3), 79–85.

Adler, Nancy J. (1984b). "Women do not want international careers: And other myths about international management," *Organizational Dynamics,* 13(2), 66–79.

Adler, N.J., & Bartholomew, S. (1992). "Managing globally competent people," *Academy of Management Executive,* 6(3), 52–65.

Adler, Nancy J., & Izrael, Dafne N. (eds.) (1994). *Competitive frontiers: Women managers in a global economy.* Cambridge, Mass.: Blackwell Publishing.

Adler, Nancy J., & Izraeli, Dafna N. (eds.) (1988). *Women in management worldwide.* Armonk, NY: M.E. Sharpe.

Adler, Nancy J., & Jelinek, Mariann. (1986). "Is 'organizational culture' culture bounds?" *Human Resources Management,* 25(1), 73–90.

Antal, Ariane Berthoin, & Izraeli, Dafna N. (1993). "Women managers from a global perspective: Women managers in their international homelands and as expatriates." In Ellen A. Fagenson (ed.), *Women in management: Trends, perspectives and challenges,* vol. 4. Newbury Park, CA: Sage.

Antal, Ariane Berthoin, & Krebsbach-Gnath, Camilla. (1994). "Women in management in Germany: East, West, and reunited." In Nancy J. Adler & Dafna N. Izraeli (eds.), *Competitive frontiers: Women managers in a global economy.* Cambridge, Mass.: Blackwell Publishing, 206–223.

Ball, Karen. (1991). "Study finds few women hold top executive jobs," *Washington Post,* August 26: A-11.

Brenner, O.C., Tomkiewicz, Joseph, & Schein, Virginia Ellen. (1989). "The relationship between sex role stereotypes and requisite management characteristics revisited," *Academy of Management Journal,* 32(3): 662–669.

Calas, Marta B. (1988). "Gendering leadership: The differe(e/a)nce that matters." Paper presented at the annual meeting of the Academy of Management, Anaheim, CA.

Calas, Marta B., & Smircich, Linda. (1992). "Re-writing gender into organization theorizing: Directions from feminist perspectives." In M. I. Reed and M. D. Hughes (eds.), *Re-thinking organization: New directions in organizational research and analysis.* London: Sage.

Calas, Marta B., & Smircich, Linda. (1993). "Dangerous liaisons: The `feminine-in-management' meets 'globalization'," *Business Horizons,* Mar.–Apr., 73–83.

Chan, Audrey, & Lee, Jean. (1994). "Women executives in a newly industrialized economy: The Singapore scenario." In Nancy J. Adler & Dafna N. Izraeli (eds.), *Competitive frontiers: Women managers in a global economy.* Cambridge, Mass.): Blackwell Publishing, 127–142.

Cheng, Wei-Yuan, & Liao, Lung-li. (1994). "Women managers in Taiwan," In Nancy J. Adler & Dafna N. Izraeli (eds.), *Competitive frontiers: Women managers in a global economy.* Cambridge, Mass.: Blackwell Publishing, 143–159.

Chusmir, Leonard H., & Mills, Joan. (1988). "Resolution of conflict: Managerial gender differences." Paper presented at the annual meeting of the Academy of Management, Anaheim, CA.

De Leon, Corinna, & Ho, Suk-Ching. (1994). "The third identity of modern Chinese women: Female managers in Hong Kong." In Nancy J. Adler & Dafna N. Izraeli (eds.), *Competitive frontiers: Women managers in a global economy.* Cambridge, Mass.: Blackwell Publishing, 43–56.

Erwee, Ronel. (1994). "South African women: Changing career patterns." In Nancy J. Adler & Dafna N. Izraeli (eds.), *Competitive frontiers: Women managers in a global economy.* Cambridge, Mass.: Blackwell Publishing, 325–342.

Fagenson, Ellen, & Jackson, Janice J. (1994). "The status of women managers in the United States," In Nancy J. Adler & Dafna N. Izraeli (eds.), *Competitive frontiers: Women managers in a global economy.* Cambridge, Mass.: Blackwell Publishing, 388–404.

Faludi, Susan. (1991). *Backlash: The undeclared war against American women.* New York: Crown Publishers.

Fierman, Jaclyn. (1990). "Why women still don't hit the top," *Fortune,* July 30, 40–62.

Fisher, Anne B. (1992). "When will women get to the top?" *Fortune,* September 21, 44–56.

Hammond, Valerie, & Holton, Vicki. (1994). "The scenario for women managers in Britain in the 1900s." In Nancy J. Adler & Dafna N. Izraeli (eds.), *Competitive frontiers: Women managers in a global economy.* Cambridge, Mass.: Blackwell Publishing, 224–242.

Hanninen-Salmelin, Eva, & Petajaniemi, Tulikki. (1994). "Women managers, the challenge to management: The case of Finland." In Nancy J. Adler & Dafna N. Izraeli (eds.),. *Competitive frontiers: Women managers in a global economy.* Cambridge, Mass.: Blackwell Publishing, 175–189.

Hearn, Jeffrey, & Parkin, Wendy P. (1988). "Women, men, and leadership: A critical review of assumptions, practices and change in the industrialized nations." In Nancy J. Adler and Dafna N. Izraeli (eds.), *Women in management worldwide.* Armonk: NY: M.E. Sharpe, 17–40.

Izraeli, Dafna N. (1994). "Outsiders in the promised land: Women mangers in Israel." In Nancy J. Alder & Dafna N. Izraeli (eds.), *Competitive frontiers: Women managers in a global economy.* Cambridge, Mass.: Blackwell Publishing, 301–324.

Izraeli, Dafna N. (1983). "Sex effects or structural effects?: An empirical test of Kanter's theory of proportions," *Social Forces,* 62(3): 153–165.

Izraeli, Dafna N. (1988). "Women's movement into management in Israel." In Nancy J. Adler & Dafna N. Izraeli (eds.), *Women in management worldwide,* Armonk, NY: M.E. Sharpe, 186–212.

Izraeli, Dafna N., & Adler, Nancy J. (1994). "Competitive frontiers: Women managers in a global economy." In N. J. Adler and D. N. Izraeli (eds.) *Competitive frontiers: Women managers in a global economy.*Cambridge, Mass.: Blackwell Publishing, 3–21.

Izraeli, Dafna N., & Zeira, Yoram. (1993). "Women as managers in international business: A research review and appraisal." *Business and the Contemporary World,* 5(3): 35–46.

Jelinek, Mariann, & Adler, Nancy J. (1988). "Women: World-class managers for global competition." *Academy of management executive,* 2(1): 11–19.

Kanter, Rosabeth Moss. (1977). *Men and women of the corporation.* New York: Basic Books.

Kavcic, Bogdan. (1994). "Women in management: The case of the former Yugoslavia." In Nancy J. Adler & Dafna N. Izraeli (eds.), *Competitive frontiers: Women managers in a global economy.* Cambridge, Mass.: Blackwell Publishing, 286–300.

Keller Brown, Linda. (1988). "Female managers in the United States and in Europe: Corporate boards, M.B.A. credentials, and the image/illusion of progress." In Nancy J. Adler and Dafna N. Izraeli (eds.), *Women in management worldwide.* Armonk, NY: M.E. Sharpe, 265–274.

Larwood, Laurie, Gutek, Barbara, & Gattiker, Urs E. (1984). "Perspectives on institutional discrimination and resistance to change," *Group and Organization Studies,* 9(3): 333–352.

Loring, Rosalind, & Wells, Theodora. (1972). *Breakthrough: Women into management.* New York: Van Norstrand Reinhold.

Mansor, Norma. (1994). "Women managers in Malaysia: Their mobility and challenges." In Nancy J. Adler & Dafna N. Izraeli (eds.), *Competitive frontiers: Women managers in a global economy.* Cambridge, Mass.: Blackwell Publishing, 101–113.

Martin, Patricia Yancey, Harrison, Dianne, & Dinitto, Diana. (1983). "Advancement for women in hierarchical organizations: A multilevel analysis of problems and prospects," *Journal of Applied Behavioral Science,* 19: 19–33.

Mintzberg, Henry. (1975). "The manager's job: Folklore and fact," *Harvard Business Review,* 53, July/Aug.: 49–61.

Moghadam, Valentine M. (1992). *Privatization and democratization in Central and Eastern Europe and the Soviet Union: The gender dimension.* Helsinki, Finland: Wider Institute of the United Nations University.

Moran, Stahl, & Boyer, Inc. (1988). *Status of Americans female expatriate employees: Survey results.* Boulder, CO: International Division.

Morgenthaler, E. (1978). "Women of the world: More U.S. firms put females in key posts in foreign countries," *Wall Street Journal,* 16 Mar. 1,17.

Muller, Helen J. (1994). "The legacy and opportunities for women managers in Zimbabwe." In Nancy J. Adler & Dafna N. Izraeli (eds.), *Competitive frontiers: Women managers in a global economy.* Cambridge, Mass.: Blackwell Publishing, 358–376.

Nieva, Veronica F., & Gutek, Barbara A. (1981). *Women and work: A psychological perspective.* New York: Praeger.

Offe, Carl. (1976). *Industry and inequality.* J. Wickham, trans. London: Edward Arnold.

Peters, Thomas J., & Waterman, Robert H., Jr. (1982). *In search of excellence: Lessons from America's best-run companies.* New York: Harper & Row.

Powell, Gary N. (1988). *Women and men in management.* Newbury Park, CA: Sage.

Puffer, Sheila. (1994). "Women managers in the former USSR: A case of too much equality," In Nancy J. Adler & Dafna N. Izraeli (eds.), *Competitive frontiers: Women managers in a global economy.* Cambridge, Mass.: Blackwell Publishing, 263–285.

Ragins, Belle Rose. (1991). "Gender effects in subordinate evaluations of leaders: Real or artifact?" *Journal of Organizational Behavior,* 12: 259–268.

Reskin, Barbara F., & Roos, Patricia A. (1990). *Job queues, gender queues.* Philadelphia: Temple University Press.

Schein, Virginia E. (1973). "The relationship between sex role stereotypes and requisite management characteristics," *Journal of Applied Psychology,* 57(2): 95–100.

Schein, Virginia E. (1975). "Relationships between sex role stereotypes and requisite management characteristics among female managers," *Journal of Applied Psychology,* 60(3): 340–344.

Segal, Amanda Troy, & Zellner, Wendy. (1992). "Corporate women: Progress? Sure. But the playing field is still far from level," *Business Week,* June 8, 74–78.

Serdjenian, Evelyne. (1994). "Women managers in France." In Nancy J. Adler & Dafna N. Izraeli (eds.), *Competitive frontiers: Women managers in a global economy.* Cambridge, Engl.: Blackwell Publishing, 190–205.

Siemienska, Renata. (1994). "Women managers in Poland: In transition from communism to democracy," In Nancy J. Adler & Dafna N. Izraeli (eds.), *Competitive frontiers: Women managers in a global economy.* Cambridge, Mass.: Blackwell Publishing, 243–262.

Siengthai, Sununta, & Leelakulthanit, Orose. (1994). "Women managers in Thailand," In Nancy J. Adler & Dafna N. Izraeli (eds.), *Competitive frontiers: Women managers in a global economy.* Cambridge, Mass.: Blackwell Publishing, 160–174.

Spillar, K. (1992), quoted in Segal, Amanda Troy, & Zellner, Wendy. (1992). "Corporate women: Progress? Sure. But the playing field is still far from level," *Business Week,* June 8, 74–78.

Steinhoff, Patricia, & Tanaka, Kazuko. (1994). "Women executives in Japan." In Nancy J. Adler & Dafna N. Izraeli (eds.), *Competitive frontiers: Women managers in a global economy.* Cambridge, Mass.: Blackwell Publishing, 79–100.

Thal, N., & Cateora, P. (1979). "Opportunities for women in international business," *Business Horizons,* 22(6), 21–27.

West, Candace, & Zimmerman, Don H. (1983). "Small insults: A study of interruptions in conversations between unacquainted persons." In B. Thorne, C. Kramerae, and N. Henley-Rowley (eds.), *Language, gender and society.* Rowley, MA: Newbury House.

Williams, Christine, L. (1992). "The glass escalator: Hidden advantages for men in the 'female professions.'" *Social Problems,* 39(3), 253–267.

Wright, Lorna, & Crockett-Tellei, Virginia. (1994). "Women in management in Indonesia." In Nancy J. Adler & Dafna N. Izraeli (eds.), *Competitive frontiers: Women managers in a global economy.* Cambridge, Mass: Blackwell Publishing, 57–78.

HUMAN RESOURCE MANAGEMENT IN FOREIGN AFFILIATES

Preface to Part III

Contingency Factors in HRM in Foreign Affiliates

Oded Shenkar Tel Aviv University, Israel
University of Hawaii-Manoa

The number of foreign affiliates continues to grow at a very rapid pace. Both wholly owned foreign subsidiaries (WOSs) and international joint ventures (IJVs) can now be found in almost every country across the globe. Also continuing to multiply are the operational problems frequently reported for those subsidiaries, many of which seem to be of a human resource nature (Arni, 1982; Vaupel & Curhan, 1969).

This preface to Part III of the book is intended to establish a frame of reference to be used in reading the country-specific reports that follow. Which human resource problems are universal to all foreign affiliates and which are unique to WOSs or to IJVs? Which problems can be found in various countries and which are country-specific? What are the other contingency factors we should take into account when analyzing human resource processes in foreign affiliates? These are some of the questions we attempt to answer in this section.

Multiple Ownership

Whereas the WOS is subordinated to a single parent, the IJV is a multipartite structure, owned (and often managed) by at least two parent firms (typically one foreign and one host). This structure depends on cooperation among at least three different entities: the foreign firm, the host firm, and the IJV itself, each having its own organization set (Evan, 1978).

197

Multiple National Affiliation

All foreign affiliates bring together individuals who differ in national origin, cultural values, and social norms; there also may be political, economic, and legal system differences among them and their environments. These differences are embedded not only in individual employees but also in organizations anchored in different national and cultural environments.

Hofstede (1980, p. 391) distinguished between multinational organizations, namely "organizations active in several countries but in which there is one dominant 'home' national culture to which most key decision makers of the organization belong," and international organizations, namely "organizations without a home national culture, in which the key decision makers may come from any member country." Hofstede suggested that the multinational organizations are easier to run than international ones because the dominant home culture implies shared value patterns and a common frame of reference. Such dominance prevails in WOSs but not in IJVs. IJVs are hybrids of the multinational and international organizations because they have two or more dominant home cultures rather than one or none, as is the case in the multinational and international organizations, respectively. Whereas international organizations may encourage pluralism because of the multiplicity of cultures, IJVs may set the stage for head-on conflict among few environmental systems struggling for dominance.

Thus, as shown in Table 1, IJVs differ from domestic JVs, in which parents operate in the same country, and they differ from the wholly owned subsidiaries of multinational corporations (MNCs), which are owned and managed by a single parent. This unique position of IJVs may promote personnel processes typical only of that type of enterprise.

TABLE 1
Ownership and Location Factors Affecting Foreign Affiliates

Country	*Ownership*	
	Single Parent	**Multiple Parents**
Same country of operation for HQ and affiliate	Local subsidiary	Domestic joint venture
Separate countries of operation for HQ and affiliate	Wholly owned foreign subsidiary	International joint venture

Source: Adapted from Oded Shenkar, and Yoram Zeira, Human resource management in international joint ventures: Directions for research, *Academy of Management Review* 12, 1987:546–557.

Human Resources in Foreign Affiliates

Foreign affiliates tend to employ different employee groups, as follows (see Table 2, which is based on Shenkar & Zeira, 1987):

1. Foreign parent(s) expatriates (i.e., nationals of the country in which the headquarters of the foreign parent(s) is (are) located, and who are assigned by that parent(s) as expatriate managers to the affiliate).

TABLE 2
Employee Groups in Foreign Affiliates

Employee Group	Country of Origin[a]	Recruiting Entity	Location	Wholly Owned Subsidiaries	International Joint Ventures
1. Foreign parent(s) expatriates	Foreign	Foreign parent(s)		Yes	Yes
2. Host parent(s) transferees	Host	Host parent(s)		No	Yes
3. Host country nationals	Host	Affiliate	Country in which the affiliate is located	Yes	Yes
4. Third country expatriates of the host parent(s)		Host parent(s)		No	Yes
5. Third country expatriates of the foreign parent(s)	Third	Foreign parent(s)		Yes	Yes
6. Third country expatriates of the affiliate		Affiliate		Yes	Yes
7. Foreign HQ executives	Foreign	Foreign parent(s)	Countries in which the HQ of parent are located	Yes	Yes
8. Host HQ executives	Host	Host parent(s)		No	Yes

[a]The country in which the employee usually resides prior to his or her association with the affiliate.

Source: Adapted from Oded Shenkar, Yoram Zeira, Human resource management in international joint ventures: Directions for research, *Academy of Management Review*, 12, 1987: 546–557.

2. Host parent(s) transferees (i.e., host country nationals employed by the host parent(s) and transferred to the affiliate from the host parent HQ or from one of the subsidiaries of that parent).

3. Host country nationals (i.e., nationals of the host country, hired directly by the affiliate and employed in it).

4. Third country expatriates of the host parent(s) (i.e., third country nationals who are neither nationals of the host country nor of the foreign parent(s) country(ies) and assigned by the host parent(s) to work in the affiliate).

5. Third country expatriates of the foreign parent(s) (i.e., third country nationals assigned by the foreign parent(s) to work in the affiliate).

6. Third country expatriates of the affiliate (i.e., third country nationals recruited directly by the affiliate, who are neither nationals of the parent(s) country(ies) nor of the country in which the affiliate operates).

7. Foreign HQ executives (i.e., policy makers at the HQ of the foreign parent(s), who play a major role in the functioning of the affiliate at HQ or a board members of the affiliate).

8. Host HQ executives (i.e., policy makers at the HQ of the host parent(s), who play a major role in the functioning of the affiliate at HQ or as board members of the affiliate).

As can be seen in Table 2, IJVs have a considerably higher number of employee groups than WOSs. This of course adds to the complexity involved in managing human resources in IJVs as compared to WOSs.

Ownership Factors: Typical Human Resource Problems in WOSs Versus IJVs

Following are the human resource problems typical of foreign affiliates. As noted in Table 3, those problems tend to differ by ownership (i.e., between IJVs and WOSs).

Staffing Friction

Because IJVs are owned by more than one firm, staffing tends to be a more significant problem there than in WOSs (Killing, 1982; Janger, 1980). Parent companies prefer to appoint their own transferees or expatriates to key positions in the venture, assuming that whoever has people in charge will control the organization or at least its key functions. Some parents insist that the staffing policy be specified in the contract and documents of incorporation, and indeed, when staffing policies are not detailed, serious friction frequently develops between parents. Some of the more experienced parents, as well as the less active ones, tend to limit the number of their expatriates. Most firms, however, prefer to staff the venture with their own personnel as long as the other parent(s) agrees. In many cases, friction also develops regarding the level of staffing, with the host parent looking at the IJV as a way of "unloading" extra staff (Lamont, 1973; Janger, 1980). In both types of foreign affiliates, however, host country nationals are typically deprived of opportunities to staff the most senior positions in the affiliate.

TABLE 3
Typical Human Resource Problems in Wholly Owned Subsidiaries and International Joint Ventures

Human Resource Problem	*Wholly Owned Subsidiary*	*International Joint Venture*
Gap between present and desired staffing of affiliate	Yes	Yes
Blocked promotions in affiliate	Yes	Yes
Blocked promotions in HQ	Yes	Yes
Difficulties of reentry to HQ	Yes	Yes
Conflict of loyalty to the affiliate vs. HQ	No	Yes
Limited delegation of authority to affiliate	Yes	Yes
Screening of information	No	Yes
Compensation gaps between employee groups	Yes	Yes
Unfamiliarity with the environment of the host country	Yes	Yes
Unfamiliarity with organizational procedures of HQ	No	Yes
Difficulties in adapting to host country	Yes	Yes
Exile syndromes of expatriates	Yes	Yes
Communication blockages in the affiliate	Yes	Yes
Communication blockages between HQ and affiliate	Varies	Yes
Communication problems between parents	No	Yes
Complexity of decision-making processes	No	Yes
Difficulties in performance evaluation	Yes	Yes
Lack of training for functioning in affiliate	No	Yes

Source: Adapted from Oded Shenkar, and Yoram Zeira. Human resource management in international joint ventures: Directions for research, *Academy of Management Review* 12, 1987:546–557.

Blocked Promotion

In both types of foreign subsidiaries, local employees are frequently frustrated by the lack of promotion opportunities to key jobs, because senior positions are reserved for "outsiders." This problem is especially serious in IJVs where the contract and/or documents of incorporation do not refer to the staffing of senior positions, leading host country nationals to believe that these posts are open to them whereas in reality this is not the case. Unlike WOS, in IJVs such "outsiders" may be not only the foreign expatriates but also transferees of the host parent (Bivens & Lovell, 1966). When such "outsiders" are abundant, local personnel may be reluctant to join, to stay, and to contribute their best to the venture, which must rely on competent local work force. The problem may be especially serious in IJVs with a limited life span.

Exile Syndrome and Reentry Difficulties

Reluctance to accept an overseas assignment because of fear of interruption of the career track back home is apparent in both WOSs and IJVs, but it tends to take on added urgency in IJVs. WOSs are usually more closely integrated in the firm's global operations, and therefore an assignment to such subsidiaries may be less disruptive. Assignees in an IJV, on the other hand, may be working with, or supervised by, employees of another company. They may not report directly to their parent company's headquarters, nor will their supervisors be in the best position to assess their performance. Hence, an assignee is more of an exile than the WOS' expatriate (Young & Bradford, 1977; Wright, 1979).

Exile syndrome may be damaging to the foreign affiliate. Those employees who wish to return to headquarters are likely to maintain frequent and direct contact with it even if this means overpassing their own supervisors in the affiliate. They may be more inclined to report achievements, rather than problems and failures, to emphasize a short-term outlook and immediate pay off. Those employees who do not wish to return may represent another problem: They may try hard to show that their continuous employment in the affiliate is essential, even if this means distorting the accurate condition of the venture.

Split Loyalty

The problem of split loyalty is quite unique to IJVs. Employees recruited by the host or the foreign parent tend to remain loyal to that parent rather than shift their loyalty to the IJV (Franko, 1971; Kobayashi, 1967a; Peterson & Shimada, 1978). The reason is simple: They usually expect to return to that parent following the end of their assignment. Even when they don't expect to return, as is the case of older Japanese executives transferred from their parent company, years of service with the parent have fostered strong ties of allegiance to that parent (Kobayashi, 1967b; Peterson & Shimada, 1978; Yoshino, 1968). As a result, IJVs tend to have a significant number of employees, especially in senior positions, whose loyalty lies not with their current organizations but with the owner organizations, a situation that increases suspicion and prevents full cooperation within the venture. This allegiance to HQ is particularly salient among the transferees and expatriates of the host parent, probably due to the IJV's proximity. The loyalty of foreign parent expatriates, on the other hand, seems to depend on a variety of factors, among them the reputation of the venture vis-a-vis the parent firms and its planned duration.

Compensation Gaps

The problem of compensation gaps also occurs in WOSs but tends to be more acute in IJVs, especially those with many employee groups. This is a problem of "relative deprivation" (Janger, 1980), where different employee groups receive different compensation packages that are not necessarily based on universal criteria, such as skills and experience, but on affiliation with a particular parent or the venture. Usually each experienced MNC has an established compensation policy, and in many cases, the differences between parents' policies are significant. Moreover, each employee group has a different perception about what is the most desired package of benefits. The result is a feeling of deprivation by those receiving lesser compensation, and, consequently reduced motivation and morale.

Blocked Communication

Effective communication among parent(s) and between them and the affiliate is frequently hampered by a combination of cultural differences and variations in organizational procedures and norms of operation (Peterson & Schwind, 1977, 1979; Wright, 1979). Such communication blockages represent an impediment to decision-making. Because of the differences in parents' objectives, communications may be distorted or withheld by their respective employees. With essential information missing, decision-making uncertainty considerably increases. The problem seems to be especially serious in IJVs with a 50/50 equity distribution.

Limited Delegation

Many parents try to maintain control of their affiliate by limiting the scope of authority and decision-making power they delegate to it (Holton, 1981; Killing, 1982; Otterbeck, 1981). This is especially true when parents have conflicting goals, when they depend on the affiliate for scarce and vital resources, and when they feel that the affiliate's staff is loyal to the host parent. Not surprisingly, under these conditions the affiliate's management finds it difficult to operate effectively, especially in a fast-changing environment.

Screening of Information

Quite frequently companies are hesitant about passing information (e.g., technology) to an affiliate (Kobayashi, 1967b). The problem is, however, much more difficult in an IJV, where parents are reluctant to pass on sensitive information to other than their own representatives in the venture (Daniels, Krug, & Nigh, 1985; Peterson & Schwind, 1977, 1979). This is understandable: They worry that such information will be used by competitors (the IJV itself or the other parent(s) may be such competitors themselves) (Yoshino, 1968). The result, however, tends to be self-defeating, with the other parent(s) limiting the information they release as well. As a result, factions tend to develop along the lines of the parent firm, making integration of IJV activities increasingly difficult.

Unfamiliarity

In both WOS and IJVs, expatriates who join the affiliate are not familiar, in most cases, with the environment in which the venture operates (Peterson & Shimada, 1978). In IJVs, however, there is another type of unfamiliarity to which most employee groups are vulnerable. This is the unfamiliarity involved in the unique structure of the IJV, especially the exposure to new and different groups of employees (Bivens & Lovell, 1966; Killing, 1982). If this unfamiliarity is not addressed at an early stage, mutual suspicion and stereotyping are likely, thus undermining the trust that is so essential to an effective operation of IJVs.

Country-Specific Factors

Ownership provides one major source of complexity in foreign affiliates, and environmental diversity across investor and target country provides the other (see Figure 1). Thus, although many of the problems identified so far can be found in the respective foreign affiliates across various countries, the magnitude of those problems can significantly vary from one country to another. For instance, disagreements over staffing have been discovered in IJVs in such diverse countries as the United States, China, Japan, Hungary and Israel, to mention just a few (Bivens & Lovell, 1966; Friedmann & Beguin, 1971; Lamont, 1973; Kobayashi, 1967a). For example, Kobayashi (1967a) suggested that Japanese transferees believe that their promotion in the parent company in Japan is blocked (Kobayashi, 1967b), a problem related to the lower status of subsidiaries in Japan (N. Kobayashi, 1967;

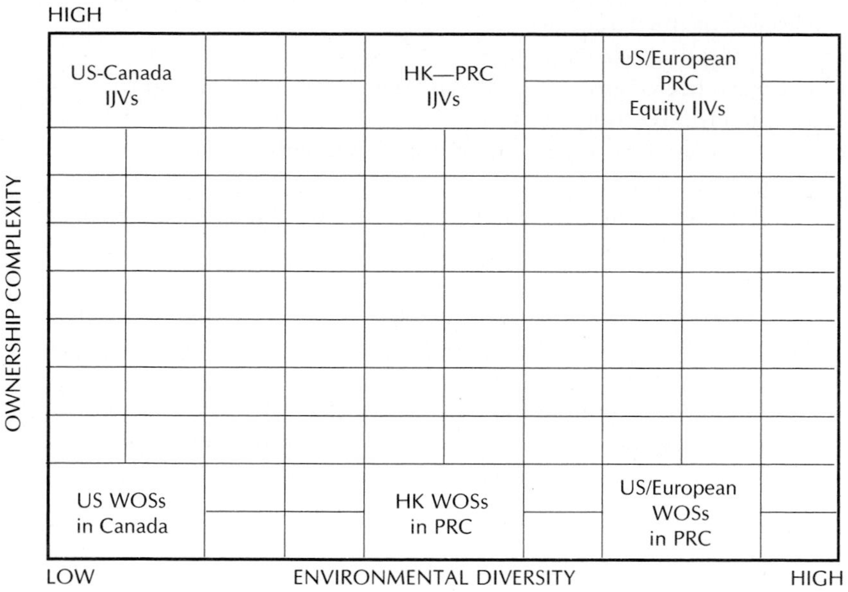

HIGH

| US-Canada IJVs | | | | HK—PRC IJVs | | | | US/European PRC Equity IJVs | |

(OWNERSHIP COMPLEXITY)

| US WOSs in Canada | | | | HK WOSs in PRC | | | | US/European WOSs in PRC | |

LOW   ENVIRONMENTAL DIVERSITY   HIGH

FIGURE 1
The Foreign Direct Investment Management Grid

Source: Oded Shenkar, International joint ventures problems in China: Risks and remedies, *Long-Range Planning*, 23, 1990: 83.

Yoshino, 1968; Wright, 1979). This problem may be less acute in other, non-Japanese IJVs, particularly those enjoying a reputation similar to that of the parent firm. Again, the very existence of problems, if not their magnitude, may be typical of a particular type of affiliate, regardless of the country involved. Thus, while most studies identifying loyalty problems in IJVs (Kobayashi, 1967; Peterson & Shimada, 1978; Yoshino, 1968; Sullivan, Peterson, Kameda & Shimada, 1981; Sullivan & Peterson, 1982) focused on Japan, where loyalty is a particularly important issue, Flick (1972) concluded that the loyalty problem is a general phenomenon in IJVs, stemming from the multiplicity of entities involved in the IJV framework. IJV employees quickly learn that promoting the goals of one entity may decrease the effectiveness or profits of the others (Franko, 1971).

Other Contingency Factors

A number of variables have been identified as distinguishing one IJV from another (see Zeira & Shenkar, 1990). They include the following:

1. The number of parent companies holding a significant share of the venture's equity.
2. The objectives of the parents in establishing or joining the venture.
3. The sector parents belong to (e.g., private or state-owned).
4. The distribution of ownership among the parents (e.g., 50/50).
5. The extent to which one parent dominates the venture.

6. The size of the parent firms.
7. The reputation of each parent.
8. The existence or absence of at least one parent with HQ in the country in which the IJV operates.
9. The contractual arrangement among the parents.
10. The parents' industry.
11. The direction of flow of resources among the IJV and the parents (this is relevant to WOSs as well).

Each of these variables can have a major impact on the staff problems in IJVs. For instance, host country nationals in IJVs dominated by a majority owner tend to look at that parent as a positive reference group and feel less loyal to other parents in minority positions. Expatriates or transferees of the minority parent(s) tend to face difficulties in adapting to the managerial style imposed by the representatives of the majority parent. Or, when the foreign parent is more prestigious that the host parent(s), there is a tendency to import managerial styles that do not fit the conditions in the local environment. Likewise, IJVs without a host parent encounter greater problems of adaptability to the regulations imposed by the foreign parents than managerial staff in IJVs with host parents, which are composed of local managers and host country transferees. In addition, foreign parent expatriates in IJVs, where profits are not reinvested but taken out entirely by the foreign parent, typically face hostile host environments that affect their adaptability to the host country.

Killing (1982) found disagreements among parent firms concerning the desired composition of the work force typical of "shared management" IJVs, a finding consistent with Janger's (1980). Both Lamont (1973) and Janger (1980) emphasized the particular staffing problems of IJVs when the host parent was a state enterprise. Frequently, state or state-owned parents perceive providing jobs to their nationals to be a more important objective than increasing profits, creating a clash with the foreign parent.

Preparation for an Assignment in a Foreign Affiliate

Although much has been written about expatriate selection (e.g., Lainer, 1979; Misa & Fabricatore, 1979; Zeira & Banai, 1984), relatively little is known about the training and preparation required for operating effectively in a specific foreign affiliate. Part III of the book provides many clues on how to adjust training to a particular environment. At the same time, we are only beginning to consider the adjustments that need to be made when moving, say, from a WOS to an IJV. Table 4 provides a starting point.

TABLE 4
Management Education in Two Types of Foreign Affiliates

Educational Focus	Wholly Owned Subsidiary	International Joint Venture
Cultural sensitivity/national	High	High
Cultural sensitivity/org. level	Low	High
Interpersonal skills	Low	High
Negotiation/bargaining skills	Med	High
Entrepreneurial skills	High	High
Leadership skills	High	High
Knowledge/global environment	High	High
Knowledge/regional	High	High
Knowledge/firm-specific	Med	Low
Knowledge/functional area	High	Med

Source:Adapted from Elaine Bailey, and Oded Shenkar. Management education for international joint venture managers, *Leadership and Organization Development Journal* 14, 1993: 15–20.

In the chapters that follow, four countries are highlighted: The United States, Mexico, Hungary, and China. Each of these countries has its own unique environment, which influences the human resource processes in the affiliate. Such processes are also influenced, however, by the various other contingency variables briefly delineated in this preface. These factors should be taken into account when drawing conclusions from the present case chapters to one's own circumstances.

References

Arni, V. R. S. (1982). *Guidelines for the establishment of industrial ventures in developing countries.* New York: UNIDO.

Bivens, K. K. and Lovell, E. B. (1966). *Joint ventures with foreign partners: International survey of business opinion and experience.* New York: National Industrial Conference Board.

Daniels, J. D., Krug, J., and Nigh, D. (1985). U.S. joint ventures in China: Motivation and management of political risks. *California Management Review,* 27(4): 46–58.

Evan, W. M. (1978). The organization-set: Toward a theory of international relations. In W. M. Evan (ed.), *Inter-organizational relations* (pp. 78–90). Philadelphia: University of Pennsylvania Press.

Franko, L. G. (1971). *Joint ventures survival in multinational corporations.* New York: Praeger.

Friedmann, W. G., and Beguin, J. P. (1971). *Joint international business ventures in developing Countries.* New York: Columbia University Press.

Flick, S. E. (1972). The human side of overseas joint ventures. *Management Review,* 61(1): 29–42.

Hofstede, G. (1980). *Culture's consequences: International differences in work related values.* Beverly Hills: Sage.

Holton, R. H. (1981). Making international joint ventures work, in L. Otterbeck (ed.), *The management of headquarters subsidiary relations in multinational corporations.* Great Britain: Biddles.

Janger, A. K. (1980). *Organization of international joint ventures.* New York: Conference Board.

Killing, P. (1982). How to make a global joint venture work. *Harvard Business Review,* 60(3): 120–127.

Kobayashi, N. (1967a). Human aspects of management. In R. J. Ballon (ed.), *Joint ventures and Japan.* Tokyo: Sophia University.

Kobayashi, N. (1967b). Some organizational problems. In R. J. Ballon (ed.), *Joint ventures and Japan.* Tokyo: Sophia University.

Lamont, D. F. (1973). Joining forces with foreign state enterprises. *Harvard Business Review* (July–Aug.): 68–79.

Lanier, A. D. (1979). Selecting and preparing personnel for overseas transfers. *Personnel Journal,* 58(3): 160–163.

Misa, K. F. and Fabricatore, J. M. (1979). Return on investment of overseas personnel. *Financial Executive,* 47(4): 42–46.

Otterbeck, L., ed. (1981). *The management of headquarters subsidiary relations in multinational corporations.* Great Britain: Biddles.

Peterson, R. B., and Schwind, H. F. (1977). A comparative study of personnel problems in international companies and joint ventures in Japan. *Journal of International Business Studies,* 7–8: 45.

Peterson, R. B., and Schwind, H. F. (1979). Personnel problems in U.S. and German international companies and joint ventures in Japan. Conference paper, Hawaii.

Peterson, R. B., and Shimada, J. Y. (1978). Sources of management problems in Japanese-American joint ventures. *Academy of Management Review,* 3(4): 796–804.

Shenkar, O., & Zeira, Y. (1987). Human resource management in international joint ventures: Directions for research. *Academy of Management Review,* (12): 546–557.

Shenkar, O. and Zeira, Y. (1991). International joint ventures: The case of Israel. *Journal of Global Marketing,* [special issue on international joint ventures], 5(1–2): 145–161.

Sullivan, J., Peterson, R. B., Kameda, N. and Shimada, J. (1981). The relationship between conflict resolution approaches and trust: A cross-cultural Study. *Academy of Management Journal,* 24(4): 803–815.

Sullivan, J., and Peterson, R. B. (1982). Factors associated with trust in Japanese-American joint ventures. *Management International Review,* 22(2): 30–40.

Vaupel, J. W., and Curhan, J. P. (1969). *The making of multinational enterprise.* Boston: Division of Research, Graduate School of Business Administration, Harvard University.

Wright, R. W. (1979). Joint venture problems in Japan. *Columbia Journal of World Business* (Spring): 25–31.

Yoshino, M. Y. (1968). *Japan's managerial system.* Cambridge, MA: MIT Press.

Young, R. G., and Bradford, S. Jr. (1977). *Joint ventures planning and action.* New York: Arthur D. Little.

Zeira, Y., and Banai, M. (1984). Present and desired methods of selecting expatriate managers for international assignments. *Personnel Review,* 13(3): 29–35.

Zeira, Y., and Shenkar, O. (1990). Interactive and specific parent characteristics: Implications for management and human resources in international joint ventures. *Management International Review* [special issue on human resource management in international joint ventures], 30: 7–22.

Management Localization in Japanese Subsidiaries in the United States

Manuel G. Serapio, Jr.   University of Colorado-Denver

Consider these organizational changes in three Japanese subsidiaries in the United States:

- Four years ago Matsushita Electric Corporation of America appointed Richard Kraft as president and chief operating officer. Kraft's appointment marks the first time in three decades that an American has been promoted to the second highest ranking position at Matsushita's North American operations.
- Nomura Securities Corporation became the first Japanese financial firm to put an American in charge of its U.S. operations with the appointment of Max Chapman as co-chairman of Nomura Securities International (NSI). Nomura Securities Corporation has also appointed several other Americans to key management positions at NSI (Shida, 1990).
- Sony Corporation appointed Michael Schulhof, Sony's highest ranking American executive, to its board of directors. This was an unprecedented move by a major Japanese company. At the time of his appointment, Schulhof was one of only two non-Japanese nationals to serve on the board of directors of Sony Corporation (Isaka 1990).

These organizational changes reflect an important development. Japanese subsidiaries in the United States, such as Matsushita, Nomura Securities, and Sony, have recently appointed Americans to key management positions and have promoted Americans to management positions held previously by Japanese nationals.

211

Longitudinal Study

Five years ago, I started a major longitudinal study to examine the organizational functioning of the U.S. subsidiaries of Japanese multinational companies. As one of my emphases, I studied the management staffing policies and practices of Japanese subsidiaries in the United States. During the course of my investigation, I found that the majority of the Japanese subsidiaries in my study that primarily employed Japanese expatriate managers had ongoing programs to appoint Americans to management positions, much like the programs of the corporations mentioned earlier. In Japanese subsidiaries in the United States, this program is referred to as *management localization*.

This chapter discusses management localization in Japanese subsidiaries in the United States. My discussion is guided by the lessons I learned from studying forty-seven Japanese manufacturing subsidiaries and monitoring the operations of several Japanese sales subsidiaries and financial companies in the United States. The manufacturing subsidiaries represented industries in transportation equipment, electronics and electrical equipment, industrial/commercial machinery, computer equipment, and food products. I visited these manufacturing subsidiaries' plants and offices in California, Georgia, Hawaii, Illinois, and Tennessee, and conducted in-depth interviews with their senior executives.1 In addition, I collected information on these subsidiaries from annual reports, organizational charts, company memorandums, and other secondary sources. Because the subsidiaries in this study asked that their identities remain confidential, I have left them anonymous.

What Management Localization Means

To put the subject matter of this article in perspective, let me begin by defining the term *management localization*, which conveys different meanings in different contexts. It may mean the transfer of ownership or control into local hands or, in the extreme, the nationalization of foreign-owned enterprises. It may also mean the adoption of local management practices or the adaptation of Japanese management practices to local conditions (Negandhi & Welge, 1984). For purposes of this study, I define *management localization* as:

- the appointment of Americans to key managerial positions in the subsidiary or the promotion of Americans to managerial positions in the subsidiary previously held by Japanese expatriate managers, and
- the involvement of Americans in key decision making in the subsidiary.

It is widely known in the United States that the U.S. subsidiaries of Japanese multinational companies have employed a large number of Japanese expatriate managers (see, e.g., Johnson, 1977; Kono, 1984; Kujawa, 1988; Negandhi & Welge, 1984; Negandi, 1985, 1987; and Yoshida, 1988). In two previous studies, Kujawa (1988) and Yoshida (1988) found that Japanese nationals primarily held the directorships and key management positions of Japanese subsidiaries in the United States. Likewise, Negandhi & Welge (1984) observed that American executives of the U.S. subsidiaries of Japanese multinational companies have had only minimal involvement in key decision making.

Because Japanese subsidiaries in the United States have traditionally relied upon Japanese expatriate managers, Americans have questioned whether this will ever change. An example of this skepticism is found in a *Business Week* article entitled "Can Japan's Giants Cut the Apron Strings?" (Borrus, 1990). However, the appointment or promotion of Americans in Japanese subsidiaries in the United States, such as the appointments at Matsushita, Nomura Securities, and Sony, demonstrates that the management staffing policies and practices of Japanese subsidiaries in the United States are in flux.

My purpose in this article is not to generalize. Not all Japanese subsidiaries in the United States have increased the localization of their management. In addition, some Japanese companies that have tried management localization have been less successful than others. However, management localization is an important emerging development in Japanese subsidiaries in the United States. (For other examples, see Gross, 1988; and Mizuni, 1990.)

Presence of Japanese Expatriate Managers: A Mixed Blessing

The presence of Japanese expatriate managers has been a mixed blessing for many Japanese subsidiaries in the United States. On the one hand, Japanese expatriate managers have played a key role in facilitating control, coordination, communication, and management and production technology transfer between the parent company and the U.S. subsidiary (Negandhi & Welge, 1984; Serapio & Negandhi, 1991). On the other hand, the concentration of management in the hands of Japanese expatriate managers has often created problems for Japanese subsidiaries in the United States. These problems have been the catalyst for several Japanese subsidiaries in the United States to increase management localization.

One of the most serious drawbacks of primarily employing Japanese expatriate managers is its demoralizing effects on U.S. nationals in Japanese subsidiaries in the United States. The U.S. business press has reported several cases of American managers quitting their jobs with Japanese companies in the United States due to a lack of career advancement opportunities or involvement in decision making. According to *Business Week* (Borrus, 1990), two senior American executives of the Flat Rock, Michigan, plant of Mazda Motors Corporation left the company because they felt they had been excluded from key decision making. In a *Fortune* article (Moffat, 1990), an unnamed American executive of a Japanese trading company said, "Japanese think of themselves as the managers and Americans as support staff. I don't ever expect to have Japanese working under me. . . . Come work for a Japanese company if you're looking for an interesting experience, but don't stay too long." According to *Fortune*, the executive was thinking of leaving her Japanese employer after working for it for nearly a decade.

Quitting their jobs has not been the only avenue through which U.S. executives or employees who have felt deprived of career advancement opportunities in Japanese subsidiaries in the United States have expressed their frustration. Others have brought discrimination suits against their Japanese employers. In the most celebrated case to date, female employees of Sumitomo Corporation charged that they had lost promotions to male Japanese co-workers. Likewise, Americans working for Sumitomo have alleged in a class action suit that the company's practice of rotating senior management positions among Japanese expatriate managers constituted discrimination against non-Japanese staff. In 1982, the U.S. Supreme Court rejected Sumitomo's claim that a treaty exempted its U.S. subsidiary from U.S. equal employment opportunity laws (because it was a foreign company) and ordered a trial. Sumitomo settled the case for an undisclosed amount and agreed to a consent decree that will increase management localization in its U.S. subsidiary ("Sumitomo Sets Accord," 1990).

Similar discrimination lawsuits have been brought against other Japanese companies, such as C. Itoh, Inc., Nippon Electric Company (NEC), Canon U.S.A., and Honda of America, Mfg., Inc. Discrimination lawsuits have concerned managers of many Japanese companies in the United States (Galen and Nathans, 1989; "Japanese Firms," 1990; and "U.S. Culture," 1990). According to the *Wall Street Journal* ("Japanese Firms," 1990), a 1989 Japanese government survey found that 57 percent of Japanese companies operating in the United States were worried about discrimination lawsuits. In recent years, Japanese subsidiaries in the United States have lost or settled about a dozen lawsuits; several others are pending.

In addition to discrimination lawsuits and the high turnover of U.S. nationals, the concentration of management in the hands of Japanese expatriate managers has made it more difficult for Japanese subsidiaries in the United States to attract new management recruits. Interestingly, in Negandhi's (1987) study of the management recruitment practices of Japanese multinational companies in developing countries, he similarly observed that Japanese employers have found it more difficult to attract local managers than have their U.S. or European counterparts.

The presence of many Japanese expatriate managers has also had undesirable political repercussions for Japanese companies in the United States. Although most of these subsidiaries would like their U.S. operations to be considered as bonafide U.S. companies, they continue to be treated as "foreign operations" because of the conspicuous presence of many Japanese expatriate managers. According to an article in *Business Week* (Mason & Hoerr, 1988), Tseuneo Tanaka, president of Hitachi America, Ltd. said, "We have to operate this company as an American company with U.S.-made policy. We have to be accepted in the U.S. market as a U.S. citizen."

Economics has played an important role in inducing Japanese subsidiaries in the United States to increase the localization of their management. Senior executives and personnel managers of Japanese subsidiaries in the United States have expressed concern about the escalating costs of posting Japanese expatriate managers in the United States. For example, the cost of employing a Japanese expatriate middle manager on a three- to five-year rotation in the United States is at least twice the cost of employing a U.S. national. A more serious concern expressed by personnel managers was the Japanese expatriate managers' temporary separation from family. The families of Japanese expatriate managers with school-age children usually stay behind in Japan so that their children can attend Japanese schools.

Management Opportunities for U.S. Nationals

Because of these problems, Japanese subsidiaries in the United States have appointed more Americans to management positions or have promoted Americans to management positions previously held by Japanese expatriate managers. Several of these subsidiaries have appointed or promoted Americans to top management positions. This has been the case at the U.S. subsidiaries of Japanese multinational companies such as Bridgestone, Nissan, Nomura Securities, Seiko Instruments, and Sony. Both Nomura Securities and Sony have gone a step further by appointing their top U.S. managers to serve as members of their corporate board of directors in Japan.

Although management localization has reached the highest management levels in several Japanese subsidiaries in the United States, its impact has been most evident at the middle- and lower-level management positions in many of the subsidiaries in this study. In the majority of the subsidiaries in this study, American nationals held the following positions: personnel manager, human resource manager, administration manager, and industrial relations manager. However, American managers held these positions in the majority of the subsidiaries both at the start of their U.S. operations and at the time of this study (see Table 1).

As shown in the table, the proportion of U.S. nationals holding selected management posts increased in the following positions: executive vice president, senior vice president, product division manager, manufacturing man-

TABLE 1

Proportion of U.S. Nationals in Selected Management Positions: At the Start of the Sample Companies' Operations vs. at the Time of This Study[a]

Management Positions	Proportion (%) of U.S. Nationals to Total Number of Managers	
	At the Start of the Sample Companies' Operation	At the Time of This Study[b]
President/General Manager/ Plant Manager	0–20%	0–20%
Executive Vice President/Deputy General Manager/Assistant Plant Manager	0–20	41–60
Senior Vice President	0–20	21–40
Treasurer	0–20	0–20
Product Division Manager	0–20	41–60
Manufacturing Manager	41–60	61–80
Marketing/Sales Manager	21–40	61–80
Personnel/HR Manager	81–100	81–100
Industrial Relations Manager	81–100	81–100
Administration Manager	81–100	81–100
General Affairs Manager	0–20	0–20
Planning Manager	21–40	21–40
Accounting Manager	0–20	21–40
Quality Control/Assurance Manager	0–20	21–40
Purchasing/Materials Manager	41–60	41–60
Production Control Manager	21–40	41–60
Production Engineer	0–20	21–40

[a]For forty-seven companies.
[b]Based on the latest information provided by the sample companies (for 1991–1992).

ager, marketing/sales manager, quality control manager, production control manager, and production engineer. More U.S. nationals were appointed or promoted to these positions for a number of reasons.

Most companies in this study that sought to increase management localization believed that an American should be appointed as head of their U.S. operations. For example, in an article in *Business Week* (Mason & Hoerr, 1988), Tseuneo Tanaka said that he expected to have an American succeed him as president of Hitachi America, Ltd. However, at the time of this study, only a few companies had appointed Americans to the positions of president or general manager. Instead, most Japanese subsidiaries that wanted more participation by Americans in top management promoted an American to the position of executive vice president or senior vice president. Interestingly, the positions of senior vice president or executive vice president existed in more Japanese subsidiaries at the time of this study compared to when these subsidiaries started their U.S. operations. Many of these subsidiaries established the positions of senior vice president or executive vice president as a means to increase the participation of Americans in top management or to serve as a training ground for prospective American top managers, or both. As one Japanese senior executive of a large consumer electronics company in this study said, "We like to have an American lead this company. We just appointed [an American] as our number two executive. We hope he will become our president in the near future."

Japanese subsidiaries that traditionally focused their business on Japanese customers but recently sought to increase their business with U.S. customers have formed divisions or departments to generate new businesses from U.S. customers. These subsidiaries have appointed Americans to these divisions as a division manager, product manager, marketing manager, sales manager, or business development manager. An automobile parts manufacturer, for example, that formerly supplied parts only to Japanese automobile transplant companies in the United States, appointed several U.S. nationals to its newly formed group that aimed to win more business from the U.S. Big Three automobile companies.

Competition helps explain why some management positions tend to be localized sooner and faster than other management positions. For example, managers of several Japanese companies in Silicon Valley have expressed concern about the difficulty of finding and retaining top-quality people in areas such as engineering, quality control, and manufacturing. Because the most qualified Americans in these areas are in demand, these companies stand to lose them unless they provide them with sufficient career advancement opportunities in their present jobs. "This is a very competitive business. If our local [American] managers and employees can get a better deal in our competitor next door, they will quit and move to the competitor next door," said a treasurer-controller of a Japanese computer company in Silicon Valley.

Barriers to Management Localization

The ability or willingness of a Japanese subsidiary to increase management localization in general and to localize specific management positions is greatly influenced by the various aforementioned factors. In addition, several factors may constrain a company's ability or willingness to increase management localization. There are three major barriers to management localization: (1) nature of the business, (2) the emphasis on personal control, and (3) turnover of American personnel.

Nature of the Business

Some Japanese subsidiaries have had more difficulty or have been deliberately slower in increasing the localization of their management than others. For example, Japanese subsidiaries that conduct business extensively with the parent company continue primarily to employ Japanese expatriate managers. In an article in the *Wall Street Journal* "Sumitomo Sets Accord," 1990), Christine Houston, an executive recruiter at Tasa International, Inc., said, "Japanese trading companies in particular have a problem promoting non-Japanese workers as managers in the U.S." The difficulty faced by the U.S. subsidiaries of Japanese trading companies in appointing more Americans to management positions is due in large part to the nature of their business. Since these trading companies conduct a major portion of their business with Japanese customers in Japan, the United States, and other countries, they employ many Japanese expatriate managers and staff personnel to deal with their Japanese customers.

Several Japanese subsidiaries that primarily conduct business with other Japanese companies have likewise been slow in appointing Americans to management positions. Japanese automotive parts suppliers, for example, which supply parts only to Japanese automobile companies in the United States, have employed primarily Japanese nationals in management because they were familiar with the operations of their Japanese customers. In fact, the senior managers of two Japanese automotive suppliers in this study were former employees of the parent company of their Japanese customers in the United States.

Japanese subsidiaries in the United States that are highly dependent on the parent company for management and production technology tend to employ more Japanese expatriate managers. This partly explains the presence of many Japanese expatriate managers in Japanese transplant companies (e.g., Japanese automobile transplant companies). That this is the case can be explained by the important role played by Japanese expatriate managers in the transfer and control of technology from the parent company to the U.S. subsidiary.

Emphasis on Personal Control

The emphasis by many Japanese companies on the personal control of their U.S. subsidiaries is one of the major stumbling blocks faced by Japanese subsidiaries in increasing management localization. As mentioned previously, Japanese expatriate managers played a key role in facilitating control, coordination, and communication between the parent company and the U.S. subsidiary (Edstrom and Galbraith, 1982; Negandhi, 1987; Rehfeld, 1990). Often the managers of Japanese multinational companies rely upon the networks of personal linkages between the managers of the parent company and the subsidiary. In the absence of these personal contacts, an American manager may find it difficult to deal effectively with his or her counterparts in the parent company.

Japanese subsidiaries that have sought to increase management localization have dealt with this issue in two ways. One approach has been to increase the formalization of control, coordination, and communication mechanisms, and to enhance the parent company's involvement in decision making. Another approach, which is favored by more Japanese subsidiaries, has been to emphasize the socialization and training of American managers. This requires that the American manager become familiar with the company's management philosophies and practices, and know important people in the parent company. To achieve this, the subsidiary usually sends the American manager to visit or work in Japan, usually for several months on up to a year. According to an article in *Fortune* (Moffat, 1990), Honda of America sends about 1,000 managers and workers to Japan every year as part of its socialization and familiarization program. In addition, the parent company may send a Japanese national to the United States to work closely with the American manager prior to the latter's appointment or promotion. Upon his return to Japan, the Japanese national becomes the American manager's personal contact and liaison with the managers in the parent company.

Japanese language proficiency was officially not required before an American can be appointed to a management position. However, most American respondents in this study maintained that a "working knowledge" of the Japanese language has made it easier for them to participate in their company's socialization and training programs. It has also helped them communicate more effectively with Japanese colleagues in the United States and Japan. (In order to help train American employees of Japanese companies in the Japanese language, schools in close proximity to Japanese companies in several states have been offering Japanese language training programs for Americans.) Interestingly, expatriate managers of several Japanese companies in this study said that although they welcome their American colleagues' desire to learn Japanese, they actually discouraged the use of Japanese in daily workplace conversations. A case in point is the policy of Shiro Takemura, the plant manager of Hitachi in Norman, Oklahoma.

According to an article in *Business Week* (Mason & Hoerr, 1988), Japanese expatriate managers were admonished if they spoke Japanese in meetings.

Turnover of American Personnel

Socialization and training work only if the American manager elects to stay with the employer. The president of a large Japanese consumer electronics company in the United States maintained that it was risky to rely solely on socialization and training of American managers: "Three years ago we sent many American personnel to Japan for management training. Sadly, only a few months after they returned to the United States, several of them left and joined our competitors."

The propensity among American managers to switch jobs has been a major cause of worry for Japanese subsidiaries in the United States. On the one hand, this factor explains the reluctance of some Japanese subsidiaries to localize management. It also explains why other Japanese subsidiaries in the United States have deliberately waited many years before promoting an American to a management position. According to the personnel manager of one of the companies in this study, tenure in the company has played an important role in their decision to promote Americans to management positions. Not surprisingly, Americans holding key management positions in several subsidiaries in this study were employed by the subsidiary for at least twelve years prior to their promotion.

The frequent turnover of American managers may prompt a Japanese company to appoint an expatriate manager to take over the position vacated by an American manager. For example, Japanese expatriate managers replaced the two American managers who quit their jobs at Mazda Motors Corporation, mentioned above. In the case of the consumer electronics company that sent American managers for training in Japan, the president said that they have become more selective and that they were sending fewer American managers each year for management training in Japan.

Three Approaches to Management Localization

Three approaches have been most commonly used by Japanese subsidiaries in appointing Americans to management positions previously held by Japanese expatriate managers. These are the *direct succession system,* the *advisor system,* and the *coordinator system.* Management localization in three Japanese subsidiaries in this study should help illustrate these various approaches.

Company A, an electronics manufacturer, employs the direct succession system to localize management. For each of the positions that has been targeted for localization, the company appoints a U.S. national as an assistant (e.g., assistant vice president, assistant manufacturing manager) to the incumbent Japanese expatriate manager. The U.S. national is expected to train under the Japanese expatriate manager and to learn all the aspects of the Japanese expatriate manager's job. At the end of a specified period (usually at the end of the Japanese expatriate manager's rotation cycle—i.e., three to seven years), the U.S. national is appointed to succeed the Japanese expatriate manager.

Company B, a manufacturer of commercial machinery, uses the advisor system to localize management. A U.S. national is appointed to each position identified by the company for localization. However, the U.S. national is directed to work closely with a Japanese expatriate manager appointed by the parent company or the subsidiary's senior manager who serves as an advisor to the U.S. national. The Japanese advisor provides counsel on many aspects of the U.S. national's managerial responsibilities. The American manager formally shares decision-making authority with the Japanese expatriate advisor. The U.S. national assumes full formal managerial authority and responsibility and the advisor is relieved of his duties only after the senior managers at the parent company or the subsidiary determines that the U.S. national has attained the expertise and experience to perform the function. Unlike the direct succession system, where the U.S. national can reasonably expect to succeed his or her superior at the end of the latter's rotation cycle in the United States, the advisor system does not specify when the U.S. national will have full managerial independence from the Japanese advisor. Moreover, the direct succession system does not involve the formal joint management responsibility between the American manager and a Japanese expatriate advisor that is common in the advisor system.

Company C, a manufacturer of automobile components, relies upon the coordinator system. U.S. nationals who have been appointed to important management positions (e.g., divisional manager and above) are assigned a Japanese expatriate manager as a counterpart in the subsidiary. The U.S. national shares management responsibility and authority with the Japanese coordinator. The coordinator also serves as one of the liaisons between the subsidiary and the parent company. Unlike the advisor position, the coordinator position is permanent. In the case of Company C, Japanese expatriate coordinators have been assigned to each important managerial position (e.g., divisional manager and above) for over twelve years.[2]

Of the three approaches, the Japanese subsidiaries in this study that employed the direct succession system have reported the least problems with management localization. In contrast, subsidiaries in this study that used the advisor system or the coordinator system have experienced communication and coordination problems. These subsidiaries had difficulty making the system of joint authority and responsibility work smoothly. In spite of the reported effectiveness of the direct succession system, however, not all subsidiaries favor it. Many subsidiaries view the approach as too abrupt and risky. "Direct succession does not always work because the local manager may not have reached the desired level of competence upon his [or her] promotion. The training period is too short. Direct succession tends to take the Japanese expatriate manager out of the picture too early," said a senior manager of Company B. Proponents of the coordinator system also argue that the presence of Japanese expatriate coordinators provides them a hedge should the U.S. national quit the company after promotion.

Involvement in Decision Making

In the majority of the companies that reported the appointment or promotion of more Americans to management positions, most of the companies also reported more involvement by American managers in decision making. However, as several American managers maintained, involvement in decision making should not be equated with complete autonomy in decision making. The difference between the two is explained by Scott Whitlock, an executive vice president at Honda of America. In a *Fortune* article (Moffat, 1990), Whitlock is quoted as saying, "If your attitude is, I want to come in [a Japanese company in the United States] and run something, I would not predict success. It's understood that one is going to achieve with other associates." Thus, insofar as decision making is concerned, American managers usually have to share decision-making authority and responsibility with other Japanese or American managers in the subsidiary. This reflects the Japanese companies' strong emphasis on teamwork.

The problems encountered by one transportation equipment company in this study in increasing management localization demonstrate the importance of expanding a manager's involvement in decision making. The company appointed several Americans to key management positions without increasing their involvement in key decision making. The Japanese coordinators still retained major decision-making powers. After several months of relying on their Japanese counterparts, several U.S. managers quit their jobs in frustration.

At the parent company–subsidiary level, subsidiary autonomy was relatively higher when the subsidiary predominantly employed Japanese expatriate managers. Direct involvement by the parent company in decision making increased as the subsidiary appointed or promoted more Americans to management positions. This is consistent with the observation, mentioned earlier. As the parent company gives up personal control over the U.S. subsidiary because of management localization, it may increase the formalization of control and enhance its involvement in decision making in the subsidiary.

Summary and HRM Implications

Although Japanese subsidiaries in the United States still employ many Japanese expatriate managers, there is an emerging trend in a number of these subsidiaries to increase the localization of management. Several factors have been catalysts for Japanese subsidiaries in the United States to increase management localization. These include the need of these subsidiaries to (1) improve the morale of their American managers and employees, (2) respond to or preempt discrimination lawsuits, (3) enhance their image as a U.S. corporate citizen, (4) increase their ability to recruit and retain American executives, and (5) trim their management payroll expenses.

On the other hand, several factors have constrained Japanese subsidiaries in the United States from increasing the localization of their management. These include (1) the company's reliance on personal control, (2) the turnover of American managers, and (3) the dependence of the subsidiary on the Japanese parent company or the subsidiary's emphasis on conducting business with other Japanese companies.

Management localization in Japanese subsidiaries in the United States presents two key human resource management implications. First, the experience of several U.S. subsidiaries of Japanese companies in this study demonstrates the importance of matching the appointment/promotion of a U.S. national with increasing his or her decision-making authority. Failure to do so often leads to more frustration on the part of the American manager.

Second, the complexities and challenges faced by Japanese subsidiaries in the United States in localizing management confirm that management localization is a decision that must be dealt with in relation to other management issues. For example, as Japanese subsidiaries appoint or promote more Americans to management positions, these subsidiaries must assess the impact this change will have on other aspects of the organization design of the company, such as communication, coordination, and control processes within the subsidiary and between the subsidiary and the parent company. It must also assess how management localization will affect other aspects of the subsidiary's human resource management systems, such as compensation and performance evaluation.

Insofar as Americans working for Japanese companies in the United States are concerned, management localization has undoubtedly opened up more career advancement opportunities for them.[3] The greatest opportunities for management advancement appear currently to be in middle and lower management. In particular, management positions in competitive areas (i.e., where top-quality American managers are in great demand) and management positions whose primary focus is to generate new business from U.S. customers have been localized much sooner and faster. In addition, the number of Americans in top management, especially in the positions of executive vice president or senior vice president is gradually increasing. Because Japanese subsidiaries in the United States generally favor internal promotion over hiring from outside the company, Americans currently employed by Japanese subsidiaries stand to benefit from their employers' decision to appoint or promote more Americans to management positions. For many of these Americans, however, promotion will most likely mean a gradual, step-by-step ascent to the management hierarchy of Japanese subsidiaries in the United States.

Acknowledgment

Support for this study was given by the Faculty Development Award Fund, Office of Research Administration, and the Summer Research Fund of the Dean's Office, College of Business and Administration, University of Colorado at Denver; and by the Office of Research Administration and Department of Business Administration, University of Illinois at Urbana–Champaign. I wish to thank the executives of the forty-seven companies that participated in my study.

Notes

1. I conducted the initial interviews between 1988 and 1989, and the follow-up discussions with the majority of the sample companies between 1989 and 1992.
2. The title or position of "coordinator," as used in this chapter should not be confused with a similar title given to Japanese expatriates dispatched by the parent company to provide technical, production, or engineering support or assistance to their U.S. plants. The latter are "staff consultants" whose assignments in the United States are temporary and typically span three to six months.
3. Although a recent trend toward downsizing may seriously slow down management localization programs in Japanese subsidiaries in the United States, it is too early to assess the impact of these downsizing activities on the management localization programs of the subsidiaries in this study.

References

Borrus, A. (1990). Can Japan's giants cut the apron strings? *Business Week*, May 14, pp. 105–106.

Boyacigiller, Nakiye. (1988). Staffing in a foreign land: A model and research design to study Japanese multinationals with operations in the United States. Paper presented at the annual meeting of the Academy of Management, Anaheim, CA, Aug.

Culture shock at home: Working for a foreign boss. (1990). *Business Week*, Dec. 17.

Edstrom, Anders, & Galbraith, Jay. (1982). Transfer of managers as a coordination and control strategy in multinational corporations. *Administrative Science Quarterly*, 27 (Sept.): 435–458.

Galen, M. & Nathans, L. (1989). White people, black people not wanted here. *Business Week,* July 10, p. 31.

Gross, Neil. (1988). The Americanization of Honda. *Business Week,* Apr. 25, pp. 90–96.

Isaka, S. (1990). Sony takes lead among Japanese firms. *Japan Economic Journal,* June 2.

Japan Economic Institute. (1989). *Japan's expanding U.S. manufacturing presence,* 1988 update. Oct.

Japan External Trade Organization (JETRO). (1981). *Japanese manufacturing operations in the United States—Results of the first comprehensive field study.* Sept.

———(1989). *JETRO special report: 1989 JETRO white paper on world direct investments.* Mar.

Japanese firms in the U.S. face personnel dangers. (1990). *Wall Street Journal,* Oct. 15, p. B1.

Johnson, Richard. (1977). Success and failure of Japanese subsidiaries in America. *Columbia Journal of World Business,* Spring, 30–73.

Kono, Toyohiro. (1984). *Strategy and structure of Japanese enterprises.* Armonk, NY: M. E. Sharpe.

Kujawa, Duane. (1986). *Japanese multinationals in the United States: Case studies.* New York: Praeger.

———. (1988). *Japanese multinationals in the United States.* New York: Praeger.

Mason, T., & Hoerr, J. (1988). Hitachi: Winning friends and influencing people in Oklahoma. *Business Week,* July 11, p. 75.

Mizuni, Y. (1990). Mitsubishi bank puts on local face globally. *Japan Economic Journal,* June 16.

Moffat, Susan. (1990). Should you work for the Japanese? *Fortune,* Dec. 3, pp. 107–114.

Negandhi, Anant. (1987). *International management,* Boston, MA: Allyn & Bacon.

———. (1985). Management strategies and policies of American, German, and Japanese multinational corporations. *Management Japan* 18(1): 12–20.

Negandhi, A. & Welge, M. (1984). *Beyond theory z: Global rationalization strategies of American, German, and Japanese multinational companies.* CT: JAI Press.

Nirenberg, John. (1986). Understanding the failure of Japanese management abroad. *Journal of Managerial Psychology,* (1)1: 19–24.

O'Reilly, B. (1988). Japan's uneasy U.S. managers. *Fortune,* Apr. 25, pp. 245–260.

Rehfeld, J. (1990). What working for a Japanese company taught me. *Harvard Business Review,* Nov.–Dec. pp. 167–176.

Serapio, M. G., Jr. & Negandhi, A. (1991). Management strategies and policies of Japanese multinational companies: A reexamination. *Management Japan,* Spring, pp. 25–32.

Shida, T. (1990). The Americanization of Nomura. *Japan Economic Journal,* May 19.

Sumitomo sets accord on job bias lawsuit. (1990). *Wall Street Journal,* Nov. 8, p. B1.

U.S. culture trips Japanese firms. (1990). *Denver Post,* Sept. 10, p. 4C.

Yoshida, Mamoru. (1988). *Japanese direct manufacturing investment in the United States.* New York: Praeger.

The Best Practices Learning Curve

Human Resource Management in Mexico's Maquiladora Industry

Mary B. Teagarden San Diego State University

Mary Ann Von Glinow Florida International University

Mark C. Butler San Diego State University

Ellen Drost San Diego State University

Jim Miller closed his office door, sat down at his desk, leaned back and stared at the ceiling. For seven months he had been operations manager of the ElectroMex maquiladora (a Mexican manufacturing or processing facility), but now the honeymoon was over. Jim had taken over an operation that was running much less efficiently than the plant at home. His job was to turn the maquiladora around.

This research was partially funded by a San Diego State University Center for International Business Education and Research (CIBER) research grant. We would like to acknowledge the valuable contribution of Professor Miguel Angel Valverde of CETYS in Tijuana, Baja California, and many of our MBA graduate students and International Business and Management undergraduate students to this project. (John Hendon; Chris Feno; Marianne Sozio; Mike Adams; Jonas Almstrup; Pom Assoratgoon, Chris Barber, Al Stark, Konrad Larson, Jeff Parkinson, John Patton, Lin Farmer, Linlee Austell and Tehseen Lazzouni).

Portions of this chapter, including Table 1 and Figure 1, appeared in M. B. Teagarden, M. C. Butler, & M. A. Von Glinow (1992), Mexico's maquiladora industry: Where strategic human resource management makes a difference, *Organizational Dynamics,* Winter, 20(3), 34–47; and M. C. Butler and M. B. Teagarden (1993), Strategic management of worker health, safety and environmental issues in Mexico's maquiladora industry, *Human Resource Management,* 32(4).

ElectroMex had been in business for six years and was US Electronic's (USE) first "off-shore" manufacturing facility. Fierce price competition in the electronics industry put pressure on USE to keep costs low. They had selected a maquiladora because Mexican labor was relatively cheap, and they would still be close to their customers who demanded fast turnaround times. The maquiladora had not lived up to USE's expectations: material cost was inexplicably high, turnaround was too slow, quality varied significantly, and to make matters worse turnover in employees was 150 percent a year.

Jim had been selected for this job on the basis of his strong technical track record at USE's headquarters in Pittsburgh. With a B.S. in electrical engineering, Jim began his career at USE as a production assistant nine years ago. During the next four years he was promoted to production supervisor and completed an MBA at night. Jim had been an outstanding production supervisor. He had been aggressive in reducing scrap and had decreased the cycle time in his department by 30 percent. Management saw him as a "rising star," and his workers saw him as tough but fair. As one said, "Miller's gruff and he'll push you real hard, but he pushes himself just as hard." When the ElectroMex operations manager position in Tijuana, Mexico, opened, Jim was management's first choice.

However, it seemed to Jim that in the past few weeks every change he tried to make was resisted. First, there was the materials use problem: Quality was very high, but material use was four times as high as it should be given the output. Then, Maria Perez, his best worker, turned down a promotion to supervisor. Jim wanted to reward her outstanding performance, and he thought that she would have been an ideal lead person because she was mature, respected by her co-workers, and had experience in every assembly job in the plant. She had been with ElectroMex since the day it opened, and Jim could not understand why she did not want to get ahead. Finally, Juan Lopez, a promising young engineer, quit without notice. His only explanation was "family reasons." Jim had been shifting a lot of responsibility onto Juan. Juan had asked to attend special training sessions offered by the university. Jim had to turn him down because, given the tight budget, USE did not pay for such training. Besides, if Juan was to become a good engineer, he had to learn to make decisions on his own, on the job. This is how Jim had been trained at headquarters, and it had worked well for him.

Jim saw himself as a go-getter, a winner, a can-do kind of a guy. When he took the assignment, he was certain that he could turn the plant around quickly. However, things that had gotten him ahead at home were not working in Mexico. He felt that if he failed at ElectroMex, his career at USE was doomed. Jim knew that some of his competitors were achieving world-class performance in their maquiladora operations. As Jim looked out over the parking lot, he decided that if he was to succeed at ElectroMex, he had a lot to learn.[1]

Introduction

Foreign firms have had almost thirty years experience using the maquiladora option to manufacture in Mexico. Now that we are in the NAFTA era, this experience is particularly valuable. In this chapter we explore what these firms have learned regarding effective management of maquiladora facilities. We begin with a discussion of Mexico's role in the global economy and emphasize the maquiladora program and related strategic challenges, many of which are human resource management (HRM) issues. The chapter shifts focus to contributions of strategic HRM and discusses traditional and strategic maquiladora HRM systems. Three HRM design philosophies are presented, and the pros and cons of each are described. The developmental, human resource-based design is identified as best practice. The chapter concludes with an exploration of the "other side" of Jim Miller's challenges and what he learned by resolving them.

Mexico and the Global Economy

The realities of a dynamic, interdependent, increasingly global economy challenge firms to increase their competitiveness. In the face of severe global price competition, one business strategy often used to gain competitiveness is that of cost minimization. The "little dragons"—Taiwan, Singapore, South Korea, and Hong Kong—have been the preferred low-cost, off-shore manufacturing sites for multinational enterprises (MNEs). Low wage rates are the most often cited benefit of off-shore manufacturing, but wage rates are only part of the overall cost picture. The cumulative effect of rising manufacturing costs—rising wage rates, labor shortages, upward pressure on other factor costs; the loss of General System of Preferences (GSP) duty-free privileges among the little dragons as of January 1989; and the hidden costs associated with recent and persistent political turbulence in the Asia Pacific Rim countries—have induced MNEs to seek alternative low-cost, off-shore manufacturing sites. The People's Republic of China (PRC), Thailand, Malaysia, Indonesia, and to a lesser extent Vietnam, have emerged as alternative sites, as has Mexico through the Border Industrialization Plan, which allows MNEs to use maquiladoras.

Mexico has also emerged as an attractive growing market and excellent platform for MNE expansion into Latin American markets.[2] Mexico's market attractiveness can only grow under the North American Free Trade Agreement (NAFTA), which went into effect on January 1, 1994. The region is more populous than the European Economic Community (EEC) and not far behind it in industrial output and gross national product. For U.S. (and Canadian) manufacturers, financial institutions and farmers the biggest advantage of NAFTA is that it will provide accelerated access to a market of over 86 million people, 20 million of whom currently have the buying power of the average U.S. consumer. Mexico is the fastest-growing market for U.S. goods and services in the world. Mexico is America's third largest customer, having bought US$41 billion of U.S. exports in 1992. If it has not already, Mexico is soon expected to surpass Japan, the United States' second largest customer. (Canada is the largest U.S. customer.) The combined value of U.S.–Mexico trade in 1992 was US$76 billion, as compared to US$30 billion in 1987. In addition, North American firms that manufacture in Mexico will be able to sell their products in Mexico without the trade restrictions they encounter under existing programs such as the Border Industrial Program. In addition, Mexican consumer preferences for American products and services are extremely strong, significantly higher than for those of other Latin, European, or Japanese products and services. NAFTA holds the promise of very positive outcomes for firms willing to skillfully take advantage of this opportunity. These skills have been well developed in the maquiladora industry.

What Are Maquiladoras?

Maquiladoras are manufacturing or processing facilities located in Mexico.[3] They have had a significant impact on the Mexican economy and the competitiveness of MNEs using this option.[4] The maquiladora "industry" is Mexico's second largest source of hard currency after petroleum sales, and it is actually an agglomeration of manufacturers from various industrial sectors, including among others, the electronics industry; the automotive supply, computer, television, and other electronic-based industries; medical supply, woodworking, furniture manufacture, and garment industries; and service providers—for example, grocery store coupon sorters and data entry facilities. Maquiladoras are formed through wholly owned subsidiaries, joint ventures, and shelter (subcontracting) agreements. The total value-added in maquiladoras in 1992 exceeded US$1.8 billion generated in more than 2,400 maquiladora manufacturing plants, which employed more than 500,000 Mexican workers. Plant sizes range from more than 2,500 employees in some automotive and electronic assembly plants to 6- to 8-person "low-tech" job shops, more common in woodworking and garment operations.

U.S. MNEs, such as Ford, Hewlett-Packard, Mattel, and Motorola, account for over 90 percent of the value of maquiladora investment and control the largest number of plants, 68 percent in 1992. Mexicans control 25 percent of the maquiladora plants and operate many industrial parks and shelter operation sites. There is an increasing presence of third country maquiladoras including those controlled by Japanese and Korean MNEs. Japanese MNEs such as Sony, Sanyo, Fujitsu, Matsushita, and Hitachi represent 4 percent of the maquiladora plants, and some of these have encouraged their suppliers from Japan—for example, Sanoh and Tocabi—to follow. Although Japanese maquiladoras are small in number, they are large in size, employing about 15 percent of the maquiladora workforce. Similarly, large Korean MNEs such as Samsung, Lucky Goldstar and Hyundai have also recently established maquiladoras. An additional small number of third country maquiladora users include MNEs from Germany (whose total foreign direct investment in Mexico surpasses that of Japan), France, Finland, Canada, and Taiwan.

Maquiladoras and Global Competition

From the short-term perspective, maquiladoras represent a source of cheap labor. The cheap labor concept, however, deserves closer inspection. If cheap labor were an MNE's only criterion, then less industrialized countries like the People's Republic of China (PRC), India, Thailand, or Viet Nam would offer more attractive manufacturing sites than Mexico because their wage rates are lower. Mexico offers additional benefits such as proximity to the United States and higher levels of productivity—in terms of output *and* quality—than these alternatives.

More than 20 percent of maquiladora production is done in plants using world-class state-of-the-art technology that affords high quality and manufacturing flexibility. Ford, General Motors, Hewlett-Packard, AT&T, and other MNEs identify Mexican plants as their highest-quality producers in the world. This sentiment is echoed by Japanese MNEs such as Sony, Hitachi, and Sanyo. German MNEs like Mercedes Benz are opening Mexican operations to take advantage of high quality at a relatively low price. Increasingly, the strategic challenge for all maquiladoras is to produce relatively low-cost, high-quality products with sufficient speed to meet consumer demands.

Mexico is currently an "off-shore" manufacturing "hot spot," and is expected to remain so, and to grow in importance under NAFTA. Attractiveness of off-shore sites, however, shifts with changes in labor cost and availability, and other related costs. Some of those costs are now "hidden" but are expected to be made clearer over time. For example, environment plays an increasing role in the cost equation. As unique as the maquiladoras are for their significant presence between two vastly different cultures, nowhere are the differences felt more than in discussions around the environment. These are politically charged and heated arguments by both sides, and it is clear that costs of environmental clean-up will be passed to the MNEs active in the maquiladoras. By all assessments, the costs will be nontrivial and borne by many who are seeking to reduce their own hefty labor rates. This is a key tension point, which as of this writing, remains indeterminate. Maquiladoras, or any other off-shore manufacturing option, remain an attractive alternative only so long as they are able to help MNEs achieve or sustain global competitiveness.

In the increasingly competitive global marketplace there appears to be a convergence of many manufacturing techniques, those traditional areas where competitiveness has been enhanced by increasing efficiencies. The "hard" techniques (and advantages) of Total Quality Management, Integrated Manufacturing and Design, Just-in-Time Inventory Control, Process Mapping, Benchmarking, and Best Practices are rapidly diffused internationally as compared to the "soft" techniques associated with HRM.[5] This diffusion has resulted in increased expectations of high quality and productivity as the new bases of competitiveness: the level of the playing field has risen for all competitors. The advent of these "hard" techniques suggest, at a minimum, the need for a more strategic focus on recruitment, selection, and training issues. However, those MNEs able to incorporate *and* move beyond the more rapidly diffused "hard" techniques to develop effective approaches for managing human resources will win future competitiveness challenges.

Strategic Benefits of Maquiladoras

Specific maquiladora benefits include low wage rates; low factor costs; proximity and ease of access to the U.S. market; abundant labor (Mexico's population is the second youngest in the world with the average age of sixteen), 100 percent foreign ownership, if desired; and the ability to staff key management and technical support positions with expatriates—who often live in the United States and commute to border plants daily.

Despite these substantial benefits, maquiladora manufacturers repeatedly cite workforce and organizational factors as being problematic. The most persistent of the problems encountered are HRM problems. "Cheap Mexican labor" is a primary benefit sought by most MNEs and seem to be a primary means for entering the Mexican market. However, labor costs are a function of the hourly wage rate *and* worker productivity or output. Strategic HRM specifically targets the productivity side of the equation and thus is the lens through which the following discussion focuses.

The Strategic Management of Maquiladora Human Resources

Strategic HRM is the design and implementation of human resource systems to support the firm's short- and long-term strategic objectives. Strategic HRM contributes to development of a capable, effective, world-class workforce. HRM serves additional, important purposes for MNEs operating internationally. International strategic HRM practices are used to enhance MNE control in foreign affiliates, and as a mechanism for bridging cross-cultural issues that are often at the heart of MNE–affiliate differences.[6] Consequently, in an international setting, strategic HRM emphasizes strategic fit issues, control issues, and cross-cultural issues.

The predominant theme in strategic HRM literature concerns the need to fit HRM strategy to the larger organizational context, specifically, to the firm's business and functional strategies. Strategic HRM promotes productivity *and* overall organizational effectiveness.[7] This is accomplished in part by increasing worker satisfaction and investing in worker development. In contrast to the traditional view of HRM, which is typically reactive, control oriented, and productivity focused, the strategic orientation is decidedly proactive in nature. Specifically, the importance of viewing traditional aspects of HRM—recruitment and selection, training, appraisal, compensation, and employee relations—from both short- and long-term perspectives affords an organization the opportunity to gain or maintain competitive advantage.

HRM-Based Strategic Challenges in Maquiladoras

Seven HRM-based strategic challenges encountered in maquiladoras have been identified in our research. These include (1) a work force comprised of young workers without previous manufacturing exposure or meaningful work experience, often from rural Mexico; (2) significant challenges based on cross-cultural differences—including expectations of paternalism, importance of family, "work to live" values, and "machismo"; (3) abundant literate but unskilled labor; (4) extensive labor law influences that commonly favor the worker; (5) family management issues that spillover to the workplace and contribute to high turnover rates; (6) the need to "Mexicanize" maquiladora management; and (7) increasing pressure to meet global quality and manufacturing flexibility standards.[8] These will discussed in more detail below.

Young "Green Hands."   Over 80 percent of the maquiladoras are located along the U.S.–Mexico border from California to Texas. Many workers have migrated to the area from the interior within the last five years and are usually without family in the local setting. Two-thirds of the maquiladora assembly workers are women between the ages of sixteen and twenty-five with little manufacturing-related work experience. Most workers have completed between six and nine years of education.[9] Maquiladora employers, especially in electronic manufacturing, explain that young women are best suited to assembly processes requiring the high levels of fine motor skills and manual dexterity that these women possess; that women are better suited to the tedious work; and that they are more stable than men. Culturally based arguments are also used by employers to explain the prevalence of young women.[10] For example, employers argue that assembly jobs are not seen as sufficiently *macho* and thus are shunned by men. These "cultural" arguments are seen as specious by some researchers who assert that young women are hired because they are docile, compliant, and hard to unionize.[11]

Gender-related maquiladora employment trends, however, are changing. For example, the employment of men in maquiladoras is increasing, from 15 percent of the work force in 1965 to 44 percent in 1990. Men are more prevalent in woodworking and furniture manufacture, leather processing, and automotive supply sectors of the maquiladora industry. Nevertheless, men are often seen as using maquiladora employment merely as a stopover on their way north.

Cross-Cultural Challenges.   Cultural differences are found among local workers, supervisors, and management.[12] For example, *machismo* is a trait closely associated with Latin American men and is characterized by behaviors such as pride, reluctance to admit error or ignorance, and an unwillingness to do "women's work." Many employers identify this trait as an obstacle when employing young men.

The importance of family and the family structure to Mexican workers is significant. As Oscar Lewis commented, "Without his family, the Mexican individual stands prey to every form of aggression, exploitation, and humiliation." Mexicans value an extended kinship system in which relatives, clans, and organizations are expected to look after, or care for, the individual and in exchange the individual owes absolute allegiance and loyalty.

In the maquiladora, paternalism is expected—the appropriate role of management is to take care of the workers. In addition, managers and supervisors are expected to be the authority—their status is respected, and in return the workers's status is also respected. From this perspective workers are the manager's "extended family" and expect to be cared for—the manager is the *patron*. When asked what they would change if they were supervisors, maquiladora assembly workers' responses included encouraging workers to share problems so that supervisors could make necessary or appropriate changes to solve them; helping the workers actually do their jobs; creating a more sociable work environment; holding social events; not making workers nervous; and allowing workers to work at their own pace. Work and the workplace have an enlarged role when compared to those in the United States.

Abundant, Unskilled Labor.   Maquiladoras are assured the right to determine their staffing needs and to recruit and fire personnel on their own, unlike, for example, in the PRC where staffing can require absorption of an unwieldy number of excess employees. Union influence is strong in some regions (especially the eastern Mexican border region). However, the influence is seen by most maquiladora employers as having a positive effect on maquiladora effectiveness: unions tend not to be militant and they supply a pool of readily available labor. Unskilled labor is abundant, and according to one employer, "We announce fifty openings on Friday, and by Monday we have five hundred applicants," some of whom will "jump" from other maquiladoras to shorten a commute or to get marginally better working conditions. Rapid growth of maquiladoras had caused some temporary labor shortages along the Texas border, but most employers now report that this is no longer a problem.

The abundance of applicants allows employers to screen for and select those most suitable for assembly jobs. Mexican workers are willing to participate in such screening because of the relatively good wages and benefits available in maquiladoras as opposed to other local employment opportunities. Maquiladoras do, however, have a difficult time recruiting skilled labor. Maquiladora managers who express satisfaction with their operations commonly engage in extensive, and often costly, training to accommodate skilled labor staffing needs.

Strong Labor Law Influences.   Mexico's labor law has a strong influence on HRM practices. It specifies vacations and holidays, acceptable reasons for termination, provisions for pregnant and nursing mothers, and seniority premium pay, among other things. Mexico controls minimum wages, which vary by region and employment classification. The work week is forty-eight hours, but many maquiladora employees work five nine-hour days (forty-five hours) and are paid for forty-eight hours. Benefits such as holiday pay, meals, housing, childcare, and production incentives can boost wages 30 percent to 100 percent above the minimum wage, although many of these benefits are optional. One week of vacation after the first year of employment is required, and this increases two days for each additional year of employment until two weeks of vacation are reached. A 25 percent premium is paid on vacation pay.

Generally, when a worker is hired, the employer has four weeks to evaluate his or her performance. After that point, the worker becomes permanent under a system that generally favors the employee. Since Mexico does not have a termination-at-will doctrine, termination can be costly. Mexican employees with permanent status have work contracts with their employers that require payment of severance pay upon termination or layoff. Maquiladora managers suggest that some workers work until they build up a sufficient amount of guaranteed severance pay benefits to see them through the year, then they take the balance of the year off.

Family Management Issues.   It is not uncommon for workers to leave on vacation or for the Christmas holidays and fail to return to work as scheduled. "Family reasons" are the most often cited reason for failing to return as scheduled and for resignation. "Family reasons" are also the most common reason for absenteeism and are often cited as the principal reason for other turnover. Some managers believe that this saves face when an employee resigns. Legitimate "family reasons" include, among other things, the need to take care of small children, sick children, brothers and sisters, and elderly parents and relatives. If the worker's family is located in the interior, taking care of "family issues" may involve returning home to resolve the problem. As discussed earlier, family is very important to Mexican workers, and from their perspective "family reasons" is a legitimate excuse for absence or resignation.

The Mexicanization of Management.   Generally, there is a glaring absence of Mexican managers in maquiladoras. The few MNEs that have been aggressive in recruiting, socializing, and retaining Mexican executives have enjoyed very positive results. These executives are able to reflect the norms and values of headquarters *and* the local facility. The lack of Mexican managers is often attributed to the perceived lack of skilled labor available in Mexico. However, on closer inspection it appears that these employers believe that they can better control the operation if they fill executive positions with managers who are "like them"—Americans in U.S. maquiladoras, Japanese in Japanese maquiladoras, and so forth. MNEs that do not share this bias usually are not willing to make the investment in development of the manager that would enable him or her to advance in the management hierarchy. Until and unless maquiladoras are willing to integrate Mexican managers into higher managerial levels in their operations, they will miss a valuable opportunity to enhance their global competitiveness.

Global Competitiveness.   Two generic competitive strategies have been identified in the literature: (1) competition based on overall cost leadership, where the firm is a low-cost producer; and (2) competition based on differentiation, where the firm competes using, for example, quality, customer responsiveness, or service.[13] Increasingly, MNEs find that remaining competitive in the global marketplace requires them to integrate these perspectives and produce high quality, low cost products with sufficient speed to meet consumer demands. As MNEs encounter these more sophisticated challenges, they find that they must shift from traditional to more strategic HRM system designs. Maquiladoras are no exception. However many, like ElectroMex, have not begun to make the transition.

Patterns of International HRM in the Maquiladora Industry: Moving Beyond Cost Reduction to Revenue Generation Using Human Assets

To meet increasingly sophisticated global competition, well-trained, loyal, committed workers are critical maquiladora resources as they are elsewhere around the globe. MNEs do not develop such workers by implementing short-term cost cutting, resorting to hiring contract wage earners rather than full-time equivalents. Indeed, what we call "IHRM thinking" requires HRM programs that enhance individual performance around the globe through selection, training, development, and attention to culturally appropriate reward systems—all dimensions associated with strategic HRM thinking. This strategic approach can be contrasted with a more traditional approach that is encountered in maquiladoras that have a short-term, cost reduction orientation as opposed to revenue generation.

There are four types of assumptions about people that underlie international human resource management (IHRM) system design identified in the research: (1) the nature of the employment contract; (2) the degree of participation in decision making; (3) internal versus external labor markets; and (4) group versus individual performance.[14] We have contrasted and extended traditional and strategic maquiladora IHRM system characteristics using these categories, as shown in Table 1.

Maquiladoras that embrace the strategic perspective invest in development of their human assets, workers who contribute to attainment of the firm's strategic objectives. For example, these firms implement training *and* development programs, share decision making regarding tasks, and develop internal labor markets. They make higher use of culturally appropriate

TABLE 1
Dimensions of Traditional and Strategic Maquiladora IHRM Systems

Characteristic	*Traditional Maquiladora IHRM System*	*Strategic Maquiladora IHRM System*
Time horizon	Short term	Long term
Employment contract	Work for pay	Meaningful work for loyal, committed service
Training objectives	Necessary task specific	Task specific *and* developmental
Decision making and power	Top-down	Shared (regarding tasks)
Labor market	External	Internal
Group vs. individual performance	Individual	Combination
Basis for control	External, mechanistic	Internal, behaviorally driven
Culturally appropriate rewards	Low use	High use
Basis for competition	Cost	Cost *and* differentiation

reward systems, and the basis for control is behaviorally driven supported by extensive socialization and a strong corporate culture. The following section identifies practices that underlie traditional and strategic HRM systems.

IHRM Practices in Maquiladoras

IHRM functional areas—recruitment and selection, reward systems, appraisal, career planning and family management issues—are the underpinnings that support traditional and strategic IHR systems. It should be noted that there are some differences between wholly owned subsidiaries and those that are joint ventures between a Mexican firm and an MNE from elsewhere. In the wholly owned subsidiary, one would expect to see fewer local nationals present in the management ranks, and as a result, the MNE would be more apt to use their own expatriate staff in directing the enterprise. Frequently, IHRM researchers observe that in the case of the wholly owned subsidiary, a schism exists between the workers and the management, which can be overcome by careful attention to strategic IHRM thinking and action on the part of the expatriate management. In the joint venture, however, usually a management team is constituted of both local nationals, as well as expatriate managers. In this case, a more balanced view of the practices may be evident from the start. Local national managers help inform their expatriate colleagues of traditional Mexican practices, that may run counter to traditional HR practices of the MNE. We will try to pinpoint differences in problems encountered, as well as solutions that have been resolved using the IHRM logic we identify. The following sections discuss the practices that have led to success in maquiladoras.

Employee Recruitment and Selection

Recruitment.   Turnover upward of 30 percent can be the result of ineffective recruitment policies. Employees are routinely recruited via word of mouth, or by signs hung outside of the maquiladoras announcing openings. It is common for family members to seek employment for relatives, and maquiladoras find this quite satisfactory. Some have suggested that maquiladora managers should take money budgeted for advertising job openings through public media like advertisements or radio, and use these funds as bonuses for employees who recruit others.[15] Regardless of the recruitment approaches that we have detailed, one must consider the true and effective use of recruitment strategies—namely, the generation of a qualified labor source in sufficient numbers to ensure effective employee selection. Maximizing this selection ratio allows maquiladora managers to stabilize what can be dramatic fluctuations in the work force. In wholly owned subsidiaries, these strategies are a bit more difficult to effect, particularly if the baseline of knowledge does not exist, relative to recruitment of family members, radio advertisement for jobs, and bonus monies for successful recruitment, for example. IJVs however in Mexico have had the benefit of local national insights on recruiting issues, and in general, have utilized these strategies more fully.

Selection.   Prospective employees are interviewed in Spanish, and a limited number of those interviewed go through additional screening. Effective maquiladoras make extensive use of screening—physical examinations and intelligence and dexterity tests—in the selection process prior to hiring. Maquiladoras using extensive screening processes report turnover rates lower than industry averages. Workers who stand out on intelligence tests but not on dexterity tests are often channeled into clerical and administrative positions. Many young women work only until they marry and start a family; and many men use maquiladoras as a stopover on the route north. Thus, retention remains an issue despite selection practices. This continues to be true for both wholly owned and joint venture enterprises, due in part to the nature of the work force: age, geographic home and pattern of employment history, and the "green hand" phenomenon.

Employee Training and Development

As mentioned, most entry-level maquiladora workers are "green hands"—untrained workers who have not had significant work experience in a manufacturing environment. Workers from the interior come from an agrarian background where there is a lack of social and economic infrastructure that supports industry. Thus, training is needed to develop basic social skills necessary in a manufacturing environment. On-the-job training is the primary vehicle used to familiarize workers with job requirements, and initial orientation stresses basics like the importance of punctuality and regular attendance. Personal contact between supervisors and the newly hired workers is reported to enhance training. In addition, total quality control and quality circles are common training topics in the electronics and automotive industries, and welding and soldering training are also common in the electronics industry.

Training is considered a highly desired reward by many maquiladora workers. In addition to job-related training, some employers offer on-site general education courses and high school equivalency training. The most progressive maquiladoras require such training as a minimum standard for promotion to leadperson or supervisor. Workers who come from the interior are removed from the social environment with which they are most familiar, and as mentioned earlier, personal problems are brought to the workplace. General education courses that target these needs include courses in budgeting family finances and basic health care practices. United States and Japanese companies, like Ford and Sony, have invested heavily in additional training for key technical personnel that often includes sending maquiladora workers to manufacturing facilities in the United States and

Japan. Maquiladoras that offer training, both job-related and general, report lower turnover rates than industry averages, and higher productivity. While training, in general, tends to emerge as a best practice for both wholly owned as well as joint venture workers, the amount tends to vary, depending on MNE country of origin. Some countries invest more heavily in training than others, so we would expect some specific country differences here.

Reward Systems Design

Wages are higher in maquiladoras than in other Mexican manufacturing alternatives, and there is considerable pressure from domestic non-maquiladora employers to keep maquiladora wages low. Consequently, perquisites are used to enlarge the compensation package. Some maquiladoras have reduced turnover and absenteeism dramatically through the use of additional perquisites targeted at specific employee needs. Allen Bradley, Pulse Engineering, Sanyo, and others offer perquisite packages that may include transportation from central urban and rural locations to the plant; employee funds based on hours worked and distributed on a scheduled basis; quality and punctuality bonuses; on-site health care clinics for workers and their families; cafeterias that serve traditional Mexican food, often free; free beverage dispensers; shower facilities for those who do not have these available at home; on-site education (in addition to work-related training); athletic activities; and packages of food and make-up for women workers. The most successful maquiladoras tailor the perquisite packages to the specific needs of their workers.

Use of reward system–based mechanisms, such as those just described, is reported by maquiladora managers to enhance overall effectiveness in these manufacturing sites. The benefits of using reward system interventions is reported to positively influence overall MNE effectiveness to the degree that they are able to maintain low manufacturing costs. There has been little systematic research, however, that explores the range and frequency of HRM design interventions used in maquiladoras, or evaluates the effectiveness of specific interventions.

A critical issue here is, "Are the rewards received by maquiladora workers tied to performance?" To the degree that the extensive array of entitlements and perquisites provided are seen as rewards, a key problem develops: Every time you give a "reward" for something other than performance—for example, just showing up for work (the punctuality bonus)—you give the employee one less reason to perform. Our observations indicate that worker expectations about the roles of employer and employee have a strong influence here: Maquiladora workers perform because the employer is providing *expected* entitlements thus filling the role of *patron*. However, performance is higher in IJV (international joint venture) maquiladoras where rewards, such as punctuality bonuses, are directly tied to quality and output performance targets.

Performance Appraisal

The apparent, or at least dominant, function of appraisal in maquiladoras at the present time seems to be very traditional. Specifically, the systems track for internal promotion purposes those individuals with the greatest demonstrated ability to supervise the efforts of other maquiladora workers, or to simply perform adequately on the job themselves. However, a more strategic look at the appraisal function provides additional and useful potential. In light of the high turnover rate experienced by most maquiladoras, the performance appraisal setting provides a unique opportunity for supervisor and employee to engage in a number of developmental activities. We have found that the loyalty maquiladora workers feel toward the firm is strongly influenced by their attitude toward their immediate supervisor.

Content analysis of open-ended responses to surveys administered in maquiladoras clearly indicated that the typical Mexican worker chronically complained that their supervisors and managers did not view them as people or as individuals, simply as workers. This is interpreted as a significant lack of respect for workers, more evident in wholly owned subsidiaries than in IJVs. Modern, strategic views regarding the performance appraisal process indicate that the performance appraisal offers a context in which many of such misperceptions or myths can be dispelled or modified. Given the limited ability of most maquiladoras to offer added wage incentives, and the increasing levels of competition between maquiladoras, positive gains could be realized when simple procedures like performance appraisal are altered to appeal to the developmental needs of employees.

Family Issues Management

Problems associated with the management of family issues have perhaps the most insidious influence on maquiladora effectiveness. As stated, family issues are the most often cited reason for both turnover and absenteeism. Effective maquiladoras have addressed these issues in various ways. For example, some maquiladoras provide on-site health care facilities for workers and their families; others have developed or coordinated childcare facilities; and others make small loans to workers to help in financially troubled times. All these options contribute to the overall cost of labor, but firms using these options feel that the benefits of stabilizing the work force outweigh the costs of the programs and that offering these perquisites makes them more attractive employers.

Career Issues Management

To the degree that the maquiladora industry remains unstable, our initial recommendation regarding career issues is simple—why bother? It is important to bother for several reasons. First, many workers we have surveyed indicate clearly that their principal interests are in being provided with career advancement opportunities. In particular, a group of workers interviewed and surveyed in the Tijuana/San Diego area indicated their preference for learning more about what their American counterparts did on the job, *even if that meant forgoing salary or wage increases.* Second, indications exist that the maquiladoras in some border regions are beginning to stabilize. For example, in the Tijuana/San Diego area, the rapid growth seen over the past decade, which reached as high as 30 percent per year, has slowed to between 16 and 18 percent per year. Furthermore, growth is projected to remain stable or to decline only slightly over the next several years even with full implementation of NAFTA. In order to remain competitive with what will become an increasingly "in demand" resource, organizations should begin now to invest in career development for their workers to create opportunities and build in incentives for longer-term commitment.

IHRM Design Philosophies and Maquiladora Effectiveness

We have found three HRM design philosophies in maquiladoras—(1) a mechanistic, control design; (2) a paternalistic, human relations design; and (3) a developmental, human resource design—which we label IHRM. Table 2 identifies the strategic outcomes for both the MNE and Mexico associated with the three HRM designs. The costs and benefits associated with each design are discussed in the following sections.

Control-Based HRM Design

As mentioned earlier, MNEs can have a short-term, low-cost productivity objective. For these MNEs, a control-based HRM design is sufficient but not without cost. Control-based HRM strategies rely on power-coercive techniques, which are primarily based on negative reinforcement approaches such as docking pay, public chastisement, and employee termination as solutions to a variety problems such as tardiness or errors.

The control HRM design is characterized by a focus on control of worker behavior—often through punishment—to achieve economies and incorporate goal-congruent behavior; little attention is paid to motivating or developing the worker; authority is top-down, as are communication patterns with the exception of task-specific clarifications, which may be bottom-up. This approach is consistent with the HRM practices of the Third Stage Controlled Growth identified by Milliman, Von Glinow, and Nathan or the Phase 3 Multinationalization stage identified by Adler and Ghadar.[16]

These control-based designs are typically implemented in a relatively short time. They are, however, also associated with high levels of conflict,

TABLE 2
Benefits of Maquiladora HRM Designs

Design		Strategic Benefits
1. Control	MEXICO	Moderate level of benefits: Job specific training & FDI.
	MNE	Moderate to low level of benefits: Variable Cost/High Quality Outputs & Very Low to Negligible Cultural Capability
2. Human Relations	MEXICO	Moderate to low level of benefits: FDI
	MNE	Low level of benefits: Variable Cost/Variable Quality Outputs & Moderate Cultural Capability
3. Developmental Human Resource	MEXICO	High level of benefits: Training and Development & FDI.
	MNE	High level of benefits: Low Cost/High Quality Outputs & Cultural Capabilities

much of it rooted in cross-cultural issues. In maquiladoras this conflict results in increases in turnover and absenteeism, and higher costs associated with selection and training. It is not uncommon for MNEs to abandon their maquiladora operation because of the costs associated with an overreliance on this conflict-laden approach. For MNEs that use this HRM design and continue maquiladora operations, reports of quality and productivity deficiencies abound.

Human Relations–Based HRM Design

The longer-term human relations–based HRM design is a middle stance in which MNEs meet both increased productivity and improved worker satisfaction objectives. Human relations–based strategies rely on rational-empirical techniques, such as training or cross-training for specific tasks, and use of culturally appropriate rewards such as subsidized lunches, make-up kits, and records.

The human relations design is characterized by a looser approach to control; absolute top-down authority and communication patterns; and rewards and promotion based on workers "being in favor" with supervisors or management. It has been characterized as relying on "paternalism" as the basis of motivation. The human relations design uses limited training that focuses on task-specific requirements, which often takes the form of a worker being assigned to observe another worker for a "couple of hours" before beginning a new task. Like the control design, this design is consistent with the HRM practices identified in Controlled Growth or Multinationalization stages with one notable exception: parental HRM control methods are rarely incorporated into the Mexican affiliate.

This design necessarily requires more time to implement than does the control-based HRM designs. An advantage to human relations–based designs is that they typically produce lower levels of conflict than do control-based designs. Since implementation of this design typically results in productivity gains and satisfaction improvements, they are also associated with lower levels of turnover and absenteeism, and with reduced selection and training costs. Given these benefits, maquiladoras that pursue this less conflict-laden design would likely emphasize both task-related and quality-focused worker training programs.

Human Resource-Based HRM Design

Finally, MNEs can simultaneously pursue productivity, satisfaction, and development objectives. In this case, a long-term human resource-based design is necessary. Such long-term HRM designs rely on normative-reeducative techniques, are process oriented, and are aimed at generating improvements in worker satisfaction and development.

The human resource design integrates control, motivation, and developmental needs. This developmental approach includes a sophisticated reward system that provides an extensive array of culturally and contextually appropriate benefits, as well as training and development programs that reduce overall cost and improve quality *and* that target developmental and general education needs of workers. Worker development is also enhanced through the developmental use of the performance appraisal system. This approach is consistent with HRM practices identified by Adler and Ghadar as a Globalization Phase IV approach or by Milliman, Von Glinow, and Nathan as a Fourth Stage Strategic Integration approach.[17] Strategy and HRM researchers alike find that the globally effective MNE must have the ability to implement the firm's overall global strategy while simultaneously being highly sensitive to the host country and its culture in order to maintain competitive advantage.[18] This is what the most effective maquiladoras do.

Although this design must be implemented over a longer time, attainment of its objectives is associated with the lowest level of conflict and with maximum gains in productivity, levels of satisfaction, and overall employee development. Consequently, turnover and absenteeism are lower in maquiladoras using this design. However, training and selection costs, at least in the short term, are likely be higher than those encountered in maquiladoras pursing shorter-term HRM designs. Nevertheless, an emphasis on training and selection results in a work force capable of producing world-class quality products that meet demanding customer schedules. Figure 1 illustrates the costs and results of these three HRM design philosophies.

FIGURE 1
HRM Strategy Costs
and Benefits

Source: M. C. Butler and
M. B. Teagarden (1993),
Strategic management of
worker health, safety and
environmental issues in
Mexico's maquiladora
industry, *Human Resource
Management,* 32(4).
Based on R. Chin and K.
D. Benne (1976), General
strategies for effecting
change in human systems,
in W. G. Bennis, K. D.
Benne, R. Chin, and K. E.
Corey (eds.), *The planning
of change,* 3rd ed. (New
York: Holt, Rinehart and
Winston).

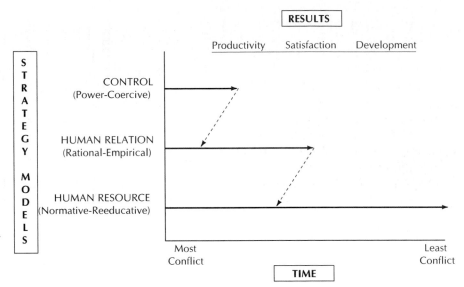

Human Resource-Based IHRM Design as Best Practice

We feel there is a compelling reason for MNEs to consider the strategic human resource–based IHRM design previously outlined in their maquiladoras: Customer preferences change over time. Customers who are satisfied with low cost now may well expect low cost, high quality and rapid delivery in the near future—especially if global competitors up the ante. Development of a work force that can deliver on these more sophisticated demands takes investment in training, development, and time. MNEs that opt for strategies that yield only short-term benefits place themselves at risk in the long-term competitive arena where ability to compete on cost, quality-based differentiation, and speed are likely to be critical.

IHRM and Strategic Capability

MNEs that embrace the human resource philosophy in their maquiladoras are building strategic capability in several ways. They are establishing "insider" status in Mexico by providing tangible benefits that go beyond foreign direct investment (FDI) into the country; they are building a work force that is capable of producing world-class quality outputs that can compete head on with outputs produced in Asian sites; and they are building cultural capability that will serve them as manufacturers and sellers in Mexico *and* throughout Latin America. When NAFTA is fully implemented, this capability will extend to the entire North American community.

Effective IHRM design has implications for MNEs *and* for Mexico that reach far beyond the maquiladora. To the degree that culturally appropriate and effective IHRM systems can be developed and implemented in maquiladoras, Mexico is the recipient of valuable "soft" technology—HRM technology—which spills over to other maquiladoras and to Mexico's domestic industry. As the application of effective IHRM practices is diffused throughout the maquiladora industry, maquiladoras become an increasingly attractive off-shore manufacturing site for MNEs, thus increasing the likelihood that higher levels of FDI and increased industry infrastructure development will occur. Also, MNEs are willing to transfer more technology-intensive manufacturing processes when they believe their affiliate will be effective. Thus, effective maquiladoras serve as a magnet for additional technology-intensive manufacturing investment.

MNEs using maquiladoras benefit in several ways as well. To the degree that maquiladoras represent an effective off-shore manufacturing option, MNEs enjoy the benefits of low labor and other factor costs; proximity and ease of access to U.S. markets and suppliers and thus low transportation costs; control enhanced by proximity to parent firms in the United States; and preferential treatment on reimported products—all of which can contribute to global competitiveness. Maquiladoras also represent an excellent incremental expansion opportunity for MNEs that plan to take advantage of NAFTA.

Finally, there are even greater benefits from effective maquiladora use that can accrue to MNEs, benefits that have implications for the MNE's long-term global competitiveness. Effective management of a maquiladora represents significant challenges to the MNE's ability to manage global diversity—the myriad cultures and contexts in which MNEs operate. As MNEs learn to be effective maquiladora managers, they also learn how to be effective managers of global diversity. Other cultures and contexts that the MNE encounters may well be very different, but the processes they use to be effective managers in the face of diversity remain the same. Ultimately, those MNEs that master the management of global diversity—those that best leverage their *human* assets wherever they are located—will be the MNEs that win the global competitiveness challenge.

The Other Side of Jim Miller's Challenges

Jim was certain that the challenges he faced were not uncommon in maquiladoras. He decided to discuss them with the group of maquiladora HR managers who met every other week for lunch. Despite the fact that they competed with one another for employees, and some even competed for customers, as a group they were dedicated to enhancing the state of HRM in Tijuana's maquiladora industry. Most of the HR managers in this group were Mexicans who had been active in the maquiladora industry for twenty years or more. They had repeatedly invited Jim to join them. Up until this time, however, Jim thought the meetings would keep him away from the plant unnecessarily, and he was suspicious of the contributions that an HR manager could make. After several meetings, Jim was able to see the other side of these challenges.

Juan Lopez.   Jim explained to the HR managers that he was shocked when Juan Lopez quit. ElectroMex was paying him well and giving him a lot of opportunity to show off his skills. Juan was a graduate of Monterrey Institute of Technology, one of Mexico's top engineering schools. Although he was young, Juan was well educated and had the promise of being an excellent engineer. However, when Juan asked to attend special quality training sessions offered by the local university, Jim had to turn him down because USE did not pay for such training. Jim had been delegating responsibility to Juan and tried to help him as little as possible so that he would learn by doing. Often, when Juan had asked for help solving a problem, Jim said he was too busy. Jim thought that this would force Juan to work through the problem and figure it out for himself. The week before Juan resigned, Jim had yelled at him in front of several production workers for making a mistake in the production schedule.

One HR manager commented that skilled workers like Juan Lopez were in very high demand, and that maquiladoras like his worked hard to retain them. He suggested that it was possible that Juan had been hired away by another maquiladora and pointed out that there were several things he would have done differently. First, yelling at a Juan, especially in front of his subordinates, was most disrespectful. The HR manager would have waited until they were alone and discussed the issues in a more respectful manner. In addition, he explained that brushing Juan off when he sought advice was probably confusing. A young engineer would expect his more senior, experienced manager to make judgment calls and to save him from making mistakes that would make him look foolish in front of his workers. In exchange the young engineer would work hard and be loyal. Finally, the HR manager explained that additional training, such as that requested by Juan, was a highly desired perquisite. It was an important sign that the recipient was appreciated and valued.

A second HR manager laughed slightly and admitted that he had hired Juan. Two of Juan's former classmates—both very good engineers—were working for his maquiladora, and they knew that Juan was not satisfied with his job. Juan felt that he was not respected by his manager. When a new engineering slot opened up, they suggested that the company take a look at Juan. They did and were delighted to be able to hire him. His compensation package was very similar to that at ElectroMex with a few important differences. Most important among these was that Juan began his new job with a three-month training program at the maquiladora headquarters in San Diego. After he returned, the company agreed to pay for completion of an MS in quality management, to be completed in the evenings at a local university. Finally, he was to participate in the mentoring program in which he would be assigned a senior engineer to mentor him during his first two years at the company. ElectroMex's loss was Juan's gain!

Maria Perez.   Maria Perez, a forty-four year old mother of six, was an outstanding worker. Maria and several children had come to Tijuana to live with her sister seven years ago after her husband was killed in a farming accident. She had worked in the ElectroMex subassembly department since the day the maquiladora opened. This was the first "real" job Maria had ever had.

Maria was mature and well respected by her co-workers. They all gravitated to her when they had problems with an assembly. Everyone knew that she had more experience with these than anyone else, and she patiently guided her co-workers through what was required. If someone fell behind in their work, Maria would cheerfully pitch in and help them catch up. When her co-workers had personal problems, she was their friend, confidante, and surrogate mother. When Jim offered her the promotion, she turned it down. She simply said, "Mr. Miller, I am a worker. What do I know about supervising? Thank you, but I like the job I have." This promotion offered a large salary increase and a lot more status. Jim was puzzled that Maria would turn down such a good opportunity for advancement.

The HR managers listened quietly as Jim explained what had happened with Maria Perez, and they appreciated his frustration. Career planning can be very challenging in the maquiladora context. One manager pointed out that there was a gigantic cultural chasm between Maria Perez and Jim Miller. Jim loves his career—he lives for his work. Maria, on the other hand, loves her family and friends—she works to live! Maria was very satisfied with her job. As a supervisor, her relationship with her co-workers would have changed. She could no longer be their friend. She would have to be their boss, and push them to meet the new production schedules, rather than help them. The higher status was not important to her. She was doing honest work and should be respected for that. In addition, the increased salary would have come at great risk. Maria had mastered the assembly jobs. She knew what to do. She did not know what being a supervisor required. From what she had seen, supervisors worked longer hours and got in trouble when there were problems. Finally, the other supervisors were younger men, most of whom had very good educations. Maria had finished sixth grade. She had not had their opportunities. She was certain that she would not fit in with the other supervisors. Maria did not want to risk losing her assembly job by taking the promotion.

Jim had been right in letting Maria remain in her old job. He decided that he could best use Maria as an informal leader. Although he now understood why Maria had turned down the promotion, he still had a supervisor position to fill. When he asked, Maria Perez suggested that he consider Lupe Cisneros, a young assembler who had been with ElectroMex for two years. She had worked for Sony for three years but took the job at ElectroMex because it was much closer to her home and three cousins worked there. Lupe was a high school graduate who spoke English and had taken quality and supervision courses at Sony and at the local technical institute. Maria said that Lupe learned very quickly. She thought that Lupe was prepared to be a supervisor and that she would enjoy the promotion. Jim offered Lupe the promotion and she accepted with enthusiasm.

The Productivity Challenge

Soon after Jim arrived at ElectroMex, he initiated a quality program on the automated lines in which supervisors were given bonuses for quality ratings above 98 percent in final inspection.[19] These supervisors, all men, were responsible for scheduling the work, adjusting malfunctioning equipment, monitoring ongoing quality of the process, and training new line workers. Jim had introduced the new program with a day-long training session to make sure that all supervisors understood their new responsibilities. At the end of the day, he asked if anyone would like more training or information. He asked, "Do you all understand what you will be doing?" All responded that they did. He asked, "Do you all understand how to do your new jobs?" Again, they all responded affirmatively. Satisfied, Jim launched the new program the next week. In the ensuing six months, Jim has seen material use double. This was perplexing because although quality ratings remained very high, production efficiencies were low and material use inexplicably high.

Discussions with the HR managers shed light on several mistakes that Jim had made. There was a consensus that the supervisors did not have enough training before implementation of the quality program. It was very likely that they did not completely understand how to carry out all the new tasks assigned to them. Most of these supervisors were young men who had not had extensive experience before being promoted. Several HR managers suggested that "machismo" would prevent these supervisors from admitting ignorance and that respect for authority would require that they respond affirmatively to please their new boss. Finally, one manager pointed out that, in this case, bonuses were being paid simply on the basis of quality. They were not linked to material use, or to overall productivity. As one of the managers said, "Jim, you get the behavior you reward—even in Mexico."

When Jim returned to the plant, he decided to spend much more time on the plant floor, observing his workers instead of asking questions. After a week it became clear that the supervisors were very good at scheduling work and fairly good at training new workers. But they did not know how to adjust malfunctioning equipment. Jim started working with them to teach them how to adjust the equipment, something he had done for years at USE. As the supervisors became more skilled working with the automated equipment, material use quickly came into line, productivity increased dramatically, and quality remained high.

In the course of this training, Jim had become particularly friendly with Pablo Martinez, who was slightly older than most of the other supervisors. One evening after work Jim told Pablo how happy he was about the improvements. Then, in confidence, Pablo told him that before the training the supervisors were secretly throwing out the bad pieces every night. Jim now realized that the Mexican supervisors were too proud to admit that they did not know how to adjust the malfunctioning equipment. So they chose to discard bad pieces. Jim now understood the productivity dilemma.

What Has Jim Miller Learned About Managing in Mexico?

Jim reflected about his learning curve regarding managing an operation in Mexico. When he accepted the challenge to turn ElectriMex around, Jim thought that his primary obstacles would be technical. He never anticipated that people issues would nearly be his downfall. To begin with, he had underestimated the importance of an effective HRM system. He was in charge of the personnel department, and it was staffed with two clerks who made sure that necessary paperwork was done. Despite his MBA, reward systems, training and development, and career paths were foreign concepts to him. To make matters worse he and headquarters were very insensitive to the very real cross-cultural differences that exist between American and Mexican cultures.

USE had given Jim no training or other preparation before posting him at ElectroMex. Jim was going to live in San Diego, just like his predecessor, and cross the border every day for work. It was not as if he was really going to be in a foreign country. When he arrived, Jim had a two-week overlap with his predecessor and was then on his own. He did not even have time to learn the new job himself before he was expected to perform. Nevertheless, it looked as if he had a good handle on turning the plant around—the productivity reports were getting better and better. But Jim decided there were several things he was going to do to ensure that things would keep moving in the right direction.

To begin with, he was going to hire an experienced Mexican HR manager for ElectroMex. Across the past few months, Jim had learned the invaluable role that these managers play in the competitiveness of the maquiladora, and he respected their expertise. He felt that if there had been a cross-cultural guide, for example, an experienced HR manager, to help him handle the people side of the operation, he would have made many fewer painful mistakes. Jim also decided to attend meetings more actively with other maquiladora managers to keep learning the best practices in the industry. He realized that he might have to change his management style a bit and that he certainly would not yell at employees in the future. Finally, he was going to learn Spanish. Jim decided that his job was in a foreign country, and that being able to talk directly with his subordinates would help ensure his success in meeting the turnaround challenge. Despite Jim's earlier doubts, perhaps USE had selected the right person for the job.

Endnotes

1. This is a composite case based on the authors' observations in numerous maquiladoras. U.S. Electronics and ElectroMex are fictitious companies.
2. Sanderson, S. W., & R. H. Hayes (1990), Mexico—opening ahead of Eastern Europe. *Harvard Business Review*, September-October, 32–42.
3. They are also called twin plants, or the in-bond industry. Twin plant stems from the belief that there would be similar plants on each side of the border; the U.S. side completing capital-intensive functions and the Mexican side labor-intensive functions. In fact, less than 10 percent of the maquiladoras have a twin plant in the United States. The in-bond term stems from the requirement that raw materials and supplies shipped to Mexico be processed and then reexported to the United States. To guarantee reexport these inputs are bonded.
4. For additional information see Teagarden, M. B., M. C. Butler, & M. A. Von Glinow (1992), Mexico's maquiladora industry: Where strategic human resource management makes a difference, *Organizational Dynamics*, Winter, 20(3), 34–47.
5. For a more in-depth discussion of this issue, see Von Glinow, M. A., & M. B. Teagarden (1988), The transfer of human resource management technology in Sino–U.S. cooperative ventures: Problems and solutions, *Human Resource Management*, 27(2), 201–229.
6. For a discussion of strategic international human resource management, see J. Milliman, M. A. Von Glinow, & M. Nathan, Organizational life cycles and strategic international human resource management in multinational companies: Implications for congruence theory, *Academy of Management Review*, 1991, 16(2), 318–339; P. J. Dowling & R. Schuler, International dimensions of human resource management (Boston: PWS-Kent, 1991); and Adler, N. J. & F. Ghadar (1990), Strategic human resource management: A global perspective (pp. 235–260), in R. Piper (ed.), *Human resource management in international comparison* (Berlin: de Gruyter).
7. See Devanna, M. A., C. J. Fombrun, & N. M. Tichy (1984), A framework for strategic human resource management (pp.33–51), in C. J. Fombrun, N. M. Tichy, & M. A. Devanna (eds.), *Strategic human resource management* (New York: John Wiley & Sons).

8. Teagarden, M. B., M. C. Butler, & M. A. Von Glinow (1991), op. cit.; M. C. Butler & M. B. Teagarden (1993), op cit.

9. See N. Clement, S. Jenner, P. Ganster, & A. Setran (1989), *Maquiladora resource guide* (San Diego, CA: Institute for Regional Studies of the Californias, San Diego State University).

10. For additional information on Mexican culture, we suggest Robert Pastor and Jorge G. Castaneda, *Limits to friendship: The United States and Mexico* (New York: Alfred A. Knopf, 1988); Eva S. Kras, *Management in two cultures: Bridging the gap between U.S. and Mexican managers* (Yarmouth, ME: Intercultural Press, Inc., 1989); Alan Riding, *Distant neighbors: A portrait of the Mexicans* (New York: Alfred A. Knopf, 1985); and Patrick Oster, *The Mexicans* (New York, Harper & Row, 1989).

11. "Cultural" arguments are refuted by J. Carillo and A. Hernandez in *Mujeres fronterizas en la industria maquiladora* [Border women in the maquiladora industry] (Mexico: SEP/CEFNOMEX, 1985); and M. P. Fernandez-Kelly, *For we are sold, I and my people: Women and industry in Mexico's frontier* (Albany, NY: SUNY Press, 1983).

12. For example, see B. Stratton, Learning the language is not enough, *Quality Progress,* January 1989, 16–21; and E. Kras (1989), op. cit.

13. See Porter, M. (1980), *Competitive strategy* (New York: Free Press).

14. See Devanna, M. A., C. J. Fombrun, & N. M. Tichy (1984), op. cit.

15. Suggested in L. Elias's article "Recruitment South of the border," *Twin Plant News,* January 1991, 9–10.

16. See J. Milliman, M. A. Von Glinow, & M. Nathan (1991), op. cit.; and Adler, N. J., & F. Ghadar (1990), op. cit.

17. Ibid.

18. This research includes M. B. Teagarden and M. A. Von Glinow's Contextual determinants of cooperative alliance effectiveness: Mexican evidence, *Management International Review,* 1990, 30 [special issue], 23–36; C. Bartlett & S. Ghoshal (1989), *Managing across borders* (Boston: Harvard University Press).

19. This challenge was suggested in M. E. Deforest, Managing a maquiladora, *Automotive Industries,* 169, May 1989, 72–74.

Human Resource Management in Foreign Affiliates in Hungary

David C. Bangert   University of Hawaii-Manoa

József Poór   Hay Management Consultants, Budapest

*I refuse to accept the stigma of the past by the term redundancy.
I refuse to be guilty. We have started work with the necessary
head count. If supply orders are received following successful
negotiations, we will hire more highly qualified workers,
although such people are hard to find in Hungary.*

Harold Codd, first CEO of the Ganz–Hunslet joint venture,
at the beginning of his regime

In socialist Hungary, the Ganz Mávag Company was an industrial giant. In 1987, in tandem with the evolution of government philosophy, the company divided into seven autonomous organizations and six smaller companies. One of the successors was Ganz Engine and Wagon Works. The Works, with its main plant in Budapest, inherited most of the debts of its predecessor—estimated at 17 billion forints (US$200 million), as compared to its estimated worth of 2 billion forints (US$25 million). Bureaucratic blundering curbed several attempted plans to salvage the company.

Hunslet, a subsidiary of a British engineering group, Telfos Holding, made an attractive offer to buy the factory and form a joint venture. The government agreed; the failing facility was acquired in late 1987. Hunslet restructured the plant at high costs in a gigantic year-long effort. Thus strengthened, Hunslet's goal was to establish a center of European railroad engine and car production.

Funding for this research was provided by the University of Hawaii's Center for International Business Education and Research and Hay Management Consultants (Budapest). We thank Linda Harris for her editorial assistance.

This marriage was necessary to the Hungarians, considering that the heavily indebted plant was on the verge of collapse. With obsolete infrastructure, poor product quality, and weak management, the company had no hope of expanding its position in the market. On the other hand, Hunslet sought to expand its global capacity. It forecasted a potential order to replace several thousand outdated British rolling stock. Also, the building of the "Chunnel" between Great Britain and France offered another market opportunity.

The Hungarian workers' attitude at the end of the 1980s was described by one of the Ganz managers as: "Everybody got a salary and everybody tried to idle as much as possible." Workers had no responsibility; their intellectual efforts were not appreciated. The quantity and quality of the output suffered.

Layoffs had begun before the arrival of the British managers. From a peak of 1,500, the workforce diminished to 1,000. The foreign managers continued the reduction to 750. From the British point of view, redundancy is not equal to layoff in the classic meaning of the term. Redundancy is necessary to ensure survival of the venture.

Although the Hungarian side agreed with the need to reduce staff, employees were upset. A conflict of values took place—the old concept of job security and "one's right to a job" clashed with the concept of cost efficiency and profitability. An assistant manager summarized the change with: "I could not sleep for two weeks. I kept thinking about telling people 'Thank you. Your work is not required.' I troubled myself a lot for every person. One of them was a good friend, another one has three children, another has worked here all his life. It was easy to find reasons against dismissing them. We had no alternative. It was a matter of life or death from the point of view of the company."

Introduction

Hungary and the rest of Eastern Europe need capital investment; managerial, marketing, and technical expertise; and access to worldwide distribution networks. The one-party political and power system collapsed in Hungary at the end of the 1980s. Hungary is well on the way from dictatorship to democracy. The dizzying speed of Hungary's four-year capitalistic renaissance has tied the country—now an associate member of the European Economic Community—more closely to the West than anytime in decades. This move to capitalism ignited a transformation of human resource management practices within Hungarian firms. Companies with foreign participation are leading the way. Firms are moving from command personnel policies to treating employees as valued resources.

There are more than 13,000 joint or wholly owned foreign ventures in Hungary. Many bring a Western style of management culture. They employ Western management philosophies, systems, and procedures. "Important international issues for a multinational corporation are the universality of accepted management practices and the proper management of human resources" (Wheelen & Hunger, 1992). Often, we find this issue overshadowed by western expatriates or consultants who cannot understand the reaction of local employees or managers to the revised management systems. They employ well-established Western management systems and forget to understand the basic features of the local management and organizational culture. The behavior, habits, and conventions of the work force cannot be changed quickly by the creation of new companies. Change takes time. Managers must deal with the full range of human resource management (HRM) issues during the transformation process. "In deciding whether to encourage a foreign populace to adjust to an international firm's accustomed practices or whether to develop new practices to fit a given population, the company should proceed with caution. Among the considerations are the cost and benefit to the firm of each alternative; the importance of the change to both parties; the possibility of participation in decision making; the way rewards for change may be allocated; the identity of opinion leaders; and the right timing" (Daniels & Radebaugh, 1989).

Challenging Hungary, inflation and budget deficits have been higher than expected. The inflation rate was 17 percent in 1989 and peaked at 39 percent during 1991. Economists expected price increases to slow down to below 20 percent in 1993. The unemployment rate increased from 2.1 percent at the end of 1990 to 8.5 percent at the end of 1991. This figure reached 10 percent at the end of 1992 and was expected to increase in 1993. Most unemployment is classified as structural. Although the labor force is generally well educated and skilled, some skills do not meet standards required by new technologies and systems. These two forces, high inflation and high unemployment, have strong, contrary effects on HRM policies, especially in compensation schemes. On one hand, high inflation presses firms and labor union leaders for higher wages so that workers can maintain their standard of living. On the other hand, high unemployment means the supply of willing workers exceeds the demand by firms for employees, a force toward lower wages.

The present economic and political changes in Hungary and Eastern Europe create a great demand for more accurate information about the region. We obtained the data for this chapter from three sources: 165 small and medium international joint ventures within Hungary (Kaucsek, Poór, & Ternovszky, 1992); six large, multinational corporations (Bangert & Poór, 1992); and observations of the forty to fifty clients of Hay Management, Budapest. The 165 international joint ventures completed a questionnaire that provided a valuable snapshot of the HRM practices in the new market economy of Hungary. To gain insight into the practices of larger firms, six in-depth, face-to-face interviews were conducted with the senior, in-country representative of multinationals that are committed to long-term presence in Hungary and Eastern Europe. Through these sources, we identified HRM trends.

Establishing an efficient HRM strategy is a complicated process. Human resource management is the term that replaces *personnel administration* or *personnel management*. The change in terminology represents the recognition that "a company's greatest asset is its people" (Kefalas, 1990). HRM is a proactive, positive force within the modern business entity, whereas personnel management is more clerically oriented and narrow. HRM has five major activities that can be divided into subtasks, as follows:

I. *Planning*
Ensuring that the organization fulfills statutory obligations.
Conducting job analyses to establish requirements for all positions.
Forecasting personnel requirements to meet the firm's strategic needs.
Developing and implementing a plan to meet these requirements.
Ensuring appropriate organizational design, growth, and synergy.

II. *Staffing*
Recruiting the required personnel.
Selecting and hiring personnel.

III. *Compensation and Benefits*
Designing and implementing compensation systems for all employees.
Designing and implementing programs that ensure employee health and safety.

IV. *Training and Development*
Orienting and training employees.
Designing and implementing management and organizational development programs.
Designing systems for appraising the performance of individual employees.
Assisting employees in developing career plans.

V. *Employee/Union Relations*
Serving as an intermediary between an organization and its union(s).
Designing discipline and grievance-handling systems (Byars & Rue, 1987; Milkovich & Boudreau, 1988).
Providing assistance to employees with personal problems that influence their work performance.
Designing and implementing employee communication systems.

The Influence of External Forces on HRM

Before discussing the major HRM activities in Eastern Europe, we will take a birdseye view of some of the forces that influence and explain the differences between Western and Eastern European HRM practices. The East Europeans often ask, "Do American or Western management practices and theory apply in Eastern Europe?" Although these practices have produced many success stories in a free market economy, there are forces and structures that limit the applicability of western practices to firms operating in Eastern Europe—regardless of ownership (Dowling & Schuler, 1991).

Former Communist System

East European economies have deeply embedded values, habits, and practices from the former system. Giles Merrit (1991) writes that "The powder train of revolution that flared across Eastern Europe in the autumn 1989 brought with it the end of an era. The significance of those events is only now becoming clearer." A poor work ethic was built on two significant foundations: (1) workers held little respect for supervisors, employers, and the party, and (2) jobs without meaning or responsibility were incorporated in order to achieve "full employment." Multinational corporations (MNCs) are caught by a tension between trying to avoid these characteristics by hiring young people who have not been influenced by the communist system and hiring seasoned managers from the former socialist enterprises with potentially valuable contacts.

Transitional Character of the Economy

East European countries are confronting two difficult challenges simultaneously: (1) the structural renewal of the economy and (2) the negative effect of a large GDP drop with high inflation and unemployment. Furthermore, the free social health system is disappearing. In response to employers and employees facing higher social and pension contributions, in-company pension funds are now starting to emerge.

Privatization

From East Berlin to Vladivostok, there are hundreds of thousands of State-owned enterprises in need of help. Change of ownership is a common therapy—selling to foreign or local investors. The new owners, attracted by seemingly low prices, forget the lessons learned from mergers and acquisitions in more stable environments. Ownership change can generate benefits only if the firm chooses to improve productivity or better product quality. Such a cultural change takes time.

Different Culture and Value System

Unlike the factory or office worker who sacrifices free time or holidays for additional pay, the worker with a peasant mentality refuses overtime. The peasant mentality drives the worker to own and maintain a small vegetable garden. Tending to that which they own (the garden) is a stronger drive than earning a better wage through overtime for an unrelated company. The people of Eastern Europe do not relate to the motivation theories of Maslow, McClelland, or Herzberg. Their world relates closer to the thinking of Freud (Hofstede, 1980).

The people of Eastern Europe are like the fox in Levitt's (1968) classic article, "The Globalization of Markets"—they are generalists. They are not hedgehogs who know everything about one thing. East Europeans are well trained. They can solve problems with basic tools. The workers were forced during the former communist system to solve shortages of spareparts while maintaining services. Many industrial giants of the communist era were manufacturing supermarkets. They had too many production profiles and services. These companies were forced to set up specific production units to solve their supply problems. Unfortunately, the economic scale of these operations was far below the world's scale.

Planning: Infrastructure of the HRM

The infrastructure of the traditional Hungarian human resources department consisted of two separate systems: white collar employees and blue collar employees. The personnel department, indirectly supervised by the chief executive officer, managed the white collar group. The labor department, supervised by the director for economic affairs, controlled pay decisions for the blue collar workers. The chief executives had no control over the wages paid to most employees; they had little control over nonwage benefits. These were directed by the State bureaucracy.

Because of the recent changes in the Hungarian economy, commercial environment, and legal framework (Labor Law, 1992), HRM has become an integrated managerial field. In many joint venture organizations, personnel managers are senior executives. In most companies with foreign ownership, the implementation of a new HRM system is directed by the foreign partner and carried out by the local HRM manager. HRM managers from the regional headquarters and outside consultants support this process.

The personnel specialists are increasingly expected to contribute to the solution of the company's strategic and mission problems. To accomplish this task, they first assess the firm's future personnel requirements. The second step is to choose a feasible combination of human resource management and developmental programs that will enable the organization to reach its stated objectives (Kefalas, 1990). The specialists establish the links between the organization's overall strategies and its human resource strategies. They are concerned with integrating all human resource decisions into a coherent human resource strategy (Milkovich & Boudreau, 1988).

Jean M. Hiltrop (1991) has studied the HRM practices of MNCs and domestic firms in Belgium and has conducted a literature search on companies in other countries. He found that foreign-owned firms are more advanced in their use of modern HRM techniques and devote more resources to HRM than do domestic firms. MNCs were especially progressive in using modern HRM practices to increase work performance, communicate financial results to employees, conduct initial orientation, and promote from within the organization. Domestic firms were better at resolving disputes and handling employee grievances.

At Ganz-Hunslet, the British management tried to change the firm's approach to HRM management. Some examples follow:

- *Benefits:* The British management rents holiday places in the country for its employees. Several hundreds of employees receive personal letters in which the personnel managers thank them for their work, offer them the use of the holiday facility, and wish them a good vacation.
- *Motivation:* The visit by Prince Charles and Lady Diana was used for building team spirit. The media covered in detail the visit of the royal couple to Ganz-Hunslet Works. On that occasion, each employee received a letter signed by the CEO together with ten sterling pounds, informing them of the visit and noting that they, too, became members of the populous Ganz-Hunslet family.
- *Team Building:* Decorated GH T-shirts and factory sports days have been implemented.

Staffing: Expatriate or Local Manager?

There are different sources for staffing subsidiaries of multinational companies. "Because of cultural differences, managerial style and practices must be tailored to fit the particular situations in other countries. Most multinational corporations therefore attempt to fill managerial positions in their subsidiaries with well-qualified citizens of the host countries" (Wheelen & Hunger, 1992). "International firms commonly categorize managers as *locals* (citizens of the country where they are working) or *expatriates* (noncitizens)" (Daniels & Radebaugh, 1989). In Hungary, the locals can be further divided in terms of whether they were or were not managers of former socialist enterprises. "The expatriate group is further categorized as *home country* and *third country nationals;* these are, respectively, citizens of the country where the company is headquartered and citizens neither of the country where they are working nor the headquarters country of the firm" (Daniels & Radebaugh, 1989). Whenever possible, MNCs prefer to fill managerial positions with qualified locals. Some reasons are the following:

- Most people do not want to leave their home country.
- Expatriates are more costly.
- Often there are legal impediments to using expatriates.
- Local managers understand the local conditions and markets.
- Local managers help sales and morale by promoting a local image.
- Expatriates tend to take shorter-term perspectives.
- If top jobs are given only to expatriates, it may be hard to attract and keep good locals.

Still MNCs employ several hundred thousand expatriates worldwide. Reasons for using expatriates include the following:

- Personnel with requisite technical, managerial, or administrative competence are in short supply.
- Multinational experience gives upwardly mobile managers new perspectives.
- People transferred from headquarters are more likely to know headquarters policies.
- Third country nationals are likely to have the advantages of the expatriates plus be knowledgeable in the language, culture, and operating conditions of the country (Daniels and Radebaugh, 1989). For example, in Hungary, a seasoned manager from Austria may be desirable.

The greatest source of locals in Hungary are managers of former socialist enterprises. To better evaluate this staffing approach, first consider the basic characteristics of management selection under the previous system. A leading executive of a state-owned firm was appointed by a superior state authority. Successful managers were promoted by moving up within the present organization or transferring to another state-controlled agency. There was no executive labor market. Career advancement depended on pleasing those at the bureaucracy's apex. Understandably, managers strove to satisfy the bureaucracy and guard against making glaring mistakes. The former socialist economic system was characterized by the permeating influence of the Communist Party, shortages in supplies, lack of incentives, negligence in fulfillment of contracts regarding quality and quantity of goods, and failure to meet deadlines. These conditions made the introduction of entrepreneurship difficult despite the individual talents of managers. Managerial techniques from the West did not thrive in the socialist organization. They provided ideas to contemplate for a talented manager in the changing Hungarian environment. For newly formed joint ventures or fully owned companies, many multinational companies hired the former CEOs. Lack of capability in the MNC's home language was not an obstacle for selecting this CEO. To support him in restructuring from a state-owned firm to a competitive venture, the multinational companies delegated staff from its headquarters.

A lessor source for staffing the managerial positions is local people with generic international experience. MNCs hire people as managers who are well educated and cosmopolitan, regardless of their managerial experience. These individuals have multiple degrees and speak one or two foreign languages fluently. They may be recruited from several fields, especially from foreign trade. The booming privatization consulting industry engages a number of these talented people. Under the former system, many business-minded people were forced to be employed as writers or editors or by government research institutions. Both general intelligence and international background provide a sufficient base to learn the culture and managerial system of the foreign multinationals. Many multinationals provide these people with training abroad.

Another source is expatriate managers, either a home country national or a third country national. The latter is a costly decision. Most of green field investments of multinational companies in Hungary are managed by foreign expatriates. In the 1980s and early 1990s, the immigration, naturalization, and employment of a foreign citizen was liberal. The new decree of the Ministry of Labor, issued on 17 October 1991, is more restrictive. It requires, for example, permission of the Ministry of Labor's Local Labor Center of the Ministry of Labor to employ an expatriate. The main reason for this new decree is the growing unemployment in Hungary.

Hunslet appointed foreigners for top management positions—for example, the CEO and the financial manager. Hungary and Ganz had touched the life of the new CEO, Harold Codd, before his appointment. The new CEO's mother was born in Hungary. Fifty years ago, his grandfather was a director of Ganz factory. Codd visited the plant at the age of six. As a birthday present, he traveled in a steam engine. This was the beginning of his lifetime devotion to railways. He accepted this job offer with pleasure because he was convinced of the importance of this business and was proud to carry on the family tradition of working in the Budapest factory.

Finance Manager Steve Kostyál, head of the accounting department, was also of Hungarian ancestry, although born in Canada. Before joining Hunslet, Kostyál, fluent in several languages, worked as Duracell's European financial control manager and paved the way for his firm's operation in Portugal. He considered his new job a professional challenge and set to work with great ambitions.

Despite their Hungarian backgrounds, Codd and Kostyál faced the same frustrations that confront virtually every western manager in Hungary: Hungarians had learned to keep their heads down and stay clear of risks and initiative under Communism. This resulted in slipshod service in commercial shops and an almost pathological inefficiency in certain service areas: Bank transactions seem interminable, and a purchase at a pharmacy requires customers to stand in three separate queues. The absence of initiative, as one British manager recalls, meant being asked what color soap should go into the washrooms.

Compensation and Benefits

Traditional Pay Practice

The state controlled the basic values of the traditional socialist pay practice. Creating of an egalitarian pay and income structure was a high priority during the early years of socialism. Another crucial priority was full employment. During the early years, when forced industrialization was the top priority in Hungary, the government tried to employ the entire population of women and men. Often, the low pay level was defended by the argument that all family expenses could be covered from the combined salaries of the wife and husband. The state-controlled pay system limited the salary increases but permitted a wage increase to any group that the management could prove received low pay.

Countries under the socialist system suffered shortages of various goods and products. These shortages dominated their economies. The strong pressures of industrialization and the existence of parallel economic structures forced the government to implement Tayloristic, quantitative-oriented incentive systems. It would be an oversimplification to believe that these values were absolute and universal. They varied with time and in different industries, sectors, and jobs. The state strongly influenced all pay decisions. This system was not comparable with Western pay mechanisms that base wages on the job market (i.e., if a particular skill is undersupplied, firms bid against each other to get employees, thus raising the wage for that skill). In the traditional system, the main decision-maker was the State Planning Office, which set up tax and penalty rules for wage and salary increases. Within this framework, the management of the enterprise attempted to find the best payment structure for itself and its employees. During the past forty years, the government paid a steadily increasing percentage of the state budget to the employee social benefits.

New Pay Environment

"Designing a fair compensation system is one of the touchiest issues in international human resource management" (Kefalas, 1990). The general characteristics of the recent compensation practices in Hungary are in flux. The minimum wage is adjusted every January. As of January 1992, it was 8,000 forints (US$100) per month. Compare this wage against the Central Statistical Office's March 1992 monthly average wage in Hungarian state and private enterprises of 22,000 forints (US$275) (see Table 1). Greater

TABLE 1
Gross Hungarian Salaries in HUF,[a] March 1992 (US$1 = 80 HUF)

Sector	Worker	Office Worker	Average
Mining	21,790	35,155	23,946
Manufacturing	17,008	31,982	20,458
Food, drink, and tobacco	17,136	30,472	19,882
Textile and leather	12,404	28,569	14,964
Timber, wood, furniture, paper printing	18,960	42,417	25,398
Chemicals	23,009	39,675	27,773
Stone, clay, glass	16,249	29,517	18,914
Metallurgy, fabricated metal	19,127	31,693	21,990
Industrial machines and equipment	17,004	28,875	20,252
Others	13,402	27,931	16,365
Electric, gas, and water supply	23,674	42,860	28,911
Industrial average	17,895	33,336	21,458
Construction	14,616	32,801	18,488
Wholesale and retail trade	15,343	42,699	26,578
Eating and drinking	14,107	36,126	20,127
Transport and telecommunications	19,149	29,126	22,410
Finance, insurance, and property	25,096	35,118	34,521
Other services	15,579	33,203	22,419
Total	17,330	34,510	22,433

[a]Hungarian forint.

Source: International Database of Hay Compnet, 1992.

pay differentials are now created by company ownership than by industry, geographical area, or size. Threefold differences in pay between privatized companies and State-owned enterprises for similar jobs is not unusual. Where there are particular skill shortages, pay pressure can be even more acute. Western-style accountants, bilingual secretarial staff, and product marketing staff are in short supply. The pay market in these areas remains volatile, and wages are likely to continue to rise until the universities and training establishments can produce a sufficiently large body of trained personnel.

New joint ventures need to establish management teams. The compensation for the executive team is the thorniest compensation problem facing the MNC. We have discussed the advantages and disadvantages of foreign expatriate and local managers. If a foreign firm chooses to use expatriate managers for a substantial period, they must pay four to five times more to a foreign manager than to a local one. This presents problems relating to salary and benefit policies in Hungary and in international headquarters.

Firms must pay enough to entice people to move, without overpaying. Living in foreign countries is more expensive because habits change slowly and the goods that support the habits may be expensive, imported products. Also, the newly assigned individuals do not know how and where to buy (Daniels & Radebaugh, 1989). Noncash benefits may exceed those of the home office and local custom. The benefits often include private (boarding) schools for children, housing subsidies, vehicle use, extra vacation days, and funds for vacation travel. This extra compensation package to expatriates may cause resentment by local managers and local officials who do business with the expatriate. In the long term, it may be a problem when the firm replaces the expatriate with a local at the prevailing local, lower salary. In Hungary, local resentment is mitigated by foreign firms paying higher wages than 100 percent Hungarian-owned firms or the state. There is a high wage inflation for Hungarians with sophisticated managerial skills. (See Table 2.)

In 1980, top managers in the private business sector earned 2.9 times more than skilled workers. In 1987, this figure had risen to 4.29. Today, managers in the state sector and in 100 percent Hungarian privatized companies earn less compensation than managers of joint ventures and 100 percent foreign-owned companies. A recent survey shows manager-to-skilled-worker wage factors of eight or twelve in many joint ventures. This figure is less than six for state-owned companies ("Hay Remuneration," 1992).

Pay Control

During the past decade, the government greatly influenced all Hungarian firms. Ninety-nine percent of the labor force worked under the pay control system. This system regulated directly between 1950 and 1968, and later indirectly, the pay decisions in enterprises. The first Hungarian joint venture was formed in 1973. The joint ventures' work forces were free of state control.

TABLE 2
Gross Salary in Different Countries

Country	Salesperson, Group Leader (US$)	Department Head Leader (US$)	Managing Director (US$)
Austria	$ 51,100	$ 98,200	$ 169,400
Belgium	47,300	93,500	157,900
France	46,870	83,200	124,300
Germany	57,300	102,200	170,800
Hungary	8,000	17,400	42,900

Source: International Database of Hay Compnet, 1992.

The former wage regulation system of companies was abolished in 1992. The new regulations apply equally to domestically and foreign owned firms. Now, if the salary increase of any company exceeds 23 percent, a new wage regulation system comes into force with a wage tax commencing with a 28 percent salary increase. This regulation does not affect companies established in 1992 or firms having fewer than ten employees.

The new labor law was introduced in Hungary on July 1, 1992. This new regulation requires that members of the company council and unions play an important role in the pay decision process, particularly at the non-managerial levels. Key elements of the law are the following (Petrik, 1992):

- The negotiated labor contract becomes the main determinant of the firm's pay scales.
- A National Collective Bargaining Council was established with representatives from the government, unions, and employers.
- Employees have the right to set up a company council. Smaller firms have the council as a committee of the whole, whereas larger firms use a system of representation.
- More than one union may represent the employee in a firm.
- Minimum benefits, such as number of holidays, health insurance copayments, and pensions, are defined.

Base Salary and Incentive Payments

At the top executive level, large bonus payments are common. The bonus may be twice as large as the annual salary. *There is a trend toward increasing base salaries and reducing the amount of bonuses paid.* At lower levels, consolidation of numerous allowances into base pay is becoming a common practice. These policies vary with sector, (e.g., the financial services sector rewards senior employees less than employees with similar jobs in industrial organizations). Within the financial sector, and in particular at top executive levels, bonus payments are a major component of total remuneration. At lower levels in the organization, the bonus is less important. The reaction to changing of compensation mixes varies. Younger employees are more willing to work for bonuses whereas older workers prefer the majority of their pay in the base. (See Table 3.)

NonCash Benefits

A new dilemma facing both employees and employers is the state's changing role in the health care and pension systems. Employees contribute 10 percent of their gross salary to cover health insurance and pension. This package of benefits does not cover higher expectations for improved benefits, especially by senior managers. The anticipation of the employees calls for the introduction of private health, pension, and life insurance.

TABLE 3
Base and Incentive Pay in Hungarian Joint Ventures

Job Title	Pay Differentials	Base Salary	Incentive	Base Salary + Incentive
General Director	14.3	81%	19%	100%
Department Head	3.2	79%	21%	100%
Bilingual Secretary	1.7	86%	14%	100%
General Administrator	1.0	84%	16%	100%
	(Base pay of study)			

Source: "Hay Remuneration Comparisons," March 1992.

Hungarian insurance institutions now provide different types of attractive policies, but companies are slow to embrace these benefits. The first US$50 of company-paid insurance is tax free in Hungary. The reasons for this slow reaction are unclear. It may reflect the low priority that Hungarian firms have traditionally afforded to HRM.

The joint ventures and foreign subsidiaries provide two types of cars: job-requirement and job-status cars. The job-requirement cars are provided because a car is essential for the job. Almost all salespeople of companies that participated in our compensation survey were provided job-requirement cars. Typical car models were VW Golf, Renault Clio, VW Passat, and Ford Fiesta 1.8L diesel. The job-status car are provided to almost all positions above deputy department manager irrespective of needs for business travel. Typical car brands are BMW, Mercedes, and Honda. In the past, the use of company cars did not attract additional taxes for employees.

There is a new trend by the state: An increasing number of elements in benefit packages will be taxed. In the extreme case, that most benefits are taxed at rates equal to cash, many companies will move to cafeteria benefit plans. Here again we see the impact of the state's redefinition of its role. Under the old system, noncash benefits were given to those favored, and the benefits were not taxed. Now, the benefit distribution is determined by the job market forces, and the state has chosen to tax the benefits.

Megatrends of the Hungarian Pay Practice

To put a number of these changes and trends into context, Table 4 summarizes the differences between the traditional Hungarian payment system and newly introduced Western-style compensation system.

Ganz-Hunslet used compensation to effect change. Due to the egalitarianism of the past 40 years, there was not much difference between the salaries of foremen and workers, and the prestige of the foreman was downgraded. Under the new management, foremen's pay can reach twice the wages of a line worker.

TABLE 4
Megatrends of the Hungarian Payment Practice

Traditional Pay Practice	*New Pay Practice*
Strong government control	Reduced government involvement
Egalitarian	Nonegalitarian
Grading structure based on hierarchy	Grading structure based on job or competency evaluation
Pay for status	Pay for performance
Pay for quantity	Pay for quality
Low base and high piecework ratio	High base and moderate piecework ratio
Tax-free benefits	Government taxation of benefits
Separate pay and personnel management	Integrated HRM, including pay

It has been a frequently reiterated principle (in fact for 40 years, although never implemented before) that the team and the individual must be rated according to performance standards and that extra work must be rewarded. Codd implemented a system commonly referred to as "autonomous teams." Workers make contracts for tasks such as assembling a chassis for a predetermined fee, which is paid to them after completing the task to standards. This compensation system allows them to earn three times the past year's income.

Compensation was not the only tool used to improve staff retention. Deliberate efforts have been made to create a climate where the people feel that the company counts on them in the long term. The management wants to achieve conditions where each person is proud of working for Ganz, feels important to the company, develops a strong awareness of "us," and builds the workers' self-esteem.

Training and Development

All organizations, after determining their human resource needs, face a "make or buy" decision. A firm that chooses a "make" strategy devotes resources to a comprehensive employee training and development program. The "buy" strategy means hiring experienced personnel by offering attractive compensation packages. In Hungary, for many job classifications, there are severe shortages. In other classifications, the personnel lack the latest technology or appropriate attitudes to produce world-class goods. Therefore, Hungarian-based firms are forced into a "make" strategy. Training and development at all levels in the organization are vital.

A survey of training practices in Hungary found a failure to determine the needs of the participants prior to commencement of the training. This lack of need identification led to some inappropriate training design. "Training is a process through which experiences are deliberately offered to trainees to enable them to absorb some new perspective, understanding, value, attitude, technique or skill" (Thomson, 1988). Some Western trainers classified the Hungarian work force as being in a category similar to that of the developing countries of Africa and Asia. Training that may lead to the successful implementation of Western marketing or engineering systems in a specific developing country may not be appropriate for the highly educated Hungarian managers. When inappropriate training is used, the Hungarians do not complain. They participate willingly as part of the program. This causes the expatriates to believe the training is appropriate.

This low profile by the Hungarians may be due to language, educational system, or the former command economic system. The number and quality of English speakers among the old and middle-aged generation is finite and variable (Stewart, 1991). During the past 45 years, Hungary belonged to the Russian-dominated Comecon. So, the former socialistic Hungarian government did not promote English-language training. Now, highly qualified engineers or managers cannot communicate effectively with their Western counterparts. Until the recent political change, the Hungarian education system followed German tradition. Business training was not a typical element of university education. During the past 40 years, the majority of the industrial workers were employed in State enterprises that were often irrational, bureaucratic, and lacking a "real owner." It encouraged laziness because work was not fairly compensated and work conditions were poor.

Challenging training has proven to be effective in Hungary. Hungarians are open-minded. Many have traveled abroad. Many others worked abroad and were successful. There has always been private economy besides the state sector (private plots for peasants, small landholders, retail shops, handicrafts made in cottage industries, and small ventures in industry and commerce). Seventy percent of the population took part in these activities where they obtained relevant work experience (Hungarian Statistical Office, 1988).

Training programs need to be planned with a view of the enterprise and the participants. The success of the training program depends heavily on an appropriate audit of the training needs of the enterprise and its employees. The implementation of the Western management systems instigates not only new methods but new behavior. Management training needs to redefine the corporate culture with the flexibility to adjust to environmental changes. Training programs are not completed after the lessons. Various operational programs need to support adopting a new approach and behavior. Joint sport activities, discussion groups, quality circles, self-learning work teams, and cultural programs help bring together managers, local people, and foreign expatriates.

Some different training approaches at Hungarian subsidiaries of the MNCs are the following:

- Training needs arose from the introduction of the parent company's management system in the field of marketing, controlling, operations, finance, computer utilization, or HRM. Often the need is satisfied by in-company training. In most cases, the training venue is in Hungary. Selected companies invite participants to their training center outside Hungary. Employees place higher value on foreign training than local training.

- Many Western MNCs buy all or part of a State-owned firm and privatize it. The privatization has significant implications on company culture. The creation of a winning team to successfully privatize the firm requires understanding between local and foreign managers. Both management groups need to form a unified management team. One- or two-day team building programs provide a good opportunity to work in teams on different problems of the newly privatized company.

- During the past few years, immense changes have occurred in Hungarian management training. Various schools (traditional universities and newly established private business schools) offer MBA or executive training programs. Various government aid programs from Western nations provide training support to talented young manager candidates. The managerial training in local institutions is now completely integrated; the curricula cover all areas of management (McNuilty, 1992).

An example of how training changed behavior can be seen at Ganz-Hunslet. The British were surprised to see that the Hungarian managers left work early or exactly at the end of the workday. Above a certain level, Western managers are inherently expected to work more than their formal working hours. When G-H took a closer look at the situation, they found that managers had less than eight hours of work assigned. A training program was implemented: British managers led the training for existing senior staff. The CEO and the financial manager gave presentations personally to the Hungarian management. Then the Hungarian management gave presentations to their respective subordinates. Work responsibilities were increased and redundancies removed. Because everyone was convinced of the usefulness of this training, it is now natural for the Hungarians to stay longer.

Employee/Union Relations

Hungary has ratified the international agreement that enables employees to establish trade unions. The state has not hindered the operations of the trade unions, nor may it interfere with their internal operations. But it is obliged to protect trade union activists. The state may not discriminate against any trade union. In Hungary, any organization may perform trade union tasks because there is no separate trade union law. For instance, several organizations are established to lobby the government for new trade union law. Other organizations are established for the achievement of trade union aims. They operate workers' councils, organizing the employees of one employer. The federation of state unions has been succeeded by a new confederation, MSZOSZ. The new unions, although separate from the Socialist party, have many of the same people in leadership positions (Jones, 1992). The goal of all these organizations is the representation of the workers' interest.

If a trade union asks for information from the employer concerning any employment-related issue, the employer has to answer. The trade union has the right to initiate a grievance. If the parties cannot negotiate settlement of the grievance, the matter is taken to a board of reconciliation. The interested parties can agree to binding or nonbinding arbitration. In case of failing to solve a conflict, the employees have the right to strike.

Trade unions often have collective agreements with companies. They cover all employees of the particular employer, including the person having concluded the agreement on the employer's behalf. Thus, from this aspect, Hungarian law treats managers the same way as any other employee.

At present, Hungary has seven major trade union groups. Their activity is not well coordinated. There are hostility and conflicts between the various unions. Trade unionism has rarely been center-stage in the Hungarian employment arena. New ventures are not obliged to recognize unions. Of the 165 international joint ventures surveyed in 1992, 93 percent did not have union representation.

At the Ganz-Hunslet plant, the role of the trade union is changing. The old trade union lost its importance and power. The former trade union secretary, who joined the plant in the 1950s as an apprentice, gave the following epitaph: "We have lost most of our strength. The trade union used to be part of the quadripartite decision making leadership of the company consisting of the management, the party organization, the trade union, and the party youth organization (KISZ). Now we are only invited to meetings concerning the whole range of employees, and I am only authorized to comment. When Codd carried out the first staff reductions, I only received some information right before announcement."

The plant used to be represented by the Vasas (Iron Workers) trade union; however, the plant's union left Vasas and even quit SZOT (National Council of Trade Unions) as of February 1, 1990, and formed a syndicate of its own. This process was strongly influenced by the British management who considered the old system unmanageable. The British suggested quitting the existing union and national council. Out of all 750 employees who might have joined the union, only 450 actually joined. There is one full-time trade union secretary paid by the British because Mr. Codd, himself, wanted a permanent contact person. The trade union and the management are on good terms; the trade union has tried not to make impossible demands, and the British management is doing its best to satisfy reasonable requirements.

The changing role of the trade union was most clearly evidenced in the handling of redundancies. To achieve staff reduction, the head count was fixed by the British, and redundancies were named by the Hungarians. The process had begun before the arrival of the foreigners ("life forced us to do it"); the British simply accelerated the process. The company carried it out fairly, without any subjective judgment, purely on professional grounds. Only 8 of the 250 dismissed persons protested through the labor arbitration committee. Their appeals were refused.

It is general opinion that the company has benefitted from staff reduction. "Since my university years we keep saying that people need some degree of job uncertainty to be motivated," a thirty-four-year-old line manager said to a British journalist. With growing unemployment, people are making an effort to keep the good jobs. Reduced staff has, thus, resulted in higher quality output.

There has also been noticeable improvement in work discipline. It seems that the poor work ethic that prevailed some years ago was a feature of the "socialist way of production" and not a Hungarian characteristic.

"When I came here as an apprentice in 1950, there was strict discipline," the head of the chassis and car assembly plant remembers. "Foremen were people who got their assignments before the war, that is, in a time when employment opportunities were limited. We had to arrive five minutes before starting the shift, prepare our tools on the bench, and keep working hard through the shift. We had a short lunch break at 2 P.M. If you did not do what you were expected to do, you were simply fired." By the time this gentleman became a foreman, people had changed. If he tried to scold somebody for being late or producing poor quality, he risked that the trade union representative, the party secretary, or the management would intervene. The working methods of foremen were often checked. Control of the workers was lost.

Conclusions

To succeed in the business world of the 1990s, firms must optimize their human resource deployment. Personnel are a firm's greatest potential source of sustainable competitive advantage. In Hungary, there are profound, important changes occurring simultaneously on national and local levels. These changes are stimulating major adjustments in HRM policies and practices.

While Hungary dramatically changes from a planned to market economy, MNCs are entering the business arena. Our research shows a definitive pattern. With time, MNCs deepen their commitment to establishing a presence in the Hungarian economy. Thus, two environmental factors have an impact on the local HRM practices: externally, the change from planned to market economy, and internally, the deepening commitment of the MNCs.

The external change process has three basic elements: price and market reform, restructuring and privatization, and redefinition of the state's role. These elements are driving changes in all major HRM activities: planning, staffing, compensation and benefits, training and development, and employee/union relations.

Price and market reform are reflected in the labor market. The price for labor is now established by the marketplace, not the State. This affects the staffing, compensation/benefits, and training/development activities. With firms actively competing for scarce skills, there is a rapid rise of managerial salaries. At the same time, the pay of the skilled, hourly workers is barely matching inflation. This increase in managerial salaries is causing firms to face a difficult decision. Should they "make" managers through training and development of their present staff? Should they "buy" managers by designing a desirable compensation and benefit package that will attract the already proficient local managers? Or should they simply transfer in expatriate managers? The options are perplexing. Local managers better understand the local environment and are less expensive. Already proficient local managers are scarce and quickly becoming as expensive as the expatriate managers. And expatriate managers know the MNC's corporate culture and have superior technological knowledge.

Restructuring and privatization compel a number of HRM adjustments. Large state-owned firms, splitting into a number of smaller entities, have a variety of owners. Often, the different owners are using different approaches to HRM. One group of owners is MNCs. Although making large capital investments and assuming ownership of Hungarian firms, MNCs are bringing in their own HRM concepts and practices. They are making the most extreme changes from the HRM practices of the former system. The greatest adjustments are to staffing and employee relations activities. International firms are avoiding unionization, thus allowing their local organizations to deal directly with their employees.

Redefinition of the state's role is easy to identify. Its impact on the prevailing HRM policies is not so easy to denote. Redefinition greatly affects the planning and compensation/benefit activities. The state has relinquished many of its functions, such as acting as the personnel office for the entire country, determining the majority of workers' pay, and staffing all important managerial positions. With the state no longer determining benefit packages for all employees, firms are filling the gap. The state is also changing the taxation regulations to treat noncash compensation as income. This may cause firms to go to "cafeteria" benefit schemes that give the employees options.

References

Bangert, David, & Poór, József (1992). Multinational involvement in Hungarian economy [in Hungarian]. *Vezetestudomany,* 2, 14–19.

Byars, Lloyd L., & Rue, Leslie W. (1987). *Human resource management.* Homewood, IL: Irwin.

Daniels, John D., & Radebaugh, Lee H. (1989). *International business, environments and operations.* Reading, MA: Addison-Wesley.

Dowling, Peter J., & Schuler, Randall S. (1991). *International dimensions of human resource management.* Boston: PWS-Kent Publishing Company.

Hay remuneration comparisons in Hungary: September–March 1992. (1992). London and Budapest: Hay Compnet.

Hiltrop, Jean M. (1991). Human resources practices of multinational organizations in Belgium. *European Management Journal,* 9 (4): 404–411.

Hofstede, G. (1980). *Culture's consequences.* Beverly Hills, CA: Sage.

Hungarian Statistical Office. (1988). *Employment in Europe in the 1980s* [in Hungarian]. Budapest.

Kaucsek, Gyorgy, Poór, József, & Ternovszky, Ferenc. (1992). Management and HRM of small and medium size joint ventures in Hungary [in Hungarian]. *Ipargazdasdag* (Feb.–Mar.): 38–44.

Jones, Derek C. (1992). Transformation of labor unions in Eastern Europe: The case of Bulgaria. *Industrial and Labor Relations Review,* 3, 452–470.

Kefalas, A. G. (1990). *Global business strategy: A system approach.* Cincinnati, OH: South-Western.

Labor law. (1992). In Hungarian Government Bulletin [in Hungarian], 30 March.

Levitt, Theodore. (1968). The globalization of markets. *Harvard Business Review,* (Nov.–Dec.).

McNuilty, Nancy G. (1992). Management education in Eastern Europe: Before and after. *Academy of Management Executive,* 4, 78–97.

Milkovich, George T., & Boudreau, John W. (1988). *Personnel–human resource management.* Homewood, IL: BPI-Irwin.

Merrit, Giles. (1991). *Eastern Europe and the USSR: The challenge of freedom.* Kogan Page.

Petrik, Ferenc, ed. (1992). *Handbook of new labor law* [in Hungarian]. Budapest.

Stewart, Allyson. (1991). If you are thinking of moving to Hungary. *Accountancy Age,* 4 July.

Thomson, George F. (1988). *A textbook of human resource management.* Institute of Personnel Management.

Wheelen, Thomas L., & Hunger, J. David. (1991). *Strategic management and business policy.* Reading, MA: Addison-Wesley.

Yin and Yang

The Interplay of Human Resources in Chinese–Foreign Ventures

Oded Shenkar Tel Aviv University, Israel
University of Hawaii-Manoa

Mee-Kau Nyaw The Chinese University of Hong Kong

Introduction

The telex, sent to Mr. Tony Fung, the Managing Director of the Ramada Renaissance Guilin hotel, and to Mr. Patrick Atlante, Vice President of Ramada International, Asia–Pacific Region, read:

> Urgent . . . Urgent . . . Urgent
>
> Re: Hotel Operation
>
> We wish to inform you on the below listed points which make it difficult to continue the operation of the Ramada Renaissance Hotel Guilin (Guilin Garden Hotel).
>
> (1) On the 21st Dec. 1987 at 0800 HRS the telephone Co. disconnected our telephone lines.
>
> Reason: Connection fee has not been paid yet.
>
> (2) On the 22nd Dec. 1987 our telex machine was disconnected,
>
> Reason: Connection fee has not been paid yet.
>
> (3) On the 24th Dec. 1987 we were informed that the electrical power would be disconnected.
>
> Reason: Bond for power plant has not been paid on which the local authorities insist. At the moment we are still being supplied with power

but since the problem has not been solved the power might be switched off at any given moment.

(4) On the 25th Dec. 1987 our water supply was cut off and the meter was removed.

Reason: Connection fee has not been paid yet.

(5) On the 31st Dec. 1987 Ramada International Inc. was refused the renewal of the management license for 1988, despite numerous meetings between the financial controller of the hotel and the official from the commerce administration bureau, where we were assured there would be no problems and the license would be renewed. . . . Despite our willingness and effort to keep the Ramada Renaissance Hotel Guilin operational we face increasing problems to do so. . . . We request urgent advice and instructions from the parties concerned as to how to proceed on this matter.

Your prompt reply will be appreciated and best regards.

> Rudolf Bruggemann, General Manager
> Ramada Renaissance Hotel Guilin

The collapse of the Ramada Renaissance Guilin hotel was anything but predictable. The hotel was conceived in 1984 as an equity joint venture (EJV)* between the Australian-based China Trade Omni-Development Center (CTODC) headed by Tony Fung, an ethnic Chinese, and China Youth Travel Service (CYTS) Guilin Branch, the local agency responsible for tourism in the Guilin area. Located at one of the most scenic spots in a city that has been a tourist mecca for centuries, the hotel, which opened May 1987, was ideally situated to benefit from a major growth in foreign tourism to China. Yet, in May 1988, *Ramada International* canceled its management contract with the hotel, citing the feud between the parties and a host of operational problems. At about the same time, the Dutch commercial bank, Hong Kong branch, recalled the mortgage on the property. In February 1989, the mortgage was paid by the Guarantor—the Guanxi International Trust and Investment Corporation (GITIC), which was to receive all fixed assets and equity. On September 5 that year, the hotel assets were put up for sale.

The fate of the Ramada Guilin hotel was the result of many factors, not least among them an ambiguous contract that led to a dispute over responsibility for utility fees and subsequent disconnection of power. The

---

*This chapter defines *equity joint venture (EJV)* as "a separate legal organizational entity representing the partial holdings of two or more parent firms, in which the headquarters of at least one is located outside the country of operation of the joint venture" (Shenkar & Zeira, 1987). Contractual joint ventures and other types of strategic alliances in which no shared equity, independent entity is formed, are excluded from the present analysis, as they are subject to a different legal framework and differ in their management structure and processes.

management of human resources was, however, a very prominent factor: A weak work ethic led to frequent thefts that went unpunished because of political pressure. Service was poor, and nepotism permeated the staffing of the local work force. When the son of a senior official in the water department, a hotel employee, was fired for stealing expensive meat from the restaurant, the water supply was cut off. In February 1988, seventy employees went on strike to protest what they claimed was an unfair withholding of new year bonuses (Lague, 1988).

Despite his experience, Tony Fung did not call into question the very wisdom of establishing an EJV in China. Himself an investor in another, successful EJV in the People's Republic of China (PRC), he announced that he has "built the hotel in the wrong place and with the wrong partners." Indeed, some of the hotel's problems have been attributed to the slow recovery of the Guanxi Autonomous Region from the Cultural Revolution, during which it suffered more than other Chinese regions and provinces, and to the combativeness of local officials, which is not necessarily typical of China as a whole.

This more balanced view of foreign–Chinese ventures is strongly supported by the available data. While certainly not the only foreign–Chinese EJV to have collapsed (for another publicized case, see the Hong Kong–based Sino On-line Corporation), foreign direct investment continues to pour into China, much of it in the form of EJVs. The *Beijing Review* (Feb. 4, 1991) reported that by the end of 1990, 4,091 EJVs had been approved by the PRC authorities, for a total of $2.704 billion of pledged investment, and $1.836 billion of actual outlays. With preliminary data showing a 131 percent increase in FDI for the first nine months of 1992 over the previous year, it is safe to assume that there are, at writing time, close to 10,000 EJVs in the PRC. This figure does *not* include an estimated 60,000 nonequity alliances. Many of these ventures have been very successful. Henley and Nyaw (1987) reported that more than 50 percent of the Shenzhen-based EJVs they studied achieved their profit objectives (see also "China Now Ripe," 1987). A similar figure was reported by A. T. Kearney, Inc. in its study of manufacturing EJVs. Davidson (1987) reports an even higher figure—over two-thirds of the EJVs in his sample achieved or surpassed their profit expectations. Successes have also been reported by the National Council for U.S.–China Trade (1987) which suggested that "only a handful" of the US–PRC ventures it had studied have failed. Campbell and Adlington (1988) report that a majority of U.S. (though not Japanese) companies surpassed their initial performance target. These achievements are all the more impressive considering the notoriously high rate of EJV failure worldwide (e.g., Young and Bradford, 1977). Beamish (1993), who has summarized twelve studies on EJVs in China, concluded that their stability rate was quite high in comparison to that of EJVs in developing country market economies, though performance has been low. A recent *Wall Street Journal* article suggested that success was the best-kept secret of PRC-based ventures. And many EJVs such as Hewlett-Packard China (HPC) and Guangzhou MC Packaging (GMCP), report reaching profitability much earlier than forecasted in their initial feasibility studies.

Although the reasons for EJV success or failure are numerous, human resource management is, without doubt, a major factor. Particularly vulnerable to the Chinese legacy of political and bureaucratic interference in enterprise affairs, human resource management became one of the major challenges facing EJVs in the PRC. Starting with early ventures, such as Tianjin-Otis (see Hendryx, 1986), the ability to resolve challenges in staffing, performance evaluation, compensation, and other human resource processes has proved to be a key to the survival and prosperity of China-based EJVs. Indeed, one of the first disputes between the parties to the Ramada Renaissance Guilin involved the staffing of important hotel jobs, a dispute that was later proved to be critical when the personnel manager, appointed by the Chinese, failed to carry out management orders pertaining to staff violations ("Partners Fight Plague," 1988).

The Institutional Context

Cultural and Institutional Encounters

All EJVs bring about a potential clash among the cultural, legal, political, and social systems of the respective environments of the venture and parents. In the case of Hong Kong, Taiwan, and overseas Chinese investors, the clash is limited to political, legal, and business practices, which partially explains why these investors are responsible for the majority of PRC–based EJVs. Although Chinese investors have a lesser cultural barrier to overcome, they must synchronize the extreme differences between the hybrid, "market socialism" planning system of the PRC, on the one hand, and the relatively free markets of their own environments, on the other.

The Western, and to a lesser extent the Japanese, investor must go appreciably beyond that. For instance, Bond and Hwang (1986, p. 229) offer that "American culture differs from Chinese culture precisely on those dimensions where the Chinese cultures cluster, namely individualism and power distance." Marked differences have also been found among the work attitudes and motivational structures of Chinese and Western employees (e.g., Shenkar & Ronen, 1987; Ronen & Shenkar, 1985), and between the interpersonal norms, and hence negotiation patterns, of the two groups (Shenkar & Ronen, 1987b). Such differences have been found not only vis-à-vis Americans but also other groups, for example, the Germans (Domsch & Lichtenbeger, 1991) and the Belgians (Van den Bulcke & Zhang, 1992), among others. Synchronizing such differences, or buffering them, is a tall task.

Governance Structure of EJVs: The Board of Directors

Bridging across multiple headquarters and frequently conflicting objectives, boards of directors in EJVs have been known to "take over" various managerial functions (Janger, 1980). They serve as a buffer to parents' demands, to reconcile divergent goals, and to translate them into a coherent management policy. In such a context, the staffing of board positions and their assigned authority become a major issue. The 1979 Joint Venture Law stipulated that "the Chairman of the board shall be appointed by the Chinese participant and its vice-chairman by the foreign participant." After the stream of foreign investment temporarily slowed to a trickle in the aftermath of the Tiananmen massacre, the PRC introduced changes in the EJV law, which, among other things, allow the foreign parent to appoint the board chairman. These changes took effect in 1990, so it is too early to estimate their impact.

Interviews conducted in Shenzhen SEZ in 1990 show that most EJVs have articles of association that stipulate the authority and responsibilities of the board. As might be expected, the articles are more detailed for larger ventures involving European or American parent firms than for smaller or medium-sized ventures with Hong Kong– or Macau–based parents. In most instances, the board decides on key personnel issues (e.g., the appointment of senior office holders such as general manager, deputy manager(s), chief engineer, and chief accountant and auditors), as well as on their authority and terms of employment.

Respondents in Shenzhen complained of a number of problems regarding the directors appointed by the Chinese authorities. First, the high turnover of PRC appointees to the board undermined the continuity necessary for effective decision making. Second, with many board chairmen simultaneously serving as heads of the administrative departments or industrial companies responsible for the EJV, they are often too busy to actively monitor the venture's affairs. Third, many board members merely serve as figureheads. Some are retired senior cadres with no business experience, whose board assignment is merely a reward for their past service to the state. Fourth, with almost every administrative department related to the EJV exercising the right to nominate a director, some genuine partners are deprived of their seat on the board and hence cannot participate in strategic decisions vis-à-vis the ventures.

The Role of Labor Unions

The Joint Venture Law stipulates that union representatives have the right to attend board meetings, albeit as nonvoting members. Such participation is not limited to human resource issues but includes operational and even strategic matters, adding to the weight of the Chinese parent by using the interlocking relationships of the union with various PRC agencies. In contrast to state enterprises, where workers are "masters of the house," trade unions are not mandatory in EJVs in the PRC. Yet, 92 percent of Shenzhen-based EJVs surveyed in 1987 had union representation. Like any enterprise in China, the EJV's union is a member of the local or industrial trade union. Unlike state enterprises, however, venture unions deal directly with the foreign parents or their representatives concerning labor disputes or grievances, and have usually opted for a consultative over a confrontational approach. When consultation fails, one or both parties can request arbitration by the local government, in accordance with the Provisions for Labor Management in Chinese–Foreign Joint Ventures. However, cases of arbitration seem to be rare because most unions appear to be cooperative and conciliatory. They organize vocational and technical activities, and educate the workers to "observe labor discipline" and to "fulfil the economic task of the enterprise." By law, EJVs have to allocate a sum equal to 2 percent of the actual wages of all staff and workers as union funds to finance these activities.

Also in contrast to State enterprises, the Joint Venture Law does not stipulate the role of the Communist Party committee. In one episode cited, the board of directors rejected a request to set up a Party organization in an EJV with no objection from the Chinese side. At the same time, the Chinese leadership seems to favor some form of Party organization in the EJV, and interviews in Shenzhen Special Economic Zone (SEZ) in 1990 revealed that party activities are carried out by the trade unions. The Party also exerts its influence via the senior trade unionists and directors, who are almost always Party members and adhere to Party line and policy. The Party's activities in the EJVs consist mainly of indoctrinating staff and workers to adhere to the Party line and to work in harmony with the investors.

Also channeled through the EJV trade unions are the activities of other mass organizations, such as the Communist Youth League, Youth Federation, and Women's Federation. Interviews revealed that the secretary of the local Communist Youth League is usually the vice president of the joint venture's trade union or a member of its executive committee. Union officials may also fill managerial positions in the EJV. At GMCP, the head of the union is an employee of the personnel department who has been transferred from one of the Chinese parents. A generalist, he delegates responsibilities in recruitment, compensation, training, and employee welfare to a number of assistants.

The Managerial Role

General managers of EJVs have close contact with the various administrative bodies and government agencies, in particular the Ministry of Foreign Economic Relations and Trade (MOFERT). After a venture is approved by the Foreign Investment Commission and is established, MOFERT or its authorized agent is responsible for guiding, assisting, or supervising the implementation of the EJV contract but is prohibited from issuing directives to the venture. For example, a venture may be assisted by government authorities to the extent of being guaranteed priority access to resources, but it will be left to work out its own production and operating plans. In the past, government departments dealt mainly with the general manager but now deal more with the board of directors. This seems to be related to the growing maturity of ventures and the gradual extension of the power of the board of directors relative to that of the general manager.

The tasks and responsibilities of a general manager are not stated in the joint venture laws or implementation regulations. The general manager of a manufacturing EJV in Shenzhen listed the following responsibilities:

1. To develop the joint venture's long-, medium-, and short-term objectives.
2. To formulate the strategy to achieve the enterprise's objectives.
3. To supervise the implementation of the strategic plan.
4. To assess immediate subordinates' performance.
5. To appoint divisional managers.
6. To readjust the organization structure to meet operational needs.
7. To arbitrate conflicts between departments or personnel.
8. To devise the major financial plan.
9. To liaise with the government, shareholders, consumers, and financial institutions, in order to promote good relations with them.
10. To deal with urgent and important matters.
11. To monitor the establishment of an effective control system.
12. To plan, implement, and control the overall development of the venture. However, in some ventures it is stipulated that a general manager has to consult with his deputies on major issues. Moreover, major documents have to be co-signed to take effect.

A recent study of managers of state and collective enterprises in Henan province, found that, although their managerial role structure was somewhat similar to that obtained from Western executives, the introduction of a political dimension had significantly altered this role (Shenkar, Ronen, Shefy, & Chow, 1993). And, especially in state units, managers had to show little initiative and had little willingness and ability to actively engage in the selection and development of human resources (Shenkar & Chow, 1989; Chow & Shenkar, 1989). We have asked Chinese general managers and deputy managers in Shenzhen what distinguished successful joint venture managers from factory directors in State-owned enterprises. They agreed on the following qualities: (1) initiative; (2) a strong background in policy and respect for the law; (3) knowledge of the relevant industry and possession of required modern management skills; (4) commitment to placing good people in appropriate positions and ability to work with them as a team.

Indeed, this is not an easy role: Around 40 percent of the Chinese partners said that substantial complexities affected their venture, and over 80 percent of the reasons given for difficulties revolved around one form or another of misunderstanding or mutual incomprehension of the other's objectives or methods. Confusion as to who had organizational authority was a particularly common source of friction.

Managing Human Resources in Chinese–Foreign Ventures

EJVs are unique in that they may have an extremely varied workforce, and China is no exception. The employees and the other "players" involved in the management of EJVs differ from each other in several respects: They come from different countries and thus hold diverse values and norms of behavior; they are recruited by different entities (i.e., the Chinese parent(s), the foreign parent(s), or the venture itself), and therefore feel a sense of allegiance to different firms; they work in separate countries (i.e., the countries where the headquarters of the foreign firms are located, or in China), and thus operate at different geographical and psychological distances from some of the major stakeholders; and they have different kinds of assignments (regular/ad hoc) and different possibilities for transfer, mobility, and promotion.

Table 1 briefly describes the many employee groups which can be found in Chinese–foreign IJVs. The exhibit illustrates the great variety of the IJV work force, and hints at potential conflicts that may arise among employee groups as a result of differences in nationality, location of employment, hierarchical echelons, and opportunities for promotion or transfer.

Staffing of Senior Positions

IJVs are owned by multiple parent firms, who typically wish to place their own transferees, expatriates, or appointees in key positions in the venture, on the assumption that whoever has the most people in charge will control the organization and guarantee fulfillment of its objectives. In many cases, friction also develops when the various parties disagree over the appropriate qualifications of personnel. The local parent may view the EJV as a way of "unloading" extra staff, leading to the appointment of underqualified, ineffective, and poorly prepared executives, who tend to flounder in the complex environment of the EJV. This tendency was nowhere more pronounced than in China, where years of Maoist indoctrination and a tradition of a centrally planned economy created a pool of passive, untrained managers, with little motivation and initiative. When assigned to EJVs, these managers face significant problems in adjusting to the more

TABLE 1
Employee Groups in Foreign–Chinese Equity Joint Ventures[a]

Employee Group	Nationality	Recruiter	Location of Employment	Level in EJV	Type of Assignment
Foreign parent expatriates	Foreign	Foreign parent	China	Upper	Regular
Chinese parent appointees	Chinese	Chinese parent	China	Upper	Regular
Foreign parent transferees	Foreign	Chinese parent	China	Top	Ad hoc
Chinese parent transferees	Chinese	Chinese parent	China	Top	Ad hoc
Chinese country nationals	Chinese	EJV	China	All levels	Regular
Third country expatriates of Chinese parent	Third	Chinese parent	China	Upper	Regular
Third country expatriates of foreign parent	Third	Foreign parent	China	Upper	Regular
Third country expatriates of EJV	Third	EJV	China	All levels	Regular
Foreign HQ executives	Foreign	Foreign parent	Foreign parent country	Top	Ad hoc
Chinese HQ executives	Chinese	Chinese parent	China	Top	Ad hoc

[a]*Source:* Developed from O. Shenkar and Y. Zeira, International joint ventures: A tough test for HR, *Personnel,* Jan. 1990: 26–31.

dynamic business environment. In its six years of operations, the Shanghai Toys Import and Export Corporation (STIEC)—an EJV between the Hong Kong–based Universal Matchbox and five Chinese organizations, led by Shanghai Toys—has had four different general managers. The first and second were Hong Kong Chinese; the third was a British national who has "tried to introduce some significant changes," but was "ignored." In a rare move for PRC-based IJVs, the Hong Kong parent (which had the authority to appoint the general manager under the JV law) then appointed a PRC national (with high school education) who may well be the first Chinese ever appointed by a foreign party to that job. The step, however, may be typical to Universal Matchbox, which has a policy of appointing locals to top management posts (the company also has manufacturing operations in Hong Kong, the United Kingdom, and Taiwan). The deputy general manager, appointed by the PRC side, has only primary education. He has worked at Shanghai Toys for 40 years.

The criteria applied by the Hong Kong party in their quest for a general manager were, in the cited order, (1) honesty, (2) capability,

(3) willingness to serve as a general manager, (4) character, and (5) good interpersonal relations. The fifth criterion is often emphasized in regard to EJVs, where multiple ownership and a diversified work force require considerable political skills. Indeed, the general manager of Shanghai Squibb suggested to us that his many years of foreign service in wholly owned subsidiaries have only partially prepared him for the intricacies and complexities involved in managing an EJV. On the other hand, the requirement that the general manager be willing to serve is quite unique to the PRC. In a study of PRC managers conducted in the early 1980s, Shenkar and Ronen (1987a) found that promotion was one of the least desired objectives for Chinese staff. This probably reflected a perception that the risk involved in taking on such a position far outweighed the relatively minor benefits accrued by it. Changing this attitude has been slow to come.

As often occurs in other types of foreign subsidiaries, local managers of IJVs are frequently frustrated by the lack of promotion opportunities to key jobs, since senior positions are reserved for "outsiders." This problem is especially serious in EJVs when the contract and/or documents of incorporation do not specify how senior positions are to be staffed, and host country nationals are thus led to believe—erroneously—that these posts are reserved for them; or, when the documents of incorporation specify that top positions are reserved for foreign parent or host parent transferees. In both these cases, the local staff is likely to become resentful and frustrated, and the venture may be plagued with low morale. In EJVs, the outsiders are not only foreign parent transferees and expatriates but also transferees and appointees of the host parent(s). In many instances when such outsiders are present in the EJV, local people are reluctant to join, stay on, or contribute their best. The damage to the morale and motivation of those employees—especially young managers and other professionals—is quite obvious, and so is the resulting damage to the venture. In EJVs that are expected to last for an indefinite period, local employees may hope the staffing policy will be changed. However, in shorter-term ventures, the problem is likely to be especially serious. Local managers and professionals may feel there is no incentive to do more than the minimum required.

As can be expected, many EJVs in the PRC started out with an extensive expatriate work force which was then reduced. The China Hotel, a Hong Kong–PRC EJV, initially employed 194 expatriates of nine countries in managerial and professional positions. The number has been halved after a few years of operation, with most of the remaining expatriate staff coming from Hong Kong. In the Shenzhen survey, about 40 percent of the sample firms did not have a foreign manager on site, reflecting the close proximity of Hong Kong and Macau to Shenzhen. Foreign managers who were involved on a day-to-day basis in management focused mainly on planning, marketing, financial control, and technology management. Only 20 percent participated in personnel management matters.

The Foreign Expatriate in Chinese EJVs.   Wholly owned subsidiaries of multinational corporations are usually closely integrated into the firm's global operations, so an assignment to such subsidiaries may be only somewhat disruptive. EJV assignees, on the other hand, are working with or supervised by employees of another company. They may not report directly to their parent company, and their supervisors may be in a poor position to assess their performance. Hence, they feel more strongly that they are "in exile" than do transferees in wholly owned subsidiaries. In the PRC, expatriates face a number of hardships. Zamet and Bovarnick (1986) report that more than in other countries expatriates in China tend to be single or at least not have children, and, with the possible exception of Beijing, lack supportive national communities. Cohen and Valentine (1987) add that many expatriates in the PRC "feel they are being consciously and systematically discriminated against in daily life because they are foreigners." Adaptation to a foreign environment is, however, a frequent problem for expatriates worldwide, particularly in less developed countries.

As in other countries, both host and foreign parents' managers who work for an EJV sometimes experience a conflict of loyalty between the venture and the parent companies (Shenkar & Zeira, 1987). In the PRC, however, ties to the parent firms tend to be much stronger than in other countries. For the foreign parent expatriate in China-based ventures, an eventual transfer to the venture or to the local parent is virtually impossible. Being far away from their job market, such expatriates are dependent on their parent company for continuous employment, and hence their loyalty lies not with the EJV but with the parent organizations—a situation that increases suspicion among the parent firms and prevents full cooperation among the various employee groups within the venture. Allegiance to the parent firm is even stronger, however, among the transferees and appointees of the Chinese parent, because of the broad scope of necessities whose provision is contingent upon the work unit. The Chinese work unit, or *danwei*, provides its members with housing (virtually unavailable on a free market basis), childcare, schooling, health care, social welfare, subsidized food staples, and the right to purchase scarce goods and services. In many respects, it can be regarded as a "total institution" rather than a business enterprise (Shenkar & Von Glinow, 1994).

Compensation is another problem for foreign expatriates in EJVs worldwide. In China, one such problem is downward pressure on expatriate salaries generated by Chinese demands for parity of pay to foreigners and Chinese employees holding similar titles (Cohen & Harris, 1986). The GMCP general manager earns somewhat more than "the Hong Kong standard," a common practice devised to compensate such expatriates for the posting away from their family and familiar environment. Another problem is the Chinese insistence on replacing expatriate personnel within a few years, which make start-up costs for such personnel much higher.

Work Force Recruitment and Selection

When the newly appointed U.S. manager of Babcock and Wilcox's EJV arrived in Beijing, he was surprised to find hundreds of beds scattered around the factory, where idle employees napped during working hours. He estimated that "out of 3,600 employees, 1,200 were working while 2,400 were loafing." Although the Joint Ventures Law specifies that the general manager "shall have the right to appoint and dismiss his subordinates," a right that was extended to allow for open recruitment in 1984, hiring authority remains constrained. The Joint Venture Labor Procedures require that ventures recruit their personnel from the pool of the Chinese parent's workers if those are "available and competent." This led to a problem of surplus workers, particularly in EJVs which took over operating plants from the Chinese parent. When production started at STIEC in 1985, 105 employees were transferred from the major Chinese parent. Often, these were workers shunned by this parent. Managing them proved to be a serious problem. Used to "the Iron Rice Bowl," these workers were not accustomed to modern management methods, nor were they much inclined to make an effort to improve. Dismissal threats were not effective because, once terminated, the employees would return to Shanghai Toys. Asked whether those transferees were still loyal to their parent organization, we were told that they were "loyal to themselves."

It is usually easier to avoid those problems in newly established facilities, as the U.S. parent has done successfully in the case of Cardio-Pace, a Baoji–based EJV, in which the Chinese wanted to staff the venture with a few dozen excess assistant managers and workers. Ramada Guilin faced pressure to hire more than eighty cadres, some of them in their fifties, and finally relented to hiring twenty. Sino On-Line also faced pressure to increase the number of what Sabina Wang, the general manager and partner, called "nonprofessional representatives." A similar problem was found in EJVs in other countries, particularly where the host parent is a state enterprise (e.g., Lamont, 1973), but it is probably more serious in the PRC, where most enterprises and state agencies have been overstaffed for years (Daniels, Krug, & Nigh, 1986). The 1986 regulation nonwithstanding, workers in state-owned enterprises can be dismissed only in exceptional cases, such as political purges or serious offenses. In contrast, a venture has the right to lay off staff and workers whose employment is considered redundant and can also fire undisciplined workers or those who have committed serious offenses. The Guangzhou-based China Hotel fired numerous workers during its first years of operation. HPC has fired nine workers and STIEC has dismissed eleven workers since its establishment in 1986, with tacit union support. Throughout its operation, five employees were fired at GMCP, and eight or nine left voluntarily. The employees fired were caught sleeping on the night shift or caused an inadvertent damage to machinery due to negligent operation, and were terminated with union approval.

At STIEC, most of the assembly workers are young girls from the areas surrounding the Special Economic Zone. This relieves the venture from the need to provide permanent housing, a considerable burden in other EJVs. STIEC employees are recruited through newspaper advertisements, as are employees of the China Hotel and Guangmei Foods, although consistent pressure from workers to bring in their relatives persists. The formal selection criteria at STIEC are educational level, language proficiency, experience, IQ, "manner," hobbies, and "family background." Once a worker has been selected, an application is made to the Shanghai Municipal Bureau. As elsewhere in China, an employee's transfer must be first approved by his or her unit of origin, which may refuse or insist on "compensation" (especially when the transfer is to a foreign-invested firm). As to the women assembly workers, their positions are advertised through the local cable TV or they are recommended through local county government offices.

GMCP currently employs more than 400 local, mostly young Chinese in three shifts. When operations were about to start, the venture advertised its positions and received about ten applicants for each post. Today there is no longer a need to advertise because the venture is well known, and 200 qualified candidates are on the waiting list. Many of those have been referred by GMCP's employees or by the Chinese parent firms. In 1989, GMCP selected four of the top 300 university graduates in Guangzhou to work for the venture. Because of need for technical skills, the venture does not employ rural work force, although it is abundant in the area and quite cheap. Only a small number (fewer than ten) of locals who used to live on the factory's site are employed as caretakers at monthly salaries of about 500 yuan.

Performance Evaluation and Compensation

Appraisal.   New recruits at GMCP begin a three-month probation period during which they must meet the "three satisfactions" of (a) the company, (b) the work unit, and (c) themselves. Failure to meet any of those results in dismissal. Performance appraisal is conducted twice yearly. The criteria used are (1) worker's attitude, (2) technical skills, (3) efficiency, and (4) initiative. The appraisal is mainly used as a morale incentive to select "Advanced Workers," but also for promotion and training purposes.

GMCP's Mr. Qin defines the company approach as a "Strong Man Philosophy" but emphasizes that it is also a "human-centered" policy that demands both hard work and close team cooperation. The company pays little attention to labor classification, and job analysis is also rarely conducted. A local manager in GMCP's personnel department noted that in comparison to his previous employer (a Chinese state firm), the EJV allowed for more open communications, relied less on seniority and more on achievement, and allowed for the development of one's potential.

Wages.   There is no single model of wage payment to staff and workers of joint ventures in China. A survey of thirty-eight EJVs conducted in Shenzhen SEZ, revealed as many as thirteen combinations of wage components. This is in line with the Provisions for Labor Management, which stipulate that the system of wage standards, types of wages, bonuses, and so on are at the discretion of the board of directors. In general, wages can be divided into the following five components: basic wage, floating wage, position wage, piece-rate wage, and bonuses. Basic wage guarantees that workers and staff can meet daily basic needs, whereas position wage varies by position and echelon. Floating wage is fully or partially tied to enterprise profitability.

According to Article 39 of Joint Ventures Implementation Regulations, a joint venture's salary and wages and bonus system should adhere to the principles of "to each according to his work," and "more pay for more work." The distribution principles are analogous to that of the Chinese state-owned enterprises that subscribe to the "socialist" principle of "from each according to his ability and to each according to his work". Article 8 of the Provisions for Labor Management in Sino–Foreign Joint Ventures in 1980 stipulates that the wage levels of the local staff and workers "shall be fixed at 120 to 150 percent of the real wages of the staff and workers of state enterprises in the locality in the same line of business." The higher levels are intended to attract competent staff and workers, as well as compensate them for the much faster work pace required in EJVs versus state (especially) and collective enterprises. In late 1990, the Chinese Ministry of Labor enacted new regulations, limiting compensation in EJVs to 120 percent more than that of comparable state enterprises, and up to 150 percent in cases of proven high profitability. Any excess payment must be approved by local labor bureaus. United States parent firms strongly opposed the measure, fearing that it could curb EJVs' attractiveness to top-level staff (Foreign Labor Trends, 1991).

According to a survey, wages of staff and workers account for about 70 percent of total labor service fees of joint ventures but vary across localities. The survey result in Shenzhen shows that workers and staff of joint ventures were generally satisfied with the amount of wages they received: Over 50 percent found compensation to be "extremely satisfactory" or "satisfactory" and only about 5 percent of workers and staff were dissatisfied. According to Mr. Qin of GMCP, the average salary of rank-and-file employees is about 600 to 700 yuan per month, with roughly half of that comprised of various bonuses. About 25 percent of workers' salary normally goes toward housing. The company purchased (on the open market) 96 apartments of various sizes that are allocated on the basis of rank and family status. Most are already occupied and are rented at a subsidized rate of 20 to 30 yuan per month. The venture's management and its parents decided on this very substantial investment (such apartments range in price from 150,000 to 170,000 yuan and are normally sold to overseas Chinese or locals with such relatives) because of the scarcity of housing in the area and as an incentive to retain good workers, although the foreign party initially opposed the purchase. At STIEC, rank-and-file employees are either in a temporary status and are paid on a piece-rate basis only (such workers normally earn between 300 and 400 yuan a month); or are on a "contract" basis, which would normally entitle them to a salary between 400 and 500 yuan, inclusive of bonuses and allowances.

Equity.   The problem of relative deprivation also occurs in wholly owned subsidiaries, but it tends to be more acute in EJVs, especially those with many employee groups. These groups typically receive different compensation packages, which are strongly biased by the employee's affiliation with a particular parent or with the venture. Frequently, these differences create feelings of deprivation among those receiving lower compensation, such as the Chinese managers in EJVs whose mandatory parity in wages with the foreign expatriates has only a partial impact on their actual paychecks. For example, GMCP's two Chinese deputies make about 80 percent of the general manager's (a Hong Kong resident) salary but, as is common in other foreign-invested firms in the PRC, a substantial part of that goes to the State. Still, these salaries are considerably higher than in Chinese State enterprises, and the apartments allocated to the two are of considerably high standard. Also, a new wage structure, such as the one instituted in the Babcock and Wilcox's venture, had the impact of reducing the gap between workers directly involved in production and engineers and managers, to the dismay of the latter. The limited differential in the wages of simple assembly workers versus foundry employees and technicians is largely a legacy of the wage structure at Shanghai Toys, which was implemented at STIEC. The system has been reformed once but needs to be reformed again, we were told, as foundry workers (whose work requires skills and a physical agility) and highly skilled technicians and tool makers have been voicing complaints about the artificial parity: In Hong Kong, tool makers earn double the salary of assembly line workers. Salaries of department managers reach 1,000 yuan monthly, including an annual bonus based on the venture's performance. Such employees would have made about 250 yuan in Shanghai Toys. Rank-and-file workers suffer less because their reference group is likely to be State enterprises where workers usually make less. However, they may feel frustrated that only a fraction of this relative advantage reaches their pockets, and if they have been transferred from the Chinese parent, may have a hard time adjusting to a competitive wage system instead of the egalitarian system of the Maoist period.

Training

Many EJVs in the PRC provide on-the-job training to their Chinese employees. Sometimes, such training takes the form of mentoring, with the foreign expatriate coaching a PRC counterpart, or with an experienced

Chinese employee coaching a younger one. Mentoring, however, creates a blurring of authority lines. At Guangmei Foods, a US–PRC EJV in Guangzhou, personnel frequently bypass their Chinese supervisor and appeal to the foreign expatriate, who may formally be in a staff position because they consider him the expert. At GMCP, the problem seems to be less pronounced, perhaps because of the frequent crossing of organizational boundaries: Employees are sent to Hong Kong to observe the Hong Kong parent's operations (which are quite similar to those in Guangzhou); foreign experts are invited to conduct workshops in the firm; and relations with Guangzhou universities are cultivated. Chinese officials involved with the venture particularly noted the support provided by the Hong Kong and U.S. parent in assisting the training of the local work force, obviously a major concern both for the Chinese and foreign parents as well as for the local officialdom. Such training, especially when provided abroad, was considered a major reward for local employees.

Training of foreign parent expatriates is another issue. As the voluminous literature on expatriates suggests, such managers must be trained for work in the unfamiliar environment of the PRC—something which, surprisingly does not always take place. Not less importantly, such expatriates are rarely trained to work in an EJV environment, which is abound with complexities and ambiguities. This appears to be a serious deficiency that should be corrected in the future.

Preparing for the Future

With foreign investment in China now growing by leaps and bounds, managers are sometimes at a loss deciding which management processes practiced at home or learned in other overseas subsidiaries, including EJVs, are transferable to PRC–based ventures. Although many of the problems described here can be found in EJVs in many countries and in a variety of industries, the exact form they take, as well as their severity, tends to vary. Variations typically depend on the characteristics of the host country, the number and characteristics of the parent firms, the nature of the work force, the life expectancy of the EJV, and the strategic importance of the venture to the host country and the parent firms, to mention just a few (for a detailed discussion, see Zeira & Shenkar, 1990). Such variations are very important when one considers the relevance of human resource policies and practices developed in EJVs in other countries for the PRC.

As in other countries, it is important for human resource managers in China–based ventures to recognize that the problems they may encounter in running EJVs notwithstanding, this form of organization frequently serves their company objectives better than any other. Although other investment vehicles—be they licensing, franchising, a wholly owned subsidiary (allowed in China for a number of years now), an international merger, an acquisition, or a partnership—abound, these other vehicles may not always provide the same level of effectiveness or as desirable incentives as those granted to the parents of EJVs. Human resource professionals must do their utmost to plan, prepare, and implement proper human resource policies and practices which will enable effective utilization of the potential embedded in EJV participation.

The experience of PRC–based EJVs suggests a number of strong recommendations regarding the management of human resources. First, virtually all foreign parents recommend "starting from scratch"—whether they have done that themselves or not. This enables the venture to avoid the problems associated with the Chinese parent transferees who bring with them lax work habits, are largely immune to sanctions, and have little to lose if the venture is not successful. If it is not possible to start anew, foreign parents must make sure that the number and qualifications of such transferees are carefully negotiated and scrutinized.

Second, human resource issues must be considered throughout the process of negotiation and partner selection. A partner that fits strategic requirements may not necessarily possess the compatible work force and personnel policy that will enable harmonious and successful cooperation. Companies should seek a match that is as suitable on the human resource front as on a strategic level. Many EJV problems arise when parent firms have conflicting objectives, a highly likely occurrence in Chinese–foreign ventures (see Shenkar, 1990). For instance, a foreign parent may enter into an EJV in order to lower its production costs, thus trying to keep training expenses to a minimum. The Chinese parent, however, may have entered the venture with the objective of obtaining a transfer of technology and may be in favor of a full training program for employees. The contract negotiations phase is the best time to identify each party's objectives for the EJV and to design human resource policies that represent the best possible compromise. Substantial evidence suggests that a carefully worded and very detailed contract reduces the uncertainty involved in human resource decisions by providing specific guidelines and criteria to be used in employee selection, promotion, and compensation. The human resource manager should ensure that the China–based EJV contract address in detail such issues as staffing levels and criteria, compensation, promotion, and performance evaluation procedures.

Third, as HPC's Dr. Liu suggests, take *initial* control of human resource functions so as to assure the institutionalization of proper practices at an early stage. The recruitment of younger, educated staff is not a guarantee of effective performance, unless it is accompanied by a well-thought-out human resource system that will instill discipline and a desirable work ethic. The time to instill such values and practices is clearly at the very beginning, before other work habits have been formed and an organizational culture has been institutionalized.

Fourth, human relations, paramount to any EJV, are critical in the Chinese cultural environment, which places a premium on such relations. Tony Fung, the Australian investor in the Ramada Renaissance Guilin, noted that "the trouble actually started" when the deputy chairman, whom he had known for five years, was replaced by the Chinese party. In EJVs with more than two parent firms, such as GMPC or Guangmei Foods, relations need to be cultivated with all parties involved. This should not deter foreign firms, however, from forming such multiple parent ventures. Common wisdom to the contrary, such ventures were found to reduce the role conflict and ambiguity of CEOs in Israel–based ventures (Shenkar & Zeira, 1992), and there is a good reason to believe that China is no exception. The CEO of Gunagzhou-based Guangmei Foods, for example, attributed the success of the enterprise to the presence of two Chinese parents in addition to the American one. One Chinese parent was a local company that contributed knowledge of the local labor scene and marketplace; the other was a Beijing company with close ties to the relevant government ministries.

Fifth, as in all organizations, the best way to eliminate, or at least to minimize, human resource problems in EJVs is to anticipate them and take preemptive action. Managers should participate in a program that explains the unique structure of EJVs, identifies the various employee groups in such ventures and the human resource problems they typically suffer from, and offers possible solutions to these problems within the special context of the Chinese environment, including its cultural and institutional attributes. Such training is most effective if provided before the venture is under way. But even EJVs that are already operational can benefit from an organization development (OD) effort that is designed to make employees aware of the complexity of the system and to sensitize them to the needs and constraints of employees in other groups, as well as those of other stakeholders in the Chinese system. A role-based intervention in which participants learn to understand the constraints faced by other "players" in the venture is particularly recommended, and will likely lead to better communication and deeper trust among the groups. Such an OD effort should begin early in the life of the venture, and if based on programs adopted for other ventures, be tailormade to fit the needs of the Chinese environment.

Finally, many successful EJVs reduce friction among parents, and between the venture and the parents, by dividing functional responsibilities. In such an arrangement, the Chinese parent typically is in charge of personnel and domestic marketing and the foreign parent controls finance and/or engineering, as well as international marketing. This arrangement has its drawbacks (e.g., integration across organizational functions is sometimes difficult), but it also has advantages in terms of establishing clear lines of authority, and should be considered as a viable option.

References

Beamish, P. W. (1993). The characteristics of joint ventures in the People's Republic of China. *Journal of International Marketing*, 1, 2, 29–48.

Beijing Review, Feb. 4, 1991.

Bond, M. H., & Hwang, K. K. (1986). The social psychology of Chinese people. In M. H. Bond (ed.), *The psychology of the Chinese people.* Hong Kong: Oxford University Press.

Campbell, N., & Adlington, P. (1988). *China business strategies.* London: Pergamon Press.

China now ripe for investment says new study. (1987). *South China Morning Post,* Aug. 19.

Chow, I., & Shenkar, O. (1989). HR practices in the People's Republic of China. *Personnel,* 66, 41–47.

Cohen, J. A., & Harris, C. H. (1986). Equal pay for equal work: Remuneration for high-level management in Chinese-foreign equity joint ventures. *China Business Review,* Jan./Feb., 10–13.

Cohen, J. A., & Valentine, S. H. (1987). Foreign direct investment in the People's Republic of China: Progress, problems, and proposals. *Roundtable on foreign direct investment in the People's Republic of China,* Beijing, 25–26 May.

Daniels, J. D., Krug, J., & Nigh, D. (1986). U.S. joint ventures in China: Motivation and management of political risks. *California Management Review* 27(4): 46–58.

Davidson, W. H. (1987). Creating and managing joint ventures in China. *California Management Review* 24(4): 77–94.

Domsch, M., & Lichtenberger, B. (1991). In search of appropriate management transfer: Leadership style of West German expatriate managers in the People's Republic of China. *International Journal of Human Resource Management,* 73–86.

Foreign labor trends: China. (1991). Washington, DC: U.S. Department of Labor, Bureau of International Labor Affairs.

Hendryx, S. R. (1986). Implementation of a technology transfer joint venture in the People's Republic of China: A management perspective. *Columbia Journal of World Business,* Spring, 57–65.

Henley, J. S., & Nyaw, M. K. (1987). The management system and organizational functioning of joint ventures in China: Some evidence from Shenzhen SEZ. Paper presented at the Chinese Enterprise Conference, Manchester, U.K., June.

Janger, A. K. (1980). *Organization of international joint ventures.* New York: Conference Board.

Lague, D. (1988). Hotel workers' threatened with violence. *South China Morning Post,* Feb. 28, 2.

Lamont, D. F. (1973). Joining forces with foreign state enterprises. *Harvard Business Review* 51(5): 68–79.

National Council for U.S.–China Trade. (1987). *U.S. joint ventures in China: A progress report.* Washington, DC.

Nyaw, M. K., & Liu, G. S. (1987). Organizational size, adjustment and managerial effectiveness of the joint ventures in Shenzhen Special Economic Zone. Paper presented at the International Conference of China's Special Economic Zones and Open Policy: Development and Perspective. The Chinese University of Hong Kong, Hong Kong, April.

Partners fight plague Guilin venture. (1988). *Asian Wall Street Journal,* Feb. 10, A1.

Ronen, S., & Shenkar, O. (1985). Clustering countries on attitudinal dimensions: A review and synthesis. *Academy of Management Review* 10(3): 435–454.

Shenkar, O. (1990). International joint ventures' problem in China: Risks and remedies. *Long-Range Planning,* April, 82–90.

Shenkar, O., & Chow, I. H. S. (1989). From political praise to stock options: Reforming compensation systems in the People's Republic of China. *Human Resource Management* 28(1): 65–85.

Shenkar, O., & Ronen, S. (1987). The structure and importance of work goals among managers in the People's Republic of China. *Academy of Management Journal* 30(3): 564–576.

Shenkar, O., Ronen, S., Shefy, E., & Chow, I. H. S. (1993). The manager as mayor: A study of PRC executives. Paper presented at the Academy of International Business annual meeting. Maui, Hawaii, October.

Shenkar, O., & Von Glinow, M. A. (1994). Paradoxes of organizational theory and research: Using the case of China to illustrate national contingency. *Management Science* [Special issue: *Management Science International: In Search of Universal Rules*] 40, 1, 56–71.

Shenkar, O., & Zeira, Y. (1992). Role conflict and role ambiguity of chief executive officers in international joint ventures. *Journal of International Business Studies* 23(1): 55–76.

Shenkar, O., & Zeira, Y. (1987). International joint ventures: Implications for organizational development. *Personnel Review* 16(1): 30–37.

Van den Bulke, D., & Zhang, H. Y. (1992). Belgian equity joint ventures in China: Some theoretical considerations and evidence. In *Proceedings of the conference on current development in joint ventures in the PRC.* Hong Kong University, June 16–18.

Young, R. G., & Bradford, Jr., S. (1977). *Joint ventures planning and action.* New York: Arthur K. Little.

Zamet, J. M., & Bovarnick, M. E. (1986). Employee relations for multinational companies in China. *Columbia Journal of World Business,* Spring, 13–19.

Zeira, Y., & Shenkar, O. (1990). Interactive and specific parent characteristics: Implications for management and human resources in international joint ventures. *Management International Review* [Special issue: *Human Resource Management in International Joint Ventures*] 30, 7–22.